DOG AND CAT
NUTRITION

DOG AND CAT NUTRITION

A Handbook for Students, Veterinarians, Breeders and Owners

Editor

A. T. B. EDNEY

Animal Studies Centre
Waltham-on-the-Wolds

PERGAMON PRESS

OXFORD · NEW YORK · TORONTO · SYDNEY · PARIS · FRANKFURT

U.K.	Pergamon Press Ltd., Headington Hill Hall, Oxford OX3 0BW, England
U.S.A.	Pergamon Press Inc., Maxwell House, Fairview Park, Elmsford, New York 10523, U.S.A.
CANADA	Pergamon Press Canada Ltd., Suite 104, 150 Consumers Rd., Willowdale, Ontario M2J 1P9, Canada
AUSTRALIA	Pergamon Press (Aust.) Pty. Ltd., P.O. Box 544, Potts Point, N.S.W. 2011, Australia
FRANCE	Pergamon Press SARL, 24 rue des Ecoles, 75240 Paris, Cedex 05, France
FEDERAL REPUBLIC OF GERMANY	Pergamon Press GmbH, Hammerweg 6, D- 6242 Kronberg-Taunus, Federal Republic of Germany

First edition 1982
Reprinted 1982, 1983, 1985

Library of Congress Cataloging in Publication Data
Main entry under title:
Dog & cat nutrition.
  Includes bibliographies and index.
  Contents: Energy balance, water balance, and the physiology of digestion and absorption./ S.E. Blaza — A simplified guide to nutritional needs/ I.H. Burger — Foods for dogs and cats/ D.W. Holme — [etc.]
  1. Dogs—Food. 2. Cats—Food. 3. Animal nutrition.
I. Edney, A. T. B.   II. Title: Dog and cat nutrition.
SF427.4.D63 1982   636.7'084   82-417
ISBN 0-08-028891-X (Hardcover)
ISBN 0-08-028890-1 (Flexicover)

Printed in Great Britain by A. Wheaton & Co. Ltd., Exeter

FOREWORD

Of the many books on nutrition, few relate to pet animals. This is surprising as, in the United Kingdom alone there are around 10 million dogs and cats. In the whole of the western world the dog and cat population is of the order of 150 million, virtually all of which need to be fed every day.

Nutrition is difficult to make readable, in spite of the obvious practical nature of the subject. Much of what is available is rather imprecise and in some cases has a liberal component of folklore. More accurate information tends to be less accessible to a general readership. There is it seems a need for a practically-orientated and above all readable account of the nutrition of dogs and cats. This book is meant to provide such a work for student veterinarians and animal nurses, those breeders of dogs and cats and all others who take a deeper interest in the feeding of their animals.

The book is structured so that the reader can progress from an understanding of the nutritional needs of dogs and cats, to the foods which are used to meet those needs. The middle section of the work is devoted to feeding in special circumstances, such as hard work, stress, orphaned puppies and various illnesses. The final chapter is included to explain how prepared foods are evaluated and validated, information which is difficult to find elsewhere. Only key references are included in the text, but a more comprehensive bibliography is given at the end of each chapter as a guide to further reading.

The contributors to this book are drawn from workers at the Animal Studies Centre in Leicestershire, and four of the world's leading authorities on dog and cat nutrition. These include Professor D. S. Kronfeld, who has kindly provided an account of his unique studies of sledge dogs as an investigation into the needs of animals doing very hard work.

The editor is pleased to express sincere thanks to Christina Loxley of the Animal Studies Centre and Dorothy Howard of Waltham for typing the manuscript and to Alison Wearne of Gwynne Hart & Associates, as well as John Lavender of Pergamon Press for progressing the work.

A. T. B. Edney

CONTENTS

LIST OF CONTRIBUTORS

Dr S. E. Blaza BSc PhD
Dr I. H. Burger BSc PhD
Mr A. T. B. Edney BA BVetMed MRCVS
Dr D. W. Holme BSc PhD NDA MIBiol
Dr P. T. Kendall BSc PhD

Animal Studies Centre
Freeby Lane
Waltham-on-the-Wolds
Leicestershire LE14 4RT
United Kingdom

Dr L. W. Hall MA BSc PhD DVA MRCVS

Department of Clinical Veterinary
   Medicine
University of Cambridge
Madingley Road
Cambridge CB3 0ES
United Kingdom

Dr Å. A. Hedhammar DVM MS PhD

Swedish University of Agricultural
   Sciences
College of Veterinary Medicine
Department of Medicine I
S 750 07 Uppsala
Sweden

Professor D. S. Kronfeld
  MVSc PhD DSc MRCVS

Professor of Nutrition
University of Pennsylvania
School of Veterinary Medicine
New Bolton Center
382 West Street Road
Kennett Square
Philadelphia
Pennsylvania 19348
U.S.A.

Professor Dr J. Leibetseder
  DrVetMed PhD

Institut für Ernährung
   der Veterinärmedizin Universität
A 1030 Vienna
Linkbahngasse 11
Austria

CHAPTER 1

ENERGY BALANCE, WATER BALANCE AND THE PHYSIOLOGY OF DIGESTION AND ABSORPTION

· S. E. Blaza

In order to live, all animals require a regular intake of food and water. Food provides both individual nutrients and energy, and in most cases it also contributes some water. Requirements for particular nutrients differ between species and also vary in the life cycle of any single animal. For example, adult dogs and cats require protein to replace that used for tissue maintenance and repair and in producing antibodies, hormones, enzymes and haemoglobin, whereas growing, pregnant and lactating dogs and cats require extra protein to produce new tissue or milk in addition to meeting the demands of normal metabolism.

The body is not a sealed unit with a fixed composition, but is in a continual state of change; meals are eaten and nutrients absorbed and utilized or excreted. The maintenance of the level of any single nutrient, or the energy or water content of the body, can be thought of in terms of 'balance'. For many of the nutrients required by mammals, such as proteins, fats, minerals and vitamins, balance is achieved largely by the control of output. It is thought that mammals eat to satisfy their requirement for energy and therefore the level of intake of particular nutrients is dependent upon their concentration in the food. However, provided that the necessary minimum intake is met, anything surplus to requirement can be lost in the faeces, or having been absorbed can be converted to another useful substance (in the liver) and used or excreted via the kidneys (in the urine). However, there are limits above which certain nutrients accumulate and become toxic, and the feeding of high concentrations, particularly of the fat-soluble vitamins, should be avoided. There are also relationships between nutrients which must be considered in the formulation of any food.

The regulation of energy balance and fluid balance is rather more complex than that of individual nutrients as both involve mechanisms which govern intake as well as output. The emphasis is different for energy and fluid, so these will be covered separately. As digestion and absorption are central to the maintenance of both, these will be considered later.

ENERGY BALANCE

An animal is said to be in energy balance when its expenditure of energy is equal to its intake; with the result that the level of energy stored in the body does not change. The following equation is derived from the Law of Conservation of Energy:

Energy stored = energy intake − energy expenditure

In the adult dog or cat energy is stored predominantly as fat with some increase in lean tissue (fat free mass). In a growing or pregnant animal, the emphasis shifts to the accumulation of lean tissue. Fat is stored as adipose tissue; these deposits are easily observed in an obese animal (Fig. 1). It is also possible to decrease energy stores, by reducing energy intake until it is less than energy output. This reverses the equation.

Expenditure − intake = loss of energy from stores

Under these conditions of negative energy balance, the body has to catabolize (break down) its own tissues to meet its energy needs; as the stores are gradually depleted the animal becomes thinner in appearance and bodyweight decreases.

Energy balance is achieved by the exact matching of input and output over long periods. A very small imbalance maintained for a long time will cause obesity (if the net difference is positive) or wasting

1

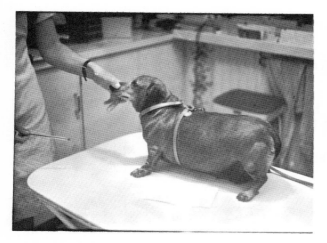

Fig. 1. Photograph of an obese dog.

(if the difference is negative). For example, imagine a Labrador Retriever which has a daily energy expenditure of 1700 kcal but an intake of 1800 kcal. The imbalance is only 100 kcal per day (1 oz of dog biscuit), but if maintained could result in an increase of 2–3 kg (4–6 lb) in bodyweight over a year. If this rate of gain continues for 2 or 3 years, even allowing for some compensation of energy output (see below) the dog will become very overweight and subject to all the problems of obesity.

Until recently it has been assumed that energy balance relied only on the exact regulation of intake and that any imbalance represented a failure to control intake appropriately. It now seems probable that both intake and output are important in the maintenance of energy balance. Intake is capable of precise control in contrast to expenditure which appears to act as a crude buffer, opposing any change to the energy content of the body.

Energy intake

Energy intake can be thought of at three different levels. These are gross energy (GE), digestible energy (DE) and metabolizable energy (ME). *Gross energy* is the total energy which would be released on complete oxidation of the food. Although a substance may have a high level of gross energy, unless the dog or cat can digest and absorb it, it is of no use to the animal. The amount which is digested and absorbed (gross energy minus faecal losses) is known as *digestible energy*. Some of the absorbed food may only be partially available to the tissues, the remainder being lost via the kidneys in the urine.

That which is utilized by the tissues is known as *metabolizable energy* and can be calculated as digestible energy minus urinary losses.

The digestible and metabolizable energy content of foods depends both upon their composition and upon the species which eats them. Ruminants, for example, are able to digest materials such as plant cell walls which would be unavailable to monogastric (single stomached) animals such as dogs and cats. To these animals such substances would simply be 'dietary fibre' or 'roughage'. There are also differences between the monogastric species, for instance the digestive systems of dogs are usually more efficient than those of cats. Therefore the same food fed to a dog or cat would yield different digestibility values. This may be partly because the dog's digestive system is proportionately longer than the cat's.

Regulation of energy balance through intake

Although very palatable foods may disturb the control of intake, many animals fed bland foods regulate energy intake very precisely. Even when the same food is given in dilute form (using water or some non-digestible material to change the energy density) compensation usually occurs rapidly and completely to a new appropriate level of food intake. There are many theories which attempt to account for this and most fit the negative feedback mechanism described in Fig. 2, to a greater or lesser degree.

The principle of negative feedback is a very simple one which can be demonstrated in many forms. For example, the control of blood pressure is dependent on negative feedback, as are many of the body's control mechanisms. It is found frequently in engineering as the example in Fig. 2 shows.

In its most straightforward form, negative feedback is a system where any change in the equilibrium of the system elicits a signal, provoking a response to oppose the initial change, and correct the error. In the example the room thermostat is the *sensor* which detects any change in ambient temperature. The

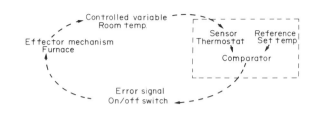

a) Principle of negative feedback

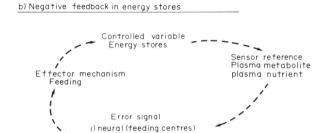

b) Negative feedback in energy stores

Fig. 2. Negative feedback.

causing peripheral hypoglycaemia (low glucose levels in the blood). Glycogen has the opposite effect to insulin, inhibiting feeding, as do oestrogens and luteinizing hormone (female reproductive hormones). As all these hormones have roles other than the stimulation or inhibition of feeding, they cannot be the sole agents governing intake.

In addition to neural and hormonal mechanisms there are other, more direct stimuli to feeding. Contractions of an empty stomach are thought to cause the sensation of hunger and provoke feeding, whereas gastric distension inhibits eating.

This model is useful in that it gives a framework to the theories on regulation of energy balance through intake, and it also allows testing of the theories. However, much of it is speculation and allowance has to be made for some contribution of energy expenditure to the regulation of energy balance. In most cases regulation is successful. Disturbances occur when highly palatable titbits are offered and the appetite for a particular food drowns out physiological satiety signals: this seems to affect dogs rather more than cats which suffer much less often from obesity.

discrepancy between the room temperature and a set reference temperature is noted by the *comparator* which signals to the boiler or *effector*, switching it on or off. The heat output from the boiler restores the room temperature, which can be thought of as the *controlled variable* and causes the comparator to cease signalling to the boiler.

In this model of the regulation of energy balance in Fig. 2, the controlled variable is the size of the energy stores. There are several feedback elements which may signal change, such as plasma nutrient and metabolite levels. Any discrepancies against set reference points indicate change in energy stores and stimulate neural and hormonal activity which may initiate or inhibit feeding.

The neural response involves 'feeding centres' in the brain which are not discrete 'hunger' and 'satiety' centres as once thought, but bundles of neurons covering several areas. Stimulation of these by electrodes can cause satiated animals to eat or prevent hungry animals from eating.

The hormonal response is more complex. Insulin stimulates feeding but it is not known whether this is a direct effect on the central nervous system or by

Energy expenditure

Since all the energy expended by the body can be measured as heat, energy output is often referred to in terms of 'heat loss', 'heat production', or in units usually associated with the measurement of heat such as watts, joules and calories. These units may also apply to the measurement of energy intake.

Energy expenditure can be divided into two parts, basal metabolic rate (BMR) and thermogenesis. BMR is the amount of energy required to keep the body 'ticking over', that is it represents the energy needed to meet the cost of essential work done by the cells and organs. This includes such processes as respiration, circulation and kidney function. Many factors determine BMR in any individual, including bodyweight and composition, age and hormonal status (particularly the thyroid hormones). As these factors change, so does the rate of basal metabolism, although such changes tend to occur slowly over long periods.

Additional energy expenditure comes under the collective title of thermogenesis. This can be the cost of digesting, absorbing and utilizing nutrients (sometimes called the 'thermic effect of food', or 'dietary induced thermogenesis'), of muscular work or exercise, of stress or of the maintenance of body temperature in a cold environment. The intake of certain drugs or hormones can also cause thermogenesis. Thermogenesis is simply any increase in metabolic rate over the basal level. In contrast to BMR the degree of thermogenesis can vary widely and quickly, and may cause large daily variations in energy output. Of the two components of total energy expenditure, thermogenesis is the part capable of rapid adaptive response to changes in the internal or external environment.

The regulation of energy balance through expenditure

When food is restricted for a long time, BMR decreases in a two-stage response. The first sharp drop is seen within days of the initial reduction in food intake and is thought to be a depression in the metabolism of individual cells, achieved through the thyroid and adrenal hormones which regulate metabolic rate. If refeeding occurs during this phase, metabolic rate recovers its initial level very quickly. The second phase takes longer to appear: this is a very gradual decline following the loss of body tissue, particularly lean tissue which is metabolically very active. Once this phase has been reached, BMR cannot be restored until the tissue has been replaced.

This decrease is a very simple form of regulation and will reduce any loss of bodyweight as a result of food restriction, although it cannot prevent it. There are important implications for the maintenance of bodyweight following a slimming regime; the level of food intake required to maintain energy balance will be less than required at the previous weight.

Similarly prolonged overfeeding results in an elevated metabolic rate which restricts the increase in energy stores. This increase in energy expenditure is partly attributable to the thermic effect of the food and to the cost of maintaining extra body tissue. However, these do not completely account for the extra expenditure, and there is still controversy over the source of the additional heat production.

There is, therefore, a rudimentary regulation of energy output which opposes any change in the status quo. Although energy output cannot completely prevent any change, it can limit its extent and this contribution should not be ignored.

WATER BALANCE

Water is often neglected as a nutritional requirement because of its ready availability in most temperate climates. However the requirement for water is at least as important as that for other nutrients; life may continue for weeks in the complete absence of food but only for days or even hours when water is not available.

Water fulfils many roles within the body. It is an excellent solvent, and this property makes possible all the complex chemistry of cellular metabolism. As the principal constituent of blood, water provides a vital transport medium, taking oxygen and nutrients to the tissues and removing carbon dioxide and metabolites. Blood also carries antibodies and white cells which protect the body from disease.

Water contributes to temperature regulation in several different ways. Firstly, the blood transports heat away from working organs and tissues, thereby preventing dangerous temperature increases. Then, by redirection of some of the blood through superficial veins, heat can be transferred to the skin and lost to the environment by radiation, convection and conduction. Heat loss may be further increased by the evaporation of water from the skin.

Water is also essential for digestion. Hydrolysis, the splitting of compounds by water, is the means by which digestion occurs. Digestive enzymes are secreted in solution, the better to disperse amongst the foodstuffs. Even the elimination of toxic metabolites via the kidney requires water as a medium. These represent only a few of the many functions of water.

There are several different fluid compartments in the body, which can be grouped together as intra- or extra-cellular fluid (ICF and ECF). ICF represents approximately 50% of the animal's total bodyweight and includes the water inside all cells from red blood cells to the neurones in the spinal cord. ECF is found bathing the tissues in between the cells, and in the blood and lymph. Movement of fluid between these compartments is continuous, different concentrations of electrolytes being maintained by the activity of cell membranes.

Water output

Water leaves the body by several routes. In the normal healthy dog and cat these include losses in expired air, in faeces, in urine and rarely also in sweat. These pathways will be discussed separately. In sick animals water loss may be increased markedly through haemorrhage (bleeding), vomiting and diarrhoea. Lactation is another instance of increased loss.

Faeces

The water content of faeces is usually very low compared with the enormous volumes of fluid secreted into the digestive tract, with enzymes, mucus and various electrolytes. The intestines have very efficient mechanisms for the reabsorption of water and it is only when these are disturbed and faeces evacuated as diarrhoea that this route makes a significant contribution to water loss.

Evaporative losses

The uptake of oxygen from inspired air is made possible by close association between the epithelium of the lung and an extensive capillary network. However, this also facilitates the transfer of water by diffusion and evaporation into the cavity of the lung, and the water is then lost in expired air. This 'respiratory water loss' is unavoidable. In hot weather evaporation is an important temperature regulating mechanism because of the body heat used to vaporize the water. This is why dogs pant and hang out their tongues, and why cats cover their coats with saliva by repeated licking. In extreme conditions there may also be some slight evaporation through the foot pads. Although these mechanisms aid temperature control, they may increase water loss considerably.

Urine

The kidney is the only organ in the body which can control water loss, and in addition to this it also regulates acid—base balance and the concentration of many electrolytes. In common with other mammals, dogs and cats have two kidneys situated in the abdominal cavity, one either side of, but ventral to (below, or in front of) the spinal column (Fig. 3). The blood supply is provided by the renal artery and vein.

The kidney consists of a network of thousands of tubules (Fig. 4). Each tubule has a blind end, or 'glomerular capsule' which envelops a knot of capillary blood vessels known as the glomerulus. There is a wide difference in pressure between the capillary and the capsule and this differential causes continuous movement of small molecules and fluid into the capsule from the capillary. Large molecules, such as proteins and the various blood cells, cannot pass into the tubule unless there has been damage to the glomerular or tubular walls. Indeed, one of the indications of kidney damage is the finding of proteins in the urine. In healthy animals therefore, the fluid

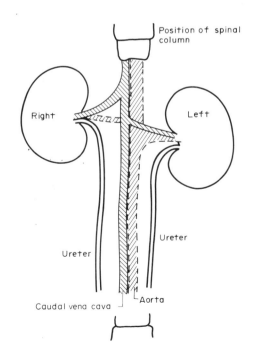

Fig. 3. Gross structure of kidneys.

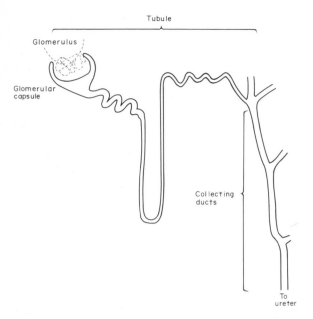

Fig. 4. Structure of kidney tubule (simplified).

which enters the tubule is an 'ultrafiltrate' of blood, and the rate of entry depends upon the difference in pressures in the two systems.

As the fluid passes down the tubule, much of it is reabsorbed by the tubular wall and returned to the blood. Reabsorption is selective, substances present in excessive quantities in the blood are not reabsorbed, nor are various waste products. Some substances can be actively secreted into the tubule by the cell walls. The tubules converge deep within the kidney in collecting ducts and the remaining contents leave the kidney via a thin-walled tube known as the 'ureter'. A ureter passes from each kidney to the bladder where urine is stored until it can be conveniently voided.

Control of the water and electrolytes lost via the kidneys occurs at several levels. There is a rudimentary form of negative feedback; if dehydration results in a loss of ECF volume, blood pressure will drop, therefore forces driving filtration into the tubule will be reduced and less filtrate will reach the tubule. This limits water loss.

Blood pressure may be partly restored by the kidney; when the blood pressure drops, the kidney releases an enzyme called renin which catalyses the conversion of an inactive plasma protein to angiotensin. Angiotensin is a potent hormone which causes constriction of the arteriolar blood vessels,

thereby maintaining a minimum pressure despite loss of volume. It also stimulates the adrenal cortex to release aldosterone, another hormone which increases the tubular reabsorption of salt and water. The rate of water reabsorption is also governed by antidiuretic hormone (ADH) which is produced by the pituitary gland in the brain in response to elevated concentrations of some of the constituents of blood. ADH acts upon part of the tubule to increase water reabsorption.

The role of the kidney in regulating electrolyte balance, particularly the level of hydrogen ions, may interfere with its role in water balance. Hydrogen ions are produced by many of the body's chemical reactions, and they cannot be allowed to accumulate, as this would change the pH of the body. As these have to be removed from the body in solution, some loss of water as urine is inevitable even in conditions of severe dehydration.

Water intake

There are several pathways along which water may enter the body. These include drinking water, the water content of foodstuffs, which may be as much as 90% of the food, and the water released during metabolic utilization of these foods.

Water content of foods

When foods are broken down during digestion, water is released together with the other end products of digestion such as sugars and amino acids. The quantity of water depends upon the type of foodstuffs; for example, commercial dry dog and cat foods may contain as little as 6% water (although some do contain more) whereas many canned foods contain up to 82% water. Milk contains approximately 88% water, and fresh fish and meat 55—75%. Therefore the amounts of water available to animals from their food can vary 10-fold.

Metabolic water

This is the water produced on chemical breakdown of the nutrients by oxidation in the tissues.

Hydrogen in the food combines with oxygen to produce water. The quantity of water released depends entirely on the class of foodstuff and the degree of oxidation (see Table 1).

Water drunk

Water taken in by drinking is under voluntary control. There are several different feedback mechanisms which stimulate drinking. Receptors in the mouth and throat send signals to the 'thirst centre' in the brain when they are dry. Similarly, certain 'osmoreceptors' feed back to the thirst centre when dehydration causes an increase in the osmotic pressure of the ECF. Severe dehydration resulting in loss of ECF volume and the consequent increase in circulating angiotensin also stimulates the thirst centre.

Fluid requirements obviously vary according to environmental conditions, the animal's physiological state and the water content of any food eaten. The dog adapts its water intake very well according to the water content of its food; the cat less quickly and completely. From a practical viewpoint, *ad libitum* access to fresh drinking water for both cats

and dogs will give them the best opportunity to meet their water requirement, particularly in warm conditions and when dry foods are fed.

DIGESTION AND ABSORPTION IN THE DOG AND CAT

The regulation of food intake has already been discussed. However, before the animal's nutritional needs can be met, there is an intermediate step to be considered. This is the breakdown of the large complex compounds in the food into a simple form which can be absorbed from the digestive tract, circulated to the tissues and used by them for maintenance, repair, growth or the provision of energy. This is the role of the digestive system.

There are three major classes of foodstuff which require digestion: carbohydrates, fats and proteins (Table 2). The purpose of digestion is to remove the linkages in the large compounds to free the small units. This is achieved by 'hydrolysis', which is the splitting of compounds by water, and it is accelerated by digestive enzymes. Enzymes are organic catalysts, produced by the body, which regulate the progress of most of the biochemical reactions in the body. Digestive enzymes have specific roles, each concerned with a particular step in the breakdown of a particular compound.

The digestive tract of the dog and cat can be thought of as a simple hollow tube, parts of which are differentiated by structure and function. Food passes down from the mouth towards the rectum, reflux being prevented by valves between each compartment. Movement of the food is assisted by muscular con-

Table 1. *Metabolic water*

Class of food	Water yield on oxidation of 100 g
Protein*	40 g
Fat	107 g
Carbohydrate	55 g

*not always completely oxidized.

Table 2. *Structure of nutrients*

Class	Common forms in food	After digestion
Carbohydrate	polysaccharides (e.g. starch) disaccharides (e.g. sucrose) monosaccharides (e.g. glucose)	monosaccharides ('simple sugars')
Proteins	protein	peptides amino acids
Fats	neutral fat	glycerol fatty acids some glycerides

tractions of the gut wall, often co-ordinated in a sequence called 'peristalsis'. This is where the wave of contraction moves down the gut, taking a bolus of food with it. Figure 5 shows a very generalized monogastric digestive system, which is applicable to both the dog and cat. The different compartments will be considered separately in the order in which they occur anatomically.

Mouth

Once the food has been caught and killed (or at least put down in a bowl within reach of the cat or dog!) the sight and smell of the food evoke the production of saliva by the salivary glands (Fig. 6). This is known as a gustatory response. Pavlov observed that saliva secretion in dogs might even be prompted by a stimulus usually associated with feeding, such as the ringing of a bell at meal times. This saliva production is reinforced when the food is taken into the mouth and taste is added to the other sensations. Saliva is a slightly acid secretion and it contains mucus which is a very effective lubricant and makes swallowing (particularly of dry foods) easier. In some animals the starch digesting enzyme salivary amylase (ptyalin) is present in saliva, but its contribution to digestion is usually negligible.

In cats, chewing allows some mechanical breakdown of the food, but many dogs bolt their food without any chewing. However, if the food is tough, both cats and dogs have the dentition associated with a carnivorous way of life, and are well equipped to tear, gnaw and chew their food.

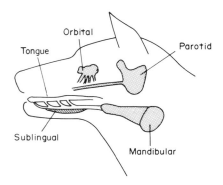

Fig. 6. The salivary glands of the dog.

Oesophagus

Swallowing transfers food from the mouth to the oesophagus, a relatively short tube which leads to the stomach. No enzymes are secreted here, but the cells of the oesophagus will add more mucus to ease movement. The presence of food stimulates peristalsis which pushes the food towards the stomach. At the base of the oesophagus, where it enters the stomach, there is a ring of specialized muscle cells, known as the cardiac sphincter.

Usually in a contracted state, this sphincter is stimulated to relax by the approach of the peristaltic wave, allowing food to pass into the stomach. However, pressure from the stomach side does not cause relaxation, so reflux is unlikely, except in the abnormal circumstances associated with vomiting.

Stomach

The stomach has many functions. It acts as a reservoir to allow food to be taken in as meals rather than continuously, it initiates the digestion of protein and it regulates the flow of material into the small intestine. Functionally, the stomach can be divided into two parts, the corpus and the antrum (Fig. 7).

The corpus has very elastic walls which can accommodate large quantities of food without any increase in pressure. The mucosa (epithelium and underlying tissue) of the corpus secretes mucus, hydrochloric acid and proteases. Proteases are protein digesting enzymes, and in the stomach they split the very

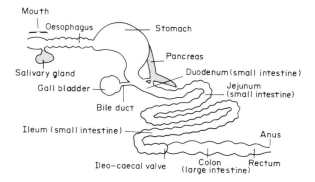

Fig. 5. Simplified monogastric digestive system.

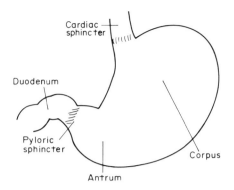

Fig. 7. Stomach of monogastric animal.

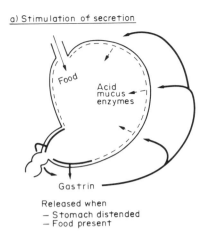

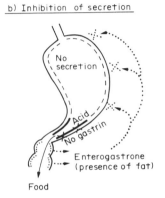

Fig. 8. Control of gastric secretion.

long protein chains into smaller polypeptides. The major enzyme, pepsin, is secreted in an inactive form, pepsinogen, to ensure that it does not digest the cells in which it is produced. Pepsinogen is converted to pepsin in the presence of hydrochloric acid, which also provides the appropriate environment for the enzymes to function at an optimum rate. The stomach is protected from pepsin by a stream of mucus which lines the walls.

The secretion of acid, mucus and enzymes depends upon the quantity and composition of the food in the stomach and is under both hormonal and nervous control (Fig. 8).

The hormone gastrin stimulates the stomach to produce acid, enzymes and also increases the motility of the stomach. It is produced in the cells of the antral mucosa and released into the blood when the stomach is distended or there is food present. Gastrin travels in the bloodstream until it returns to the stomach where it has its effect on the mucosa of the corpus. The release of gastrin is eventually self-regulating; as the acid secretion causes the pH to drop, the release of gastrin is inhibited. As the stomach empties into the small intestine, the presence of fat stimulates the release of the duodenal hormone entergastrone, which causes the stomach to cease acid production.

The nervous control of gastric secretion is rather more direct. There is a simple stretch reflex which stimulates secretion, and also a gustatory response to the sight, smell and taste of food, which evokes a secretion rich in proteases and acid, in readiness for the food to reach the stomach.

The antral mucosa, by contrast, produces a solution which is alkaline and low in enzymes. This is mixed with the food before entry into the small intestine. Mixing waves originate in the corpus and gradually increase in strength as they reach the muscular antrum where thorough mixing occurs. By this stage the stomach contents form a thick milky liquid known as chyme.

The rate at which the stomach releases chyme into the duodenum (upper part of the small intestine) is influenced by several factors, allowing the optimum conditions for digestion. The mechanisms involved are very simple. At the distal (far) end of the stomach is a tight ring of muscle called the pyloric sphincter, which like the cardiac sphincter is normally constricted. When very strong peristaltic waves approach, the sphincter relaxes and allows chyme to enter the duodenum. The presence of acids, irritants, fat or chyme in the duodenum inhibits peristaltic movement by the stomach and therefore reduces the rate of emptying.

Fluid chyme passes through the sphincter more easily, which means that the passage of well-mixed, partially digested liquid chyme is favoured, particularly when there is none present in the intestine already. This ensures that the small intestine does not receive more chyme than it can cope with efficiently, and also that the gastric enzymes have sufficient opportunity to work in an acid environment.

Small Intestine

(a) DIGESTION

More enzymes are added to the chyme in the duodenum. Some of these originate from the duodenal mucosa, others from the pancreas. The pancreas is important not only as an exocrine gland in digestion (i.e. a gland which secretes externally), but also as an endocrine gland (a gland which secretes hormones into the bloodstream) in producing insulin. It also secretes large volumes of bicarbonate salts in the gut, neutralizing the acid chyme from the stomach, and providing the optimum pH for the pancreatic and intestinal enzymes. The pancreatic enzymes include inactive proteases, lipases (fat digesting) and amylase (carbohydrate digesting). Intestinal enzymes generally catalyse the later stages of digestion.

Regulation of the pancreatic output is largely under the control of two hormones, secretin and pancreozymin (Fig. 9). They are both produced by cells of the intestinal mucosa and, under certain conditions, released into the bloodstream. Secretin is released in response to acid in the gut and stimulates the release of larger volumes of bicarbonate from the pancreas. In contrast, pancreozymin release is provoked by the presence of partially digested food and it stimulates the release of juices rich in enzymes. The complementary role of these hormones ensures the least wasteful use of the pancreas.

Bile is also added to chyme in the duodenum. Bile is a fluid which is produced continuously by the liver; in some animals (e.g. horses, rats) it trickles directly into the duodenum via the bile duct. However, in other species (e.g. man, dogs, cats) it is stored in the gall bladder, to be released into the

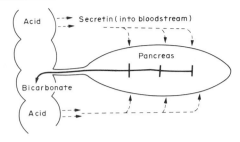

a) Through secretin

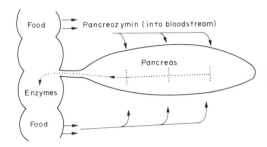

b) Through pancreozymin

Fig. 9. Regulation of pancreatic secretion.

duodenum when required. Bile contains bile salts and pigments and various waste products of the liver such as hormone and drug metabolites. Bile salts are not enzymes although they have several important roles in digestion and absorption. The most important is the emulsification of fat, bile acting upon the fat rather like a detergent, splitting it into many tiny globules with a large surface area on which the lipases can act. Some of the lipases are also activated by the presence of bile, in a similar way to the activation of proteases by acid in the stomach.

Secretin, the duodenal hormone, increases the bicarbonate content and rate of flow of bile. Another duodenal hormone, cholecystokinin, causes contraction of the gall bladder and release of the stored bile (Fig. 10).

The small intestine is so called because of its narrow bore, for although its diameter is much less than that of the 'large' intestine, it is several times as long. Digestion is completed in the small intestine, all the digestible protein, fat and carbohydrate being reduced to amino acids, dipeptides, glycerol, fatty

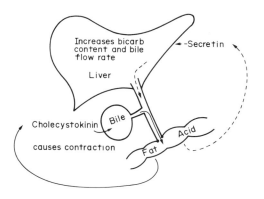

Fig. 10. Bile production and release.

acids and monosaccharides. As these are released they are absorbed, as are the minerals, vitamins and water.

(b) ABSORPTION

Absorption is the transfer of digested material from the lumen of the gut into blood or lymphatic vessels. Although some absorption occurs from the stomach and large intestine, by far the greatest proportion takes place across the mucosa of the small intestine. The surface area over which this can take place is greatly enlarged by folds and numerous small finger-like projections called villi (Fig. 11). In some dogs the surface area of the small intestine may be equivalent to the floor of a small room. Independent mixing movements of the gut wall and villi ensure that there is a good supply of materials to the epithelial surfaces, and the dense capillary network ensures

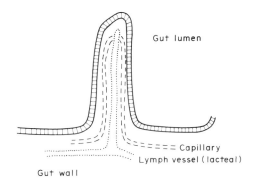

Fig. 11. Intestinal villus (simplified).

that there is no accumulation of absorbed nutrients which might hinder further absorption.

There are several different ways in which nutrients are absorbed. Absorption may be 'passive', according to the concentration or osmotic gradient, or 'active' requiring the expenditure of energy to run 'pumps' across cells or membranes. Amino acids and monosaccharides demonstrate some passive diffusion but this is very limited. Amino acids are absorbed actively by several different transport systems into the mucosal cells, then diffuse into the bloodstream. Some of the digested protein is absorbed as dipeptide (two amino acids) by active systems, the dipeptide bond being broken within the villus cell wall, and the two amino acids released singly into the bloodstream. Newborn animals are also able to absorb intact proteins (e.g. maternal antibodies in colostrum) by an enfolding action of the cell, known as pinocytosis.

The active uptake of monosaccharides is linked to a carrier complex which depends on sodium uptake. Other minerals (e.g. calcium) are also linked to the movements of monosaccharides. Sugars and amino acids are absorbed into the villus capillaries and from there converge on the portal vein which shunts the blood through the liver before returning to the heart for recirculation. The liver converts much of the absorbed glucose into glycogen (regulated by the level of circulating insulin) and stores it until a drop in blood glucose calls for the conversion of some of the stored glycogen to glucose (regulated by glucagon). The circulating level of glucose has to be maintained in order to provide a ready supply of available energy for the tissues, particularly the brain. Amino acids circulate in the blood and are absorbed by the cells as required; surplus amino acids are either converted to others as needed or broken down in the liver to urea, which is then excreted by the kidney.

The absorption of fat differs from that of protein and carbohydrates; fatty acids and glycerol are absorbed only rarely into the villus capillary, the bulk being absorbed into the villus lymphatic system. The products of fat digestion, fatty acids, glycerol and triglycerides, are insoluble in water. However, they form micelles with bile salts and lysolecithin and these can disperse freely in the fluid in the gut. Long chain fatty acids associate with bile salts to form choleic acids which are soluble in water. The bile salts and lysolecithin are not absorbed with the fat but return to the gut lumen. After absorption resynthesis occurs in the mucosal cell, triglycerides and phospholipids are formed and released into the lymphatic system, whereas glycerol and short chain fatty acids may travel in the portal system. Lymph eventually rejoins the venous circulation near the heart.

Minerals are usually absorbed in an ionized form. The means of absorption varies slightly according to the site; for example in the jejunum sodium uptake is linked to the active uptake of glucose, in the ileum it is entirely an active process, and in the large intestine it is very active (i.e. can operate against very strong concentration gradients) and entirely independent of glucose movement. The absorption of minerals depends on their levels in the body (which will influence concentration gradients) and on various hormonal factors.

Water soluble vitamins (B group) are usually absorbed passively but there may be some active absorption. Vitamin B_{12} can only be absorbed after binding to a protein known as the intrinsic factor, which is produced by the gastric mucosa.

Fat soluble vitamins (A, D, E and K) are made soluble by combination with bile salts and this aids their absorption. Where there is normal fat digestion and absorption, there should be normal fat soluble vitamin uptake.

Water is absorbed passively by diffusion down an osmotic gradient. The bulk of water is absorbed in the small intestine, with a little in the stomach and large intestine. If water uptake is impaired, dehydration may occur very quickly as all the watery secretions in the gut will be lost, in addition to water drunk and that contained in food.

The large intestine

The contents of the gut enter the large intestine through the ileo-caecal valve. Little of the food and water taken in at the mouth reaches the large intestine, that which does is mostly destined for evacuation as faeces.

The large intestine has no villi, so its surface area is limited, and although it is capable of taking up water and some electrolytes, it has none of the transport mechanisms needed for organic nutrients. Water is absorbed differently here, being drawn into the intercellular spaces by the setting up of gradients. The degree of absorption is affected by the fluid status of the body, reflected by the presence or absence of the hormones aldosterone and angiotensin. The ileum and colon (part of the large intestine) are particularly sensitive to these. There is also a slight inhibitory action of secretin, gastrin and pancreozymin on water uptake.

The bacterial colonies resident in the large intestine are able to partially digest some of the protein and fibre residue. The products of this digestion give the faeces their characteristic smell and colour. Any residues left undigested, together with water, minerals and dead bacteria, are stored in the rectum until evacuation. Defaecation is usually under voluntary control, involving the relaxation of an anal sphincter, but diarrhoea or illness may override this control.

An understanding of physiology of the digestive tract helps in the interpretation of gastro-intestinal disease. Thus poor absorption of water, either from some impairment of the mechanisms, or by too rapid a transit time, results in diarrhoea. If too much absorption occurs, the faeces become hard, difficult to evacuate and constipation results. Vomiting may be caused by toxins or poisons which irritate the stomach wall, or by disease of the pyloric sphincter. Swallowing of foreign bodies may also cause vomiting.

Persistent diarrhoea and vomiting may prove fatal because of the loss of inorganic ions and the effect of dehydration. They may be an indication of serious damage or disease in some part of the digestive tract. However, occasional nausea and loose faeces may be caused by nothing more serious than a sudden change in dietary regime, or a period of overfeeding.

CHAPTER 2

A SIMPLIFIED GUIDE TO NUTRITIONAL NEEDS

I. H. Burger

Like any other living creatures dogs and cats require food to stay alive and healthy. Food may be defined as 'any substance which is capable of nourishing the living being'. A more complete description is that food is any solid or liquid which when swallowed can supply any or all of the following:

(a) energy-giving materials from which the body can produce movement, heat or other forms of energy;

(b) materials for growth, repair or reproduction;

(c) substances necessary to initiate or regulate the processes involved in the first two categories.

The components of food which have these functions are called nutrients, and the foods or food mixtures which are actually eaten are referred to as the diet. The structure of the major nutrients has already been discussed in Chapter 1 so the discussion here will be restricted mainly to that of function and requirements. The main types of nutrients present in foods are:

Carbohydrates — these provide the body with energy and may also be converted into body fat.

Fats — these provide energy in the most concentrated form, releasing about double the amount of energy per unit weight than either carbohydrates or protein. Fats also act as vehicles for the fat-soluble vitamins and for certain types of fat usually referred to as the essential fatty acids (EFA) which as their name suggests, are required for certain important body functions and are as important as individual vitamins or minerals. The EFA will be discussed in more detail later in this chapter.

Proteins — these are important because they provide amino acids which are involved in the growth and repair of body tissue. The amino acids can also be metabolized to provide energy.

Minerals and trace elements — the 'major minerals' are substances like calcium and phosphorus which are used in growth and repair, but this category also includes substances required in smaller quantities such as iron, copper and zinc. The latter group are usually referred to as trace elements.

Vitamins — these help to regulate body processes and are usually considered as two categories, the fat soluble and water soluble groups. In the former are vitamins A, D, E and K; the latter group includes vitamins of the B complex (such as thiamin) and vitamin C. The other important constituent of food is water and although this is not generally regarded as a nutrient it is essential to life.

The need for water is second only to the need for oxygen, the other vital element not included in the list above.

Hardly any foods contain only one nutrient: most are complex mixtures which consist of a variety of carbohydrates, fats and proteins together with water. Minerals and vitamins (especially the latter) are usually present in much smaller amounts.

REQUIREMENTS AND RECOMMENDATIONS

An adequate intake of nutrients is essential for the health and activity of the animal, but how much is adequate? Compared with the requirements of the adult dog or cat, there are additional needs for the more demanding stages of the life cycle such as growth, pregnancy and lactation. In the case of the dog and cat, it is possible to investigate their needs for nutrients and to obtain more precise values than is possible for man. The minimum amount of a nutrient which is necessary each day for proper body metabolism is usually referred to as the minimum daily requirement (MDR). However, even when it has been possible to determine these values by careful, lengthy investigation, they cannot allow for the individual variation of needs which exists even between animals of the same species, breed, weight, sex and physical activity. Instead it is more common to use values of recommended daily allowance (RDA) as the guide for nutritional adequacy. These recommendations are designed to ensure that the needs of virtually all healthy dogs or cats are covered. It follows that the RDA will always be in excess of minimum daily requirement (except for energy which is discussed in the next section) and the actual nutrient requirements of animals will be less than the recommended intakes. It is possible therefore, that a diet may contribute *less* than the RDA, but still provide an adequate nutrient intake.

A more important aspect is the application of RDA (or MDR) to a given food or mixture of foods, i.e. the diet. RDA and MDR will initially be measured as the quantity of nutrient ingested by the animal each day and will generally have units of g per kg bodyweight per day. But ultimately the most useful and relevant way to express this value is as a concentration in the diet. This raises the question of the quantity of different types of foods eaten by different animals. Foods vary in their composition (from canned to dry) and animals, particularly dogs, show a wide variation in size from breed to breed. The link between these variables is the energy content of the diet.

ENERGY

Energy is different to other nutrients in that appetite normally controls intake and keeps it close to requirements. Intakes in excess of requirements are undesirable and eventually lead to obesity. The energy content of a diet is derived from carbohydrates, fats and protein, and the amount of each nutrient in a food will determine its energy content. Water has no energy value so the energy density of food varies in an inverse relation to its moisture content. Energy is usually expressed in terms of kilocalories (kcal) where 1 kcal is defined as the quantity of heat required to raise the temperature of 1 kg of water by 1 centigrade degree. A more recent convention is to express energy in terms of the joule (J) which is more difficult to define in familiar terms and is based on a mechanical or electrical equivalent of heat. For the purposes of this discussion it is necessary only to realize that 1 kcal is equivalent to about 4.2 kilojoules (kJ).

The body obtains energy by oxidizing ('burning') food but, unlike the burning process in a boiler or engine, the energy is released gradually by a series of complex chemical reactions each carefully regulated by an enzyme.

Enzymes are special proteins which control the rate of chemical reactions and more importantly, enable these complex changes to take place in the relatively mild conditions of the body. To bring about the same changes in a typical industrial process would require much more extreme conditions of temperature and pH or highly reactive ingredients. Many enzymes require the presence of vitamins or minerals to function properly and this aspect will be discussed in more detail when these nutrients are considered.

The dog and cat like all animals, are not totally efficient at extracting all the energy from food. The amount available to the body, the so-called metabolizable energy (ME), is less than that obtained by burning the food (gross energy). There will also be variations between individual animals in their own metabolic efficiency so the only way to obtain a meaningful measurement of the ME content of a food is to feed it to as large a group of dogs or cats as possible and measure (by combustion) the energy provided by the food and the energy lost in faeces and urine. The ME of the food is the difference between intake and losses. This technique although perfectly feasible, is time-consuming and costly, and is not possible unless specialized animal facilities are available. Therefore over the years a simple formula has been developed, using data from many mammals including man, which gives a reasonably good approximation of the ME in a food from its carbohydrate, fat and protein contents, allowing for the losses in absorption and efficiency. It is generally accepted that:

1 g dietary carbohydrate (calculated as monosaccharides) provides 3.75 kcal or 16 kJ;

1 g dietary fat provides 9 kcal or 37 kJ;

1 g dietary protein provides 4 kcal or 17 kJ.

This is a very rapid and useful technique for obtaining an estimate of the ME of a food or diet.

But it must be remembered that it is only an approximation and will not necessarily apply with the same accuracy to all foods or food mixtures. Recommendations for food intake based on this measurement generally take these limitations into account.

Energy is used to perform muscular work, processes such as breathing and activity to maintain body temperature. Like man, the dog and cat maintain their body temperature at around 40°C, normally well above the environmental conditions, and large amounts of energy are required to achieve this. Thus the first requirement of the animal from its diet is energy. The energy density of the diet must be high enough to enable the dog or cat to obtain sufficient calories to maintain energy balance and is the principal factor determining the quantity of food eaten each day. Therefore in the following sections nutrient requirements are usually expressed in terms of the calculated ME concentration so that the values are applicable to any type of food or diet regardless of its water content, nutrient content or overall energy value.

The National Research Council (NRC) of the National Academy of Sciences of the U.S.A. has compiled a list of the recommended dietary levels of most nutrients and frequent reference to these values will be made throughout the chapter.* The recommendations are summarized in Table 3 and are stated in terms of 400 kcal ME. At first sight this may seem a rather arbitrary figure to use but the reason is that most commercial dog and cat foods contain approximately 400 kcal per 100 g dry matter, i.e. with all the water removed. So the values used in Table 3 (and elsewhere in the text) can also be considered to approximate to a concentration per 100 g of diet dry matter.

NUTRIENTS: FUNCTIONS AND REQUIREMENTS

Carbohydrates

There is no known minimum dietary carbohydrate requirement for either the dog or cat. Based on investigations in the dog and with other species it is

*The NRC will be publishing a new edition of the *Nutrient Requirements of Dogs* in 1983.

likely that dogs and cats can be maintained without carbohydrate if the diet supplies enough fat or protein from which the metabolic requirement for glucose is derived. Nevertheless it has recently been reported that the consumption of a high fat carbohydrate-free diet by bitches during gestation substantially reduced the survival of their puppies compared with a control group receiving a diet containing 44% ME as carbohydrate. The effect was attributed to a severe hypoglycaemia in the former bitches at whelping. On this occasion the carbohydrate source was cooked starch and there is little doubt that this substance is readily digested by both dogs and cats. Individual disaccharide sugars such as sucrose (cane sugar) and lactose (milk sugar) are less well tolerated. The ability to metabolize these sugars is governed respectively by the amounts of the enzymes β-fructofuronidase (sucrase) and β-galactosidase (lactase), present in the intestine. Sucrase and lactase activity is certainly present in adult dogs and cats although it is known to be higher in kittens and declines with increasing age. If adult or young dogs and cats are suddenly given *large* amounts of sucrose or lactose (for example a large bowl of milk) they may exhibit diarrhoea which is due partly to osmotic purgation and partly due to bacterial fermentation (in the large intestine) of carbohydrate escaping digestion. Despite this small quantities of these carbohydrates (say 5% of total calories) can be well tolerated by most animals although there will obviously be variations in the efficiency of individual animals in utilizing these substances.

Some recent work with dogs has suggested that a carbohydrate-free, high fat diet confers some advantages for prolonged strenuous running in racing sledge dogs compared with diets containing up to 38% of calories as carbohydrate. These advantages included a higher oxygen carrying capacity in the form of more red blood cells and haemoglobin. However for normally active dogs and cats the inclusion of 40—50% of calories as dietary carbohydrate is unlikely to represent any disadvantage compared with a total fat/protein diet, and may actually be beneficial as indicated earlier, see Chapter 5.

Fat

Dietary fat serves as the most concentrated source

Table 3. *Recommended dietary levels of nutrients for the dog and cat*

Nutrient	Units	Dog	Cat	Notes
Protein	g	22	28	a
Fat	g	5	9	
Linoleic acid	g	1	1	b
Arachidonic acid	g	NR*	0.1	
Calcium	g	1.1	1	
Phosphorus	g	0.9	0.8	
Potassium	g	0.6	0.3	
Sodium chloride	g	1.1	0.5	
Magnesium	g	0.04	0.05	
Iron	mg	6	10	c
Copper	mg	0.73	0.5	
Manganese	mg	0.5	1	
Zinc	mg	5	3	c
Iodine	mg	0.15	0.1	
Selenium	μg	11	10	
Vitamin A	IU*	500	1000	
Vitamin D	IU*	50	100	d
Vitamin E	IU*	5	8	e
Thiamin	mg	0.1	0.5	
Riboflavin	mg	0.22	0.5	
Pantothenic acid	mg	1	1	
Niacin	mg	1.14	4.5	
Pyridoxine	mg	0.1	0.4	
Biotin	μg	10	5	f
Folic acid	μg	18	100	f
Vitamin B_{12}	μg	2.2	2	
Choline	mg	120	200	g
Taurine	mg	NR*	50	h

All values are expressed in terms of 400 kcal ME, which approximates to 100 g dry matter in commercial foods.

*Abbreviations: IU = International Units; NR = not required.

(a)   Amounts are dependent on amino acid content of the dietary protein. See also Table 4.

(b)   No requirement for fat apart from need for EFA and as carrier of fat soluble vitamins. Recommendations for linoleic and arachidonic acids are probably above actual requirements for these two nutrients.

(c)   Iron and zinc requirements can be increased by vegetable (especially soy) protein in the diet. Zinc recommendation for dogs may be close to the requirement and provide only a small margin of safety.

(d)   Probably required only for growing animals as adults can manufacture sufficient amounts in skin under the action of ultra-violet (u.v.) light. Some recent evidence suggests that cats require little if any vitamin D during growth, even in the absence of u.v. light.

(e)   Requirement is dependent on levels of selenium and polyunsaturated fats in the diet, and is increased by higher amounts of the latter.

(f)   In normal healthy animals a large proportion of the requirement for these vitamins is provided by bacterial synthesis in the intestine.

(g)   Choline requirement is largely dependent on methionine level in the diet. In cats it has been shown that increased methionine can completely substitute for choline.

(h)   Latest estimate of requirement (published 1981).

of energy in the diet and lends palatability and an acceptable texture to dog and cat foods. Like carbohydrates, fats are compounds of carbon, hydrogen and oxygen. Chemically, food fats consist mainly of mixtures of triglycerides where each triglyceride is a combination of three fatty acids joined by a unit of glycerol. The differences between one fat and another are largely the result of the different fatty acids in each. There are many different fatty acids found in foods and their chemical structures are characterized by the number of carbon atoms and double bonds. Saturated fatty acids have no double bonds whereas the unsaturated variety have one or more; those containing more than one double bond are referred to as polyunsaturated. Most fats contain all of these types but in widely varying proportions.

It is difficult to give a precise requirement for total dietary fat for dogs and cats. The only demonstrable need for fat (apart from its role as a carrier of fat soluble vitamins) is as a provider of EFA. The NRC recommended levels for fat are 5% and 9% dry matter for dogs and cats respectively. This represents approximately 11% and 20% of calories but these values are based largely on the need for a certain level of fat to provide the necessary energy density and palatability in the diet.

There are three generally recognized EFA, linoleic, α-linolenic and arachidonic acids, all of which are polyunsaturated. Because of the complex nature of these compounds it is usual to designate their structure by the number of carbon atoms and double bonds they contain; thus linoleic acid which contains 18 carbon atoms and two double bonds is written 18:2. The EFA cannot be synthesized by the body and are therefore essential nutrients which must be supplied in the diet. Linoleic and α-linolenic acids are the parent compounds from which the more complex, longer chain compounds (derived EFA) can be synthesized by the body. EFA are important for the general health of the animal and are involved in many processes including skin and kidney function and reproduction. It is in the formation of the EFA that an important difference between dog and cat nutrition is evident, a contrast between the two animals which is repeated for other nutrients and in which the cat is atypical, in that the dog follows the pattern for most other mammals but the cat does not. It has recently been reported that cats have only a limited ability to convert the parent EFA into the longer chain derivatives; the lion also appears to lack this ability. As a result, the Felidae may require a dietary source of preformed 20:3 or 20:4 acids which in practical terms means a certain need for EFA of *animal* origin. At the present time it is difficult to give a precise figure for the cat's requirement for derived EFA, and it is possible that the cat also requires linoleic acid in its diet. Current NRC recommendations for linoleic and arachidonic acids for the cat are 1% and 0.1% dry matter (approximately 2.3% and 0.23% of calories) respectively but these allowances are probably fairly generous. The recommendation for the dog is 1% linoleic acid and this too is probably more than the animal really needs. EFA requirements in the cat are the subject of current enquiry and it is possible that the recommended dietary levels for parent and derived EFA will be more closely defined in the near future.

Protein and amino acids

All proteins are compounds of carbon, hydrogen and oxygen but unlike carbohydrates and fats they always contain nitrogen. Most proteins also contain sulphur. Proteins are very large molecules which consist of chains of hundreds (or perhaps thousands) of much smaller sub-units called amino acids. Although there are only about 20 amino acids used in the composition of proteins, the variety of sequences in which they can be arranged is almost infinite and this results in the wide variety of proteins which occur in nature. Cats and dogs need dietary protein to provide the specific amino acids that their tissues cannot synthesize at a rate sufficient for optimum performance. These amino acids are then reformed into new proteins which are essential constituents of all living cells where they regulate metabolic processes (in the form of enzymes), provide structure and are therefore required for tissue growth and repair.

Amino acids can be conveniently divided into two classes: essential (indispensable) and non-essential (dispensable). As their name suggests, the essential amino acids cannot be made by the body in sufficient amounts and must therefore be present in the food. The non-essential amino acids can be made from excesses of certain other dietary amino acids, although, as components of body proteins, they are as important as the essential varieties. The following amino acids have been established as essential for maintenance of the adult dog (quantitative requirements are listed in Table 4):

Threonine	Phenylalanine
Valine	Histidine
Methionine	Tryptophan
Isoleucine	Lysine
Leucine	

The requirements for the adult cat have yet to be determined but it is unlikely that it will be any different to the dog with regard to the amino acids listed. Where the adult cat is different to the dog (and also the rat and man) is that it requires a dietary source of the amino acid arginine. Arginine deficiency in the cat rapidly results in severe adverse effects because of an inability to metabolize nitrogen compounds (via the urea cycle), which then accumulate in the blood stream as ammonia (hyperammonaemia) and in serious cases, can lead to death within several hours. It seems that there is no other essential dietary component (including water) whose deficiency has

such a drastic effect upon the animal. The rapidity of the effects is second only to a lack of oxygen. This unique requirement appears to be due to an inability to synthesize the amino acid ornithine (also a component of the urea cycle) since the latter protects cats against the adverse effects of arginine deficiency.

Essential amino acid requirements for the growth of puppies and kittens have been the subject of much study in the U.S.A. over the last few years. The most recent estimates of these requirements are summarized in Table 4. As indicated the needs for methionine and phenylalanine can be partially met (up to 50%) by cystine and tyrosine respectively. However in addition to a need for individual amino acids every animal has a requirement for total protein to supply sufficient dietary nitrogen for the body pool. Clearly the value obtained for this requirement is dependent on the essential amino acid content of the protein or proteins in question. A protein which contained all the amino acids in the exact amounts required by the dog or cat could obviously be used at a much lower level in the diet than one containing a low concentration of one or more essential amino acids. This is one of the ways

Table 4. *Recommended amino acid levels for dogs and cats*

Amino acid	DOG		CAT
	Adult	Growing	Growing
Threonine	264	600	680
Valine	325	450	510
Cystine[a]	88	350	380
Methionine	180	450	380
Cystine + methionine[a]	268	800	760
Isoleucine	302	800	510
Leucine	544	600	1020
Tyrosine[a]	211		425
Phenylalanine	304		425
Tyrosine + phenylalanine[a]	515	1000	850
Histidine	132	130	255
Tryptophan	79	150	125
Lysine	368	650	680
Arginine	NR[b]	1000	900

All values are expressed as mg per 400 kcal ME, which approximates to mg/100 g dietary dry matter in commercial foods.

[a] The values shown for cystine and tyrosine reflect the extent to which these amino acids can substitute for the total requirement for methionine and phenylalanine respectively.

[b] NR = not required. Arginine is, however, required by the adult cat.

in which proteins differ in their nutritional quality. Animal proteins generally have a more balanced amino acid profile than plant proteins which are often low in one or two essential amino acids.

Nevertheless if all the essential amino acids are being provided there is still a need for additional nitrogen and this has also been the subject of recent investigations in the U.K. and U.S.A. For example it has recently been reported that if all essential amino acid requirements are met, *total* protein requirements for the growing kitten can be provided by about 16% protein calories. However these figures were obtained using a synthetic diet based on individual amino acids which cannot be considered typical of food proteins. The NRC recommendation for dietary protein for the cat is 28% of calories for all stages of the life cycle, i.e. including the most nutritionally demanding events of growth and pregnancy and lactation. The contrast between this recommendation and the value obtained from the synthetic diet illustrates the care which must be exercised in extrapolating results obtained in the laboratory to the domestic situation. The nutritional attributes of protein must be considered in terms of essential amino acids and the supply of these in practical diets will almost invariably be as pre-formed protein. The amino acid profile may vary considerably from one diet to another and this must be taken into account when recommendations are made. It is a good example of the difference between a precise requirement determined under carefully defined experimental conditions and a recommendation which must apply to a very large number of animals eating a wide range of foods. The cat is a particularly appropriate animal to use to explain this aspect of nutrition because it has traditionally been regarded as having a very high protein requirement, much higher than other animals. Yet a series of feeding trials (using a semi-synthetic diet) has recently been carried out which suggests that only about 10% protein calories are required to maintain an adult cat in protein balance when the essential amino acid profile has been adjusted to provide known adequate amounts using kitten growth values. Could this level of protein provide enough essential amino acids using a *conventional* protein source?

Whole egg is generally regarded as the most nutritionally balanced, highest quality protein. The essential amino acid profile of a diet containing whole egg at a level of 10% protein calories is given in Table 5. Comparing this with values for kitten growth in Table 4 it is doubtful whether this diet would supply adequate quantities of all amino acids even allowing for the fact that the figures in Table 5 are for an adult maintenance diet.

Despite these qualifications, experiments to determine the precise protein and amino acid requirements of the dog and cat are important steps in refining the formulation of diets for these animals at a time when protein is an expensive raw material and one which should be used as efficiently as possible.

Taurine

No discussion of the amino acid requirements of the dog and cat would be complete without at least a brief explanation of the importance of taurine. Strictly speaking taurine is not an amino acid but an amino-sulphonic acid which is *not* part of the polypeptide chain of a protein. Taurine is an end product of sulphur amino acid metabolism and is normally produced from the sulphur-containing amino acids methionine and cystine. It is involved in several functions but the one of greatest interest is in the structure and functioning of the retina. A deficiency eventually results in retinal degeneration and an impairment in the visual response, although the changes can take a

Table 5. *Essential amino acid composition of diet containing 10% protein calories based on whole egg protein*

Amino acid	Concentration in diet (mg per 400 kcal ME)
Threonine	512
Valine	752
Cystine	176
Methionine	320
Cystine + methionine	496
Isoleucine	560
Leucine	832
Tyrosine	400
Phenylalanine	512
Tyrosine + phenylalanine	912
Histidine	240
Tryptophan	176
Lysine	624
Arginine	608

long time to occur and obvious clinical signs of a visual defect may not be obvious until a year or more on a taurine-deficient diet. Unlike most other mammals, cats cannot synthesize enough taurine from the sulphur amino acids. The enzyme responsible for the conversion is not totally absent in the cat but its activity is not high enough to supply all of the cat's needs.

The special sensitivity of the cat is heightened by its total dependence on taurine for the formation of bile salts; unlike other species it cannot also use glycine for this purpose (see Chapter 1). This is yet another example of an important nutritional difference between the dog and cat. Research on the precise dietary taurine needs of the cat is still proceeding but the latest estimate puts the minimum requirement at about 0.05% of dry matter, i.e. about 50 mg per 400 kcal. The richest sources of taurine are animal-derived raw materials; little is found in plant tissues.

Minerals and trace elements

The recommended dietary concentrations of these are shown in Table 3. These values incorporate minimum requirements for the dog and cat (where data have been assembled) and findings with other animals.

Minerals

CALCIUM AND PHOSPHORUS

Calcium and phosphorus are closely inter-related nutritionally and will therefore be discussed together. They are the major minerals involved in giving bones and teeth structural rigidity. Calcium is also involved in blood clotting and in the transmission of nerve impulses. The level of calcium in the blood plasma is crucial to these functions and is very carefully regulated. Phosphorus also has many other functions (more than any other mineral element), and a complete discussion of phosphorus metabolism would require coverage of nearly all the metabolic processes in the body. Phosphorus is a component of many enzyme systems and is also involved in the storage and transfer of energy in so-called 'high energy' organic phosphate compounds.

Of perhaps the greatest importance in the requirement for calcium and phosphorus is their ratio in the diet. The optimum calcium to phosphorus ratios for dogs and cats lie between 1.2 to 1.4 : 1 and 0.9 to 1.1 : 1 respectively. Imbalance in this ratio, where calcium is much less than phosphorus, leads to a marked deficiency of calcium in relation to bone formation. There is also evidence that a very high ratio is harmful although this is less serious than a calcium deficiency. The metabolism of calcium and phosphorus is closely linked with vitamin D and this will be discussed later in the chapter.

POTASSIUM

Potassium is found in high concentrations *within* cells and is required for nerve transmission, fluid balance and muscle metabolism. A deficiency causes muscular weakness, poor growth and lesions of the heart and kidney. However potassium is widely distributed in foods and naturally occurring deficiencies are extremely rare.

SODIUM AND CHLORIDE

In contrast to potassium, sodium occurs mainly in the extracellular fluids, but like potassium, it is important for normal physiological function and these three substances represent the major electrolytes of the body water. Common salt (sodium chloride) is the most usual form of these two minerals added to food, so the dietary recommendation is normally expressed in terms of sodium chloride. As with potassium, it is most unlikely that normal diets will be deficient in these two minerals.

MAGNESIUM

Magnesium is found in the soft tissues of the body as well as bone. Heart and skeletal muscle and nervous tissue depend on a proper balance between calcium and magnesium for normal function. Magnesium is also important in sodium and potassium metabolism and plays a key role in many essential enzyme reactions, particularly those concerned with energy metabolism. A deficiency of magnesium is characterized by muscular weakness and in severe cases convulsions. Nevertheless a dietary deficiency of magnesium is very unlikely.

In contrast very high intakes of magnesium by cats are associated with an increased incidence of the so-called feline urological syndrome (FUS). FUS is characterized by dysuria, haematuria, cystitis and urinary tract obstructions by solids precipitated out of the urine. The most common crystalline component of feline uroliths is magnesium ammonium phosphate hexahydrate (struvite), and there is much evidence that high concentrations of dietary magnesium (ten times, or more, the recommended level) increase the frequency of FUS. However it must be remembered that this disease is associated with many risk factors of which high dietary magnesium is only one. An adverse dietary calcium to phosphorus ratio (either much greater or less than one) has also been reported to increase the incidence of FUS. It is possible that increasing the level of salt (sodium chloride) in the diet (up to 4% dry matter, 4 g per 400 kcal) alleviates some of the symptoms of FUS by increasing water intake, thereby increasing urinary volume and decreasing the urinary magnesium concentration. It is also possible that salt inhibits the formation of struvite in the urinary tract as a result of the increased quantity of chloride ions in the urine. It is worth noting that these opposing effects of magnesium and salt in relation to urolithiasis have also been reported in other animals, sheep, calves and goats for example, although in dogs urolithiasis is normally associated with urinary tract infection rather than diet.

Trace elements

IRON

Iron is probably the best known trace element and much research has been carried out on its functions and requirements, particularly in the dog. Iron is a component of haemoglobin and myoglobin which play an essential role in oxygen transport; it is also an essential part of many enzymes (haem enzymes) which

are involved in respiration at the cellular level, i.e. the oxidation of nutrients to form chemical energy.

The absorption of iron is known to be influenced by a number of factors. Ferrous iron is better absorbed than ferric iron, and iron contained in foods of animal origin tends to be better absorbed than that from vegetable sources. Some recent evidence from studies in man suggests that the inclusion of soy protein in a diet reduces the absorption of iron and other trace elements (zinc and manganese) and it may be important to ensure that the concentration of iron in products containing high levels of soy protein is always above the recommended allowance.

A deficiency of iron results in anaemia with the typical clinical picture of weakness and fatigue. Conversely iron, like most trace elements, is toxic if ingested in excessive amounts. Iron toxicity in dogs has been extensively studied, and is associated with anorexia and weight loss. Of the iron salts investigated ferrous sulphate was the most toxic, presumably because its absorption is high; iron oxide was less dangerous.

COPPER

Copper is involved in a broad range of biological functions and is a constituent of many enzyme systems including one which is necessary for the formation of the pigment melanin.

Copper is very closely linked with iron metabolism and its deficiency impairs the absorption and transport of iron and decreases haemoglobin synthesis. Thus a lack of copper in the diet can cause anaemia even when the intake of iron is normal. Bone disorders can also occur as a result of copper deficiency and in this case the cause is thought to be a reduction in the activity of a copper-containing enzyme leading to diminished stability and strength of bone collagen.

Ironically *excess* dietary copper may also cause anaemia which is thought to result from competition between copper and iron for absorption sites in the intestine. Bedlington terriers are known to display an unusual defect which results in toxic excesses of copper in the liver. The disorder results in hepatitis and cirrhosis and appears to be inherited. For this particular breed of dog it is probably a good idea to exclude foods with high copper contents and to avoid the use of copper-containing mineral supplements.

MANGANESE

Although little is known about the specific manganese requirements of dogs or cats, a considerable amount of evidence has accumulated that this trace element is essential in animal nutrition and there is no reason to suppose that the dog and cat are any different in this respect.

Manganese is known to activate many metal—enzyme systems in the body and is therefore involved in a wide variety of reactions. A deficiency of manganese is characterized by defective growth and disturbances in lipid metabolism. These effects, like those of copper deficiency, are probably caused by inactivation or malfunction of one or more of the enzyme-catalysed reactions associated with these physiological processes.

Although manganese is reported to be one of the least toxic of the trace elements, toxicity has been reported in several species, including cats, where it caused poor fertility and partial albinism in some Siamese. One of the other effects of excess manganese is on haemoglobin formation where its action is thought to be similar to that previously described for copper, i.e. competition with iron at the absorption sites in the alimentary tract.

ZINC

On the basis of current biochemical knowledge, the functions of zinc can be divided into two broad categories: enzyme function and protein synthesis. Zinc is known to be required by dogs and cats and recent research in the cat suggests that a vegetable protein-based diet may dramatically increase the zinc requirement — up to about 10 mg per 400 kcal. Perhaps this effect is related to that reported for iron absorption in man. Zinc is also known to be antagonized by dietary calcium although the mechanism for this is not clear. A zinc deficiency was reported in dogs receiving a diet containing 3.3 mg of zinc per 100 g and 1.1% calcium (on dry matter). In view of this and other factors influencing zinc absorption the NRC recommended values given in Table 1 may be close to the actual *requirement* and higher concentrations might be advisable to provide a greater margin of safety.

Zinc deficiency is characterized by poor growth, anorexia, testicular atrophy, emaciation and skin lesions. At high intakes zinc is relatively non-toxic. It interferes with the absorption and utilization of iron and copper (especially the latter) so the severity of effects is dependent on the levels of these two elements in the diet. Nevertheless with normal dietary levels of iron and copper it appears that concentrations of zinc up to at least 30 mg per 400 kcal will produce no adverse effects.

IODINE

The only recognized function of iodine is in the synthesis of the thyroid hormones which are released by the thyroid gland and regulate the metabolic rate of the animal. One of the factors which influences the output of the thyroid hormones is the availability of sufficient iodine, and in the absence of the requisite amount the thyroid gland increases its activity in an attempt to compensate for the iodine deficiency. As a result the gland (which is located at the neck region of the animal) enlarges and becomes turgid, a condition known as goitre which is the principal sign of iodine deficiency. Nevertheless there are other factors which are important in the occurrence of goitre. These include infectious agents, naturally occurring substances in the diet (goitrogens) which inhibit the synthesis, release or general effectiveness of the thyroid hormones, and genetically determined defects in the enzyme systems responsible for the biosynthesis of these hormones.

Severe reduction in thyroid activity (hypothyroidism) is usually referred to as cretinism when it occurs in young animals, and myxoedema in the adult. Both have been reported in dogs and iodine deficiency has also been observed in zoo felids and domestic cats. Clinical signs include skin and hair abnormalities, dullness, apathy and drowsiness. There can also be abnormal calcium metabolism and reproductive failure with foetal resorption. Excessive iodine intakes can be toxic. Hypothyroid cats given high doses of iodine (about 50 times the recommended allowance) were reported to show adverse effects which included anorexia, fever and weight loss. In other animals very large doses of iodine have been reported to produce acute effects similar to those of a *deficiency*. The high doses in some way impair thyroid hormone synthesis and can produce so-called iodine myxoedema or goitre.

SELENIUM

Ironically attention was first focused on selenium because of its toxicity. The discovery that it is an essential nutrient for mammals took place fairly recently, about 25 years ago. Any discussion of the biochemical role of selenium has to take into account the close interrelationship of this element with vitamin E and the sulphur-containing amino acids methionine and cystine. The link with vitamin E is particularly important since one nutrient can 'spare' a deficiency of the other. Nevertheless it has been demonstrated in many animals, including the dog, that selenium cannot be replaced completely by vitamin E and has a discrete unique function. Selenium is known to be an obligatory component of an enzyme called glutathione peroxidase which is thought to protect cell membranes against damage by oxidizing substances (notably lipid peroxides) which can be released by various metabolic processes in the body. Sulphur amino acids are required to form the enzyme; vitamin E is thought to act within the membranes preventing oxidation of the lipids. In this way the functions of these three nutrients are closely linked.

The interactions of selenium are obviously highly complex and much is still unknown about this substance. It may for example be involved in processes unrelated to its role as a component of glutathione peroxidase. It has been reported to protect against lead, cadmium and mercury poisoning and has even been implicated as an anti-cancer agent in both experimental and epidemiological studies.

Selenium deficiency has many effects but one described in dogs is degeneration of skeletal and cardiac muscle. Effects of deficiency in other species include reproductive disorders and oedema.

As mentioned earlier, selenium is highly toxic in large doses and the available evidence suggests that the difference between the recommended allowance and the toxic dose may be quite small. Injudicious supplementation of foods is therefore particularly dangerous.

COBALT

Cobalt is a component of vitamin B_{12} and this may be its only biological function in the dog and cat. Under laboratory conditions cobalt can replace zinc in a few zinc-containing enzyme systems but whether this is of biological importance is not known. In ruminants vitamin B_{12} can be synthesized by gut bacteria in the presence of cobalt in the upper intestine from which the vitamin is then absorbed. In non-ruminants like the dog and cat this synthesis may be of only limited use because it occurs mainly in the lower part of the intestine where absorption is minimal. It is likely that to be of significant nutritional value cobalt must be ingested by the dog and cat principally as vitamin B_{12}. With an adequate supply of the vitamin it is very doubtful whether any additional cobalt is required. Vitamin B_{12} will be discussed later in the chapter.

OTHER TRACE ELEMENTS

A number of other trace elements have been demonstrated as necessary for normal health in mammals, although specific requirements have not been established for the dog and cat. These elements are listed in Table 6 with a brief summary of their functions. From work with other animals it appears that the amounts required in the diet are very low, usually well under 1 mg per 400 kcal, although silicon may be needed at a concentration of around 5 mg per 400 kcal.

The likelihood of a deficiency of any of these nutrients in a normal diet is almost non-existent. Conversely, as with the majority of the trace elements these substances are all toxic if fed in large quantities, although the amounts which can be tolerated vary. Arsenic, vanadium, fluorine and molybdenum are the most toxic, whereas relatively large amounts of nickel and chromium can be ingested without adverse effects.

Table 6. *Summary of functions of some trace elements*

Element	Involvement
Chromium	Carbohydrate metabolism, closely linked with insulin function.
Fluoride	Teeth and bone development. Possibly some involvement in reproduction.
Nickel	Membrane function; possibly involved in metabolism of the nucleic acid RNA.
Molybdenum	Constituent of several enzymes one of which is involved in uric acid metabolism.
Silicon	Skeletal development, growth and maintenance of connective tissue.
Vanadium	Growth, reproduction, fat metabolism.
Arsenic	Growth; also some effect on blood formation, possibly haemoglobin production.

Vitamins

Recommended dietary levels for vitamins are shown in Table 3 and these incorporate results obtained from species other than the dog and cat.

The vitamins may be conveniently divided into two sub-groups: fat soluble and water soluble. Apart from the obvious chemical difference the degree of storage in the body also differs, fat soluble vitamins being stored to a greater extent than the water soluble type. A regular daily supply is therefore less critical in the case of the fat soluble vitamins.

Fat soluble vitamins

VITAMIN A

The term vitamin A is now used to describe several biologically-active compounds but retinol is the substance of primary importance in mammalian physiology. In nature vitamin A is found to a large extent in the form of its precursors, the carotenoids, which are the yellow and orange pigments of most fruits and vegetables. Of these, β-carotene is the most important 'provitamin A' because it has the highest activity on a quantitative basis, consisting essentially of two vitamin A-type molecules linked together, which most animals can convert to two molecules of the active vitamin.

Here we find yet another important difference between the dog and cat, as it has been shown that the cat is unable to convert β-carotene to vitamin A whereas the dog can effectively use carotene for this purpose. Cats therefore require a pre-formed dietary source of vitamin A of which the most common forms are derivatives of retinol, (retinyl acetate and retinyl palmitate). The practical consequence of this peculiarity is that the cat must have at least some animal-derived raw material in its diet since *preformed* vitamin A compounds are not present in plants.

The best known function of vitamin A is in vision. It is found in the retina combined with a specific protein called opsin. The compound is called rhodopsin (visual purple) and on exposure to light is split into opsin and a metabolite of retinol. It is the energy exchange in this process which produces nervous transmissions which are sent via the optic nerve to the brain and which result in visual sensations. Although the splitting of rhodopsin is reversible, a fresh supply of vitamin A is required to reform the visual pigment completely and so allow the process to continue. Vitamin A is involved in many other physiological functions one of the most important being the regulation of cell membranes; this vitamin is essential for the integrity of the epithelial tissues and the normal growth of epithelial cells. Vitamin A is also involved in the growth of bones and teeth.

As might be expected a deficiency of vitamin A has many far-reaching effects on the body and has been observed in many animals, including cats and dogs. The symptoms include xerophthalmia (excessive dryness of the eye), ataxia, conjunctivitis, opacity and ulceration of the cornea, skin lesions and disorders of the epithelial layers, e.g. the bronchial epithelium, respiratory tract, salivary glands and seminiferous tubules.

An *excess* of vitamin A is as harmful as a deficiency. A crippling bone disease with tenderness of the extremities associated with gingivitis and tooth loss has been described in cats given prolonged excessive doses of this vitamin either as vitamin A itself or by feeding large quantities of raw liver. Similar effects have been seen in dogs given large doses of vitamin A. Thus inclusion in the diet of foods containing large quantities of this vitamin, e.g. liver and the fish liver oils, must be very carefully controlled. Supplementation of an already adequate diet is not only unnecessary but potentially dangerous and should be avoided.

VITAMIN D

There are several compounds which have vitamin D activity but the two most important are called ergocalciferol (vitamin D_2) and cholecalciferol (vitamin D_3). Both of these forms are effective in dogs and cats as sources of vitamin D activity. There has been a large amount of research conducted recently on the metabolism of vitamin D in other mammals and it is now known that this vitamin undergoes a series of biochemical conversions in the kidney and liver before it becomes physiologically active. It is a dihydroxy derivative of the parent compounds that is the most potent metabolite. Vitamin D is often called the 'bone vitamin' and its most clearly established function is to raise the plasma calcium and phosphorus levels to those required for the normal mineralization of bone. In the small intestine vitamin D stimulates the absorption of calcium and phosphorus and is also involved in the mobilization of calcium from bone to maintain a normal plasma calcium concentration. In fact the biochemical synthesis of the active metabolite is triggered by a fall in plasma calcium.

It is clear that the requirements for vitamin D are closely linked to the dietary concentrations of calcium and phosphorus and to the calcium/phosphorus ratio.

As vitamin D is involved in the absorption of calcium it is most crucial during the growth and development of bone, i.e. in the young growing animal. A deficiency of this vitamin causes rickets. However there is evidence that dogs and cats, in common with other mammals, can form vitamin D_3 from lipid compounds in the skin in the presence of the ultra-violet component of sunlight and it is likely that adult animals need little if any *dietary* supply of this vitamin. Furthermore some recent work suggests that cats are almost totally independent of a dietary source of vitamin D, even during growth and shielded from ultra-violet light, assuming they are fed a diet with adequate concentrations and a correct ratio of calcium and phosphorus. This appears to be because the cat mobilizes stores of vitamin D_3 which it acquires during suckling.

As with vitamin A, excessive amounts of vitamin D cause adverse effects in dogs and cats, notably extensive calcification of the soft tissues, lungs, kidneys and stomach. Deformations of the teeth and jaws can also occur and death can result if the intake of the vitamin is particularly high. Supplementation of vitamin D is therefore potentially hazardous, and for the cat the requirement may be so low that any reasonable diet is bound to supply more than enough of this nutrient.

VITAMIN E

The function which was first ascribed to this vitamin was that of preventing foetal resorption in animals that had been fed a diet containing rancid lard. The chemical name for this vitamin (α-tocopherol) is derived from the Greek word 'to bring forth offspring'. However in recent years research on vitamin E has revealed much more of its role in the body although the complete details of its function remain obscure.

It acts as an anti-oxidant and is important in maintaining the stability of cell membranes; in this its function is closely linked to that of the trace element selenium which was discussed earlier. The requirement for vitamin E also depends on the level of polyunsaturated fatty acids (PUFA) in the diet. Increasing PUFA increases the vitamin E requirement and this effect has been shown in many animals including the dog and cat. It is difficult therefore to be precise about recommendations for dietary vitamin E; the levels stated in Table 1 are based on the recommended levels for selenium and PUFA. Rancid fats should be avoided because they are particularly destructive to this vitamin.

Deficiency of vitamin E under experimental conditions presents a more bewildering range of physical abnormalities than is encountered with any other vitamin. These effects may be divided into four main areas: the muscle, reproductive, nervous and vascular systems. In dogs, a deficiency has been associated with one or more of these effects including skeletal muscle dystrophy, degeneration of the germinal epithelium of the testes, and failure of gestation. In cats, inflammatory changes in body fat (steatitis — 'yellow fat disease') occurs when low levels of vitamin E are fed in the presence of PUFA. In fact so wide is the range of the vitamin E deficiency syndrome that some workers contend that a nutrient as (apparently) vital as this must have other function(s) unrelated to its anti-oxidant effect. It remains to be seen whether further research proves this correct.

There is only very limited information on the effects of high vitamin E intakes in the dog and cat. No deleterious effects were reported when about ten times the recommended level was fed to weaned Beagle puppies for 15 weeks. However in other species some adverse reactions on thyroid activity and blood clotting have been noted with high vitamin E intakes. Therefore high levels of this nutrient must be considered potentially harmful although it is far from being as dangerous as vitamins A and D in excess.

VITAMIN K

Vitamin K describes a group of compounds, the quinone derivatives, which regulate the formation of several factors involved in the blood clotting mechanism. A requirement for vitamin K has been demonstrated in the dog and it is unlikely that the cat is any different in this respect. Nevertheless the requirement in dogs was demonstrated under experimental conditions where the animals were made vitamin K deficient by the use of anti-coagulant drugs (such as the coumarin compounds) which antagonize the action of this nutrient. In normal healthy animals a vitamin K deficiency is very rare because dogs and cats, like other mammals, obtain most if not all of their daily requirement from bacterial synthesis in the intestine. It is only under abnormal conditions such as depression of bacterial synthesis (for example by drug treatment) or interference with the absorption or utilization of vitamin K that a dietary supply will be necessary. A diet containing only 60 μg/kg dry matter (about 66 μg per 400 kcal) was fed to adult male Beagles and cats for 40 weeks with no signs of deficiency although the

same diet resulted in haemorrhages when fed to rats. A concentration of 0.1 mg per 400 kcal has been suggested as a recommended dietary level, although in view of the bacterial synthesis of this substance, this must represent a very large margin of safety.

Very large intakes of vitamin K may produce anaemia and other blood abnormalities in young animals but it does not appear to be particularly toxic.

Water soluble vitamins

The water soluble vitamins of importance in dog and cat nutrition are all members of the B complex and nearly all are involved with the utilization of foods and the production or interconversion of energy in the body.

In these processes the B vitamins are used by the animal to form coenzymes (sometimes also called cofactors). These are relatively small organic molecules, associated with larger enzyme molecules, which are necessary for the enzymes to catalyse biochemical reactions effectively. The coenzymes often act by combining with and then releasing molecules or fragments of molecules, rather like a biochemical 'relay station'. Sometimes minerals and trace elements are also involved in these reactions as has been discussed earlier in the text.

The B vitamins are now usually known by their chemical names, rather than by a letter/number combination, but this alternative nomenclature will be mentioned for vitamins where it is still in common use.

THIAMIN (*ANEURIN, VITAMIN B$_1$*)

Thiamin is a sulphur-containing compound which participates as a coenzyme in the form of its pyrophosphate (TPP), sometimes referred to as cocarboxylase. TPP is involved in several key conversions in carbohydrate metabolism and the thiamin requirement is dependent on the carbohydrate content of the diet. A high fat, low carbohydrate diet will spare the need for thiamin as less of this vitamin is required for fat metabolism than in carbohydrate utilization.

Thiamin deficiency has been described in dogs and cats. Its primary result is a 'biochemical lesion' with impaired carbohydrate metabolism with abnormal accumulation of the intermediate compounds of the metabolic pathway. The deficiency expresses itself clinically by anorexia, neurological disorders (especially of the postural mechanisms) followed ultimately by weakness, heart failure and death. In man thiamin deficiency is known as beri-beri. Thiamin is a particularly important vitamin from the aspect of dietary formulation because it is progressively destroyed by cooking and may also be inactivated by naturally occurring substances called thiaminases which are found in a number of foods, particularly raw fish.

Thiaminases are themselves inactivated by heat so the maintenance of an adequate thiamin intake must take all of these various factors into consideration. For commercially-prepared foods the normal practice is to supplement with a large enough quantity before processing so that even if particularly serious losses occur the amount remaining in the finished product will still meet or exceed the dietary recommendations.

Like the other water soluble vitamins thiamin is of low toxicity. Although intravenous *injection* of thiamin in dogs produces death due to depression of the respiratory centre the *oral* intake needed to cause the same effect is some 40 times the intravenous dose and represents a level many thousands of times the recommended dietary concentration.

RIBOFLAVIN (*VITAMIN B$_2$*)

Riboflavin is a yellow crystalline compound which shows a characteristic yellow-green fluorescence when dissolved in water. Riboflavin is a constituent of two coenzymes, riboflavin 5-phosphate and a more complex chemical called flavin adenine dinucleotide. These coenzymes are essential in a number of oxidative enzyme systems. Cellular growth cannot occur in the absence of riboflavin.

Riboflavin requirements have been investigated in dogs and cats and a deficiency is associated with eye lesions, skin disorders and testicular hypoplasia. There is some evidence that part of the requirement for riboflavin can be met by bacterial synthesis in the intestine and that this is favoured by a high-carbohydrate, low-fat diet. However the daily needs for the vitamin are certainly greater than any possible

contribution by this route so a regular dietary intake is necessary.

PANTOTHENIC ACID

This substance is a constituent of coenzyme A which is an essential component of enzyme reactions in carbohydrate, fat and amino acid metabolism. A need for pantothenic acid has been demonstrated in dogs and cats. There are many deficiency signs, including depression or failure of growth, development of fatty liver and gastrointestinal disturbances including ulcers. In dogs, but not cats, alopecia has also been observed. These deficiency signs were produced using semi-purified diets. Under normal circumstances, using a mixture of foods, a deficiency of pantothenic acid is extremely unlikely as it is very widespread in animal and plant tissues, as implied by its name which means 'derived from everywhere'.

NIACIN (*NICOTINIC ACID*)

Niacin is rapidly converted in the body to the physiologically active derivative nicotinamide (niacinamide). Nicotinamide is a component of two very important coenzymes, the nicotinamide adenine dinucleotides, which are required for oxidation—reduction reactions necessary for the utilization of all the major nutrients. In mammalian species including the dog the requirement for niacin is influenced by the dietary level of the amino acid tryptophan which can be converted to the vitamin. In cats this conversion does not occur but, unlike the other differences between the dog and cat, this is not due to lack of an enzyme. It occurs because the reaction sequence for the breakdown of tryptophan can go one of two ways and in the cat the enzyme responsible for the alternative 'non-niacin' pathway has a very high activity and effectively abstracts the tryptophan metabolites from niacin synthesis. This alternative pathway eventually breaks down the metabolites to supply energy, similar to the utilization of carbohydrates.

Niacin deficiency has been described in dogs and cats and is accompanied by inflammation and ulceration of the oral cavity with thick, blood-stained saliva drooling from the mouth, and foul breath. The deficiency syndrome is referred to as blacktongue in the dog and pellagra in man. Niacin is sometimes referred to as the pellagra-preventing vitamin or PP factor.

Large doses of niacin (but not nicotinamide) produce a flushing reaction in many animals including dogs. Thus if large therapeutic quantities of this vitamin need to be administered it is preferable to use the amide form. Nevertheless, neither of the two forms of this vitamin could be described as highly toxic.

PYRIDOXINE (*VITAMIN B₆*)

There exist three related compounds under this heading with essentially equally effective activity: pyridoxine, pyridoxal and pyridoxamine. All three occur naturally and are interconvertible during normal metabolic processes. The biologically active compound is pyridoxal and the coenzyme form is pyridoxal 5-phosphate, which is involved in a large number and variety of enzyme systems almost entirely associated with nitrogen and amino acid metabolism. In fact pyridoxal is considered essential for practically all enzymic interconversions and non-oxidative degradations of amino acids. Some of these reactions have already been discussed in relation to other nutrients; for example, the synthesis of niacin from tryptophan involves this vitamin. As might be expected, a high protein diet exacerbates vitamin B_6 deficiency, an effect which is comparable to the effect of high carbohydrate diets on thiamin deficiency.

Pyridoxine has been shown to be required by dogs and cats; a deficiency results in weight loss and a type of anaemia. In cats irreversible kidney damage can also occur with tubular deposits of calcium oxalate crystals (pyridoxine is required in the conversion of oxalate to glycine). Dermatitis and alopecia have occasionally been reported in pyridoxine deficiency in dogs.

Like the other water soluble vitamins, pyridoxine and its derivatives are not considered highly toxic.

BIOTIN

Like other B vitamins, biotin is presumed to function as a coenzyme and is necessary for certain reactions involving the metabolism of the carboxyl (CO_2) group which is initially bound to the biotin before transfer to an 'acceptor' molecule. In biotin deficiency there is a reduction in amino acid incorporation into proteins, apparently due to a fall in the synthesis of dicarboxylic acids. Impairment of glucose utilization and fatty acid synthesis have also been reported. In the early stages of deficiency the principal clinical sign seems to be a scaly dermatitis. Although these effects were initially investigated using other animals, it is now known that biotin is required by dogs and cats, and similar deficiency signs have been described. However, it is very difficult to produce biotin deficiency with a normal diet because most, if not all of the daily requirement can be met via synthesis by the gut bacteria. Deficiency signs have been produced in the dog and cat only when antibiotics were given to suppress bacterial action, and large quantities of whole egg white were included in the diet. Egg white contains a protein called avidin which forms a stable and biologically inactive complex with biotin. Avidin will also 'neutralize' biotin in food as well as that produced by bacteria. Avidin itself is relatively heat sensitive so if eggs are included in the diet they should always be fed cooked, not raw. It is also important to realize that some drug treatments can increase the requirement for vitamins like biotin which are manufactured by the intestinal bacteria. Nevertheless the likelihood of a naturally occurring biotin deficiency is remote.

FOLIC ACID (*PTEROYLGLUTAMIC ACID, FOLACIN*)

Folic acid is usually found in nature in the form of conjugates with the amino acid, glutamic acid. The biologically active coenzyme is the tetrahydro derivative, often abbreviated as THFA or FH_4, and there are several other forms of THFA with coenzyme activity all of which are usually grouped under the generic name of the folates or folate coenzymes. The folates are involved in the transfer of single carbon groups (e.g. methyl and formyl) which are important in several ways but perhaps the most significant reactions are those necessary for the synthesis of thymidine, an essential component of the nucleic acid DNA. Lack of an adequate supply of DNA prevents normal maturation of primordial red blood cells in bone marrow and the typical signs of folic acid deficiency are therefore anaemia and leukopaenia. Folic acid deficiency has been described in dogs and cats but usually only when semi-purified diets were fed in the presence of antibiotics. It is likely that most of the daily requirement for folate is met by bacterial synthesis in the intestine.

VITAMIN B_{12}

This vitamin is unique in being the first cobalt-containing substance shown to be essential for life and is the only vitamin that contains a trace element. Vitamin B_{12} is also known as cobalamin but is usually isolated in combination with a cyanide group linked to the cobalt atom. This form is known as cyano-cobalamin and is sometimes used as a synonym for vitamin B_{12} itself. The active coenzyme form is yet another derivative where a new chemical group replaces cyanide in the parent molecule. Like the folates vitamin B_{12} is involved in the transfer of one carbon fragments and its function is closely linked to that of folic acid.

Vitamin B_{12} is also involved in fat and carbohydrate metabolism and in the synthesis of myelin, a constituent of nerve tissue. The typical signs of a B_{12} deficiency in many ways resemble those of folate deficiency but characteristically also involve neurological impairment as a result of inadequate production of myelin. Vitamin B_{12} is only poorly absorbed from ingested food unless a protein, 'intrinsic factor', is present in the intestine. This factor presumably facilitates transfer of the vitamin across the mucosal membrane. Failure to absorb B_{12} due to lack of intrinisic factor results in pernicious anaemia with neurological degeneration.

These effects have been described in other animals including man, but less information is available for the dog and cat. The vitamin has been shown to be needed by these two species but a quantitative requirement has not been determined. Based on data from other mammals the amount required in the diet is likely to be very small.

CHOLINE

Choline forms part of the phospholipids which are essential components of cell membranes, it is the precursor of acetylcholine, one of the body's neurotransmitter chemicals, and it is an important methyl donor, that is it supplies single carbon fragments for metabolic conversions, the significance of which have already been discussed in the previous sections dealing with folic acid and vitamin B_{12}. A deficiency of choline causes several abnormalities including kidney and liver dysfunction which in the dog and cat are usually manifested as fatty infiltration of the liver. The precise mechanism for this is not known but may be linked to inadequate biosynthesis of specific types of phospholipids leading to impaired rates of lipid transport.

The requirement for choline in the diet can be modified by a number of factors, in particular the dietary concentration of methionine. Since methionine can also act as a methyl donor in intermediary metabolism, an increased dietary supply of one tends to spare the need for the other. Some recent work with cats has shown that methionine can completely replace the dietary need for choline if supplied in adequate amounts. The values given in Table 1 are based on a negligible contribution from methionine and therefore represent a considerable margin of safety. In view of the sparing effect of methionine and the widespread distribution of choline in plant and animal materials it is most unlikely that a dog or cat will become choline deficient under normal circumstances.

ASCORBIC ACID (*VITAMIN C*)

Unlike man, dogs and cats do not need a dietary supply of this vitamin because they are able to synthesize it from glucose. Nevertheless some researchers have claimed that a number of diseases of the dog can be ameliorated by ascorbic acid. Furthermore skeletal diseases such as hypertrophic osteodystrophy, hip dysplasia and a number of others, particularly those common in the large and giant breeds, have been said by some to resemble ascorbic acid deficiency (scurvy). However other research groups have consistently failed to show any benefits of vitamin C in either alleviating or preventing these diseases. On the available evidence it would appear that there is no need to include this particular nutrient in foods for dogs and cats.

CONCLUDING REMARKS

This completes the list of nutrients important to the dog and cat. All those substances which, on current evidence, are known (or likely) to be involved in the metabolism of these two animals have been included.

Naturally it is still possible that future research will reveal other chemical compounds with nutritional activity, but what is much more likely is that additional information will be obtained on the functions, interactions and precise requirements of the nutrients listed here. Although it is always difficult to highlight a few themes from a relatively large mass of data there are three which are worthy of at least a brief mention.

The first is that no nutrient functions in isolation. In fact the various interactions between them represent one of the most fascinating and interesting aspects of nutritional requirements, and one which is always changing as we increase our knowledge of nutrient utilization and metabolism. Their number is so large that it is difficult to pick out a few examples but those between calcium, phosphorus and vitamin D, selenium and vitamin E, choline and methionine, and tryptophan, niacin and pyridoxine represent a fairly broad selection.

The second and perhaps most important message is that all nutrient requirements are finite: enough is enough. No magical, health-promoting or life-prolonging properties result from an excessive intake of any nutrient. Unjustified supplementation is not only unnecessary but can be downright dangerous, particularly in the case of the trace elements and fat soluble vitamins. Furthermore, although the discussion of requirements has always been in terms of a daily intake of nutrients, this should not give the impression that dogs and cats must receive the precise recommended intake every day without fail. Even for the water soluble vitamins which are not stored to any extent in the body, slight fluctuations can be tolerated by the healthy animal without any ill-effects as long as the *average* amount ingested over say, a few days is sufficient. It is only in extreme cases like very low concentrations (or total absence) of a nutrient or an unusual metabolic effect (e.g. arginine deficiency in the cat) that the animal is likely to come to harm.

Lastly what is probably the most interesting aspect of dog and cat nutrition, namely the differences between their requirements, in particular the atypical metabolism of the cat. The overall theme is that the cat is dependent on a supply of at least some animal-derived raw materials in its diet and must be regarded as an obligate carnivore. Why should it not possess fully active enzyme systems responsible for the production of taurine, EFA and vitamin A? Is it possible that during the course of evolution these have been lost because of the ability of the cat family to catch prey and live off what is an almost entirely animal-based diet? Alternatively, were the early mammals obligate carnivores and the cat family represents an early branch of the evolutionary tree with such an efficient predatory lifestyle that it was subjected to little or no environmental pressure to develop mechanisms to utilize plant raw materials? Perhaps an investigation of the nutritional requirements of a primitive placental mammal like the hedgehog would reveal some interesting facts to contribute to the discussion!

Whatever the reasons for these differences between the dog and cat it must always be remembered by those involved in any aspect of pet feeding that, nutritionally and biochemically, a cat is not just a small, highly agile dog that climbs trees.

BIBLIOGRAPHY

Romsos, D. R., Palmer, H. J., Muiruri, K. L. and Bennink, M. R. (1981) Influence of a low carbohydrate diet on performance of pregnant and lactating dogs. *J. Nutr.* **111**, 678–689.

Morris, J. G., Trudell, J. and Pencovic, T. (1977) Carbohydrate digestion by the domestic cat (*Felis catus*). *Br. J. Nutr.* **37**, 365–373.

Kronfeld, D. S., Hammel, E. P., Ramberg Jnr., C. F. and Dunlap Jnr., H. L. (1977) Haematological and metabolic responses to training in racing sled dogs fed diets containing medium, low or zero carbohydrate. *Am. J. Clin. Nutr.* **30**, 419–430.

Rivers, J. P. W. and Frankel, T. L. (1980) Fat in the diet of cats and dogs, in *Nutrition of the Dog and Cat* ed. by R. S. Anderson, pp 67–99, Pergamon Press, Oxford.

Sinclair, A. J., McLean, J. G. and Monger, E. A. (1979) Metabolism of linoleic acid in the cat. *Lipids* **14**, 932–936.

Rivers, J. P. W., Hassam, A. G., Crawford, M. A. and Brambell, M. R. (1976) The inability of the lion, *Panthera leo,* to desaturate linoleic acid. *FEBS Lett.* **67**, 269.

Morris, J. G. and Rogers, Q. R. (1978) Arginine: an essential amino acid for the cat. *J. Nutr.* **108**, 1944–1953.

Anderson, P. A., Baker, D. H., Sherry, P. A. and Corbin, J. E. (1980) Nitrogen requirement of the kitten. *Am. J. Vet. Res.* **41**, 1646–1649.

Burger, I. H., Blaza, S. E. and Kendall, P. T. (1981) The protein requirement of adult cats. *Proc. Nutr. Soc.* **40**, 102A.

Twedt, D. C., Sternlieb, I. and Gilbertson, S. R. (1979) Clinical, morphologic and chemical studies on copper toxicosis of Bedlington terriers. *J. Am. Vet. Med. Assoc.* **175**, 269–275.

Ludwig, J., Owen Jnr., C. A., Barham, S. S., McCall, J. T. and Hardy, R. M. (1980) The liver in the inherited copper disease of Bedlington terriers. *Lab. Invest.* **43**, 82–87.

Robertson, B. T. and Burns, M. J. (1963) Zinc metabolism and the zinc-deficiency syndrome in the dog. *Am. J. Vet. Res.* **24**, 997–1002.

Rivers, J. P. W., Frankel, T. L., Juttla, S. and Hay, A. W. M. (1979) Vitamin D in the nutrition of the cat. *Proc. Nutr. Soc.* **38**, 36A.

Anderson, P. A., Baker, D. H., Sherry, P. A. and Corbin, J. E. (1979) Choline–methionine inter-relationship in feline nutrition. *J. Anim. Sci.* **49**, 522–527.

Nutrient Requirements of Dogs (1974) National Research Council, National Academy of Sciences, Washington, D.C.

Nutrient Requirements of Cats (1978) *Ibid.*

Ward, J. (1975) Investigation of the amino acid requirements of the adult dog. PhD Thesis, University of Cambridge.

Ha, Y. H., Milner, J. A. and Corbin, J. E. (1978) Arginine requirements in immature dogs. *J. Nutr.* **108**, 203–210.

Milner, J. A. (1979) Assessment of indispensable and dispensable amino acids for the immature dog. *J. Nutr.* **109**, 1161–1167.

Milner, J. A. (1979) Assessment of the essentiality of methionine, threonine, tryptophan, histidine and isoleucine in immature dogs. *J. Nutr.* **109**, 1351–1357.

Milner, J. A. (1981) Lysine requirements of the immature dog. *J. Nutr.* **111**, 40–45.

Hardy, A. J., Morris, J. G. and Rogers, Q. R. (1977) Valine requirement of the growing kitten. *J. Nutr.* **107**, 1308–1312.

Baker, D. H. (1980) Some essentials of kitten diet. *Petfood Industry,* **22**, (2), 20–34.

Costello, M. J., Morris, J. G. and Rogers, Q. R. (1980) Effect of dietary arginine levels on urinary orotate and citrate excretion in growing kittens. *J. Nutr.* **110**, 1204–1208.

Paul, A. A. and Southgate, D. A. T. (1978) *McCance and Widdowson's The Composition of Foods.* Fourth edition, p. 280, H.M.S.O., London.

CHAPTER 3

FOODS FOR DOGS AND CATS

D. W. Holme

Dogs and cats are carnivores, which taken literally means flesh eaters. The carnivores are an order of mammals distinguished by the arrangement of their teeth and by a feral, predatory way of living. They have long pointed canine teeth at the front corners of the upper and lower jaws, well-suited for holding and piercing their prey. The rear teeth are carnassials; short, pointed teeth adapted for slicing food into swallowable pieces rather than grinding, not at all like the molar teeth of humans or ruminants. It is likely that they evolved on a diet consisting mainly of other animals which they caught and killed. This does not mean that meat or other parts of animal bodies are the only suitable food for present-day, domesticated dogs and cats. Indeed it is quite possible to maintain dogs and cats in good health on diets which do not contain any meat as such, but consist only of nutrients provided as pure chemicals with 'protein' supplied as amino acids only or as mixtures of amino acids with isolated protein of vegetable origin. Such purified or semi-purified diets made from sugar and starch, fat, vitamins, minerals and amino acid mixtures, are not foods as we generally recognize them and are mentioned only to emphasize the fact that cats and dogs can be provided with adequate supplies of nutrients in a variety of ways and that no single food is necessarily the 'best' or most suitable for them.

In considering what it is that makes some foods clearly unsuitable for dogs and cats and others more or less suitable, we have to be aware of several factors. Some depend on the nature of the animal, some on the food itself and some on the expectations which people have about foods.

Animals eat to sustain themselves and food is the source of the energy and the major and minor nutrients of which their bodies are made. Any material which can provide nutrients or energy is a potential food source but the nutrients in food only become available to the animal through the processes of digestion and absorption which take place in the alimentary canal or gut. So unless the digestive system of the dog or cat is capable of breaking down and absorbing the nutrient content of a substance, it is not going to be suitable as a food. Dogs generally have a greater capability than cats to digest food, except for very highly digestible materials (Kendall, 1981). However, both species are unable to digest plant cell wall materials which consist for the most part of cellulose and hemicellulose. So many fibrous foods of vegetable origin are of little or no value as sources of nutrients although they may have other roles to play and are suitable as food for other species. Examples are grass, hay, sugar beet pulp, raw green vegetables and wheat bran.

Cats also have deficiencies of some enzyme systems possessed by dogs and other mammals which render them incapable of using normal metabolic pathways to synthesize certain nutrients within the body. These have to be supplied pre-formed in the diet. Examples are vitamin A, arachidonic acid (an essential fatty acid) and taurine, an amino-sulphonic acid. These essential nutrients are not found in vegetable materials and entail provision of at least part of the diet as food of animal origin. Whilst dogs can be maintained on a vegetarian diet, it is almost certain that cats cannot. Both species show a distinct preference for animal protein, animal fat and flesh.

Food is not just a source of nutrients and energy. In the context of feeding domestic pets, other characteristics or attributes must be considered and may be thought by some to be more important.

Dog and cat owners are concerned to maintain the health, activity and life of their pets for as long as possible. Feeding is seen as an occasion to be enjoyed by both, and unless food is eaten with obvious enjoyment, some of the reward and good feelings of being a provider may be lost to the owner and his or her opinion of the food's suitability lowered. It is inappropriate to evaluate foods *only* in terms of nutrient content and cost. Other factors such as safety, apparent enjoyment by the dog or cat, acceptance, suitability for feeding in the home which involves smell and appearance, keeping quality, convenience in purchasing, storage and preparation are all important to varying degrees.

Safety as a quality of a food is usually taken for granted but it is important that foods do not contain toxic components or contaminants including food spoilage organisms. Cooking and processing of food material is done mainly to ensure safety. It may also improve the appearance, taste, texture and digestibility of some foods, but the main objective of cooking is to make food safe to eat. The application of heat kills bacteria and moulds (food spoilage organisms) and also destroys most of the toxins or poisons which they produce. It kills parasites such as the eggs, larvae and encysted larvae of worms, and destroys many of the naturally occurring toxic materials present in some vegetable foods, for example, the goitre-causing substances in some brassicas, the trypsin inhibitors in soya beans and the cyanogenetic glucosides in tapioca or cassava. Cooking also destroys bacteria like *Salmonella* and *Botulinum* which can cause severe food poisoning. It also improves digestibility of foods for dogs and cats, particularly of starchy, vegetable foods like cereals by bursting the starch granules and exposing them to the action of digestive enzymes.

It usually softens and tenderizes meat containing large amounts of collagen but probably does not increase the digestibility of proteins to any marked degree. Overcooking can be harmful in destroying protein structure, some vitamins, and in causing loss of vitamins and minerals by leaching into cooking gravies or liquors.

Palatability and acceptance by dogs and cats are attributes which are hard to describe but easy to recognize. They are very important. Unpalatable, unacceptable food which remains uneaten obviously has no nutritional value and food which animals appear to eat with less than avid enjoyment and gusto is likely to be rejected by the owner unless factors such as cost and convenience are more important.

In the domestic situation the needs of the owner are important — does the food need to be cooked before feeding? Is it pleasant and convenient to handle and store before and after cooking or messy and unpleasant like green tripe? Owners have prejudices about foods and so some foods which are quite acceptable and useful for one person are completely unacceptable to another.

The total diet of a dog or cat may consist of a single food fed every day or it may be any number of combinations of mixtures of foods fed regularly or intermittently. It will be satisfactory if it is sufficiently palatable to be eaten in quantities which supply enough available nutrients to meet the needs of the animal. Foods which are good sources of some nutrients but deficient in others may be completely unsuitable as a sole food but excellent foods for feeding in a mixed diet.

What then are suitable foods for cats and dogs? This is a very difficult question and depends upon the meaning applied to the word 'suitable'. Suitability relates to fitness for the purpose intended. In the context of food it covers a very wide range of qualities, for example food which may be quite suitable for an adult dog may be quite unsuitable for a young kitten. As a rule of thumb it is almost true to say that if a food is suitable for people, it is also suitable in some degree for cats and dogs.

This does not help us in choosing foods for cats and dogs and so the following sections of this chapter attempt to describe the characteristics of several classes or types of foods in terms of nutrient content and availability, palatability and other aspects which allow a judgement to be made on their place in the construction of satisfactory feeding regimes.

MEAT AND MEAT BY-PRODUCTS

Meat as we usually think of it consists of the muscle tissue of animals together with the associated intramuscular fat, the connective tissue of muscle sheaths and tendons and blood vessels. It may also include various amounts of subcutaneous fat overlying the muscle, and marbling fat which is contained within the lean meat but between muscles. The relative proportions of muscle fibres and connective tissue have a big influence on the toughness or texture of the meat but the real differences in nutrient content between meat from different parts of the carcase depend on the proportion of fat present. Lean muscle devoid of fat has much the same proportions of water and protein, 75% water, 25% protein, no matter whether it is from different parts of the same animal or even from different animals or birds such as cattle, sheep, pigs or poultry. A most comprehensive collection of data on the nutrient content of meats and other foods is contained in Paul and Southgates' 1978 revision of *McCance and Widdowson's The Composition of Foods.*

Raw lean meat (including intramuscular fat) from pork, beef, lamb, veal, chicken, turkey, duck or rabbit, is very similar in composition and has average water, protein and fat contents ranging from about 70–76%, 20–22%, and 2–9% respectively. Fat is the major variable, the 'white' meats of poultry, veal and rabbit having rather less fat (2–5%) than lamb and pork (7–9%), but being very little different from lean beef.

Because the proportions of lean to fat vary widely between different joints of the same carcase and different animals, it is impossible to make accurate estimates of the protein, fat and energy content of an individual piece of meat using food composition tables. Lamb and pork are generally fattier than beef carcases. Boneless edible meat from a modern beef animal contains on average about 24% fat with individual joints having from as little as 10–11% (stewing steak) up to 25–26% (fore-rib and brisket). Breast of lamb or loin chops may contain 35–36% and the whole edible carcase averages about 30–32%. The leg may contain as little as 18% fat. Protein content of beef ranges from 16–18% for rib up to about 20% for steak.

The protein quality of meat from all the animals and birds mentioned is of high value. There is therefore little to choose in terms of nutrient supply between meat from different meat animals, once allowance has been made for the fat content and this varies as much or more between parts of the same animal as it does between species.

Fat from poultry and pigs is likely to be more unsaturated (that is, contains more double bonds) than that from beef and sheep but in practice, this has little effect on the digestibility or availability to dogs and cats.

Offal meats or meat by-products are generally similar in nutrient content no matter what species they are from. They tend to have more water and less protein than lean meat and a variable fat content. Table 7 shows some typical water, protein and fat contents of various meats and offals with calcium, phosphorus and energy values. Tables of food composition should be consulted for more detailed information. For all practical purposes meat is devoid of carbohydrate because energy reserves are present mostly as fat rather than sugar or starch. Muscles do contain small amounts of glycogen but this is rapidly depleted after slaughter and so the content of carbohydrate is negligible.

All meats are very low in calcium and have very adverse calcium : phosphorus ratios of about 1 : 15 or 1 : 20. This leads to very severe problems of bone under-mineralization if meats are fed as the major part of the diet without proper supplementation. All muscle meats and most offals and meat by-products are deficient in vitamins A and D and in iodine. Liver and to a lesser degree kidney are frequently good sources of these vitamins. Liver can in fact contain so much vitamin A (retinol) that cats in particular have had very serious ill effects when fed almost nothing else.

Meats generally are good sources of good quality protein and fats, iron, some of the B group vitamins, particularly niacin, thiamin, riboflavin and B_{12}. They are highly palatable to dogs and cats and generally of high digestibility which means that their nutrient content is readily available. When properly supplemented with sources of calcium, phosphorus, iodine and vitamins A and D they make excellent foods.

Among the meat by-products are materials like blood, bone, whole rabbit or chicken carcases, pigs' and sheep's heads and feet, poultry carcases from which most of the flesh has been used in the preparation of human foods. Because they may include bones, they often have high calcium and phosphorus values which complement the deficiencies of meats like lungs and livers. They are less suitable for use in home-made foods because they are difficult to handle and prepare but are used in the manufacture of prepared foods.

FISH

Fish are commonly divided into fatty fish and

Table 7. *Typical nutrient content of some meats and meat by-products (g/100 g)*

	Water	Protein	Fat	Calcium	Phosphorus	Energy (kcal)
Raw lean meats						
pork	71.5	20.6	7.1	0.008	0.20	147
beef	74.0	20.3	4.6	0.007	0.18	123
lamb	70.1	20.8	8.8	0.007	0.19	162
veal	74.9	21.1	2.7	0.008	0.26	109
chicken	74.4	20.6	4.3	0.01	0.20	121
duck	75.0	19.7	4.8	0.012	0.20	122
turkey	75.5	21.9	2.2	0.008	0.19	107
rabbit	74.6	21.9	4.0	0.022	0.22	124
Frozen meats (raw)						
lean beef	74.8	12.9	10.8	0.01	0.13	149
lean pork	75.7	10.7	12.2	0.01	0.16	153
Frozen raw by-products						
udders	72.4	11.0	15.3	0.26	0.24	182
fatty lungs	73.1	17.2	5.0	0.01	0.19	114
sheep lungs	76.0	16.9	3.2	0.01	0.20	96
brains	79.4	10.3	7.6	0.01	0.34	110
stomachs (pig)	79.1	11.6	8.7	0.03	0.11	125
spleen	75.9	17.0	6.5	0.03	0.22	126
kidney (beef)	79.8	15.7	2.6	0.02	0.25	86
heart	70.1	14.3	15.5	0.02	0.18	197
heart (trimmed)	76.3	18.9	3.6	0.005	0.23	108
liver	72.6	18.9	4.8	0.04	0.29	119
liver (fresh)	68.6	21.1	7.8	0.001	0.36	155
green tripe	76.2	12.3	11.6	0.01	0.1	154
dressed tripe	88.0	9.0	3.0	0.08	0.04	63

white fish. White fish like cod, haddock, plaice, whiting, sole or halibut, usually contain less than 2% fat whereas the oily or fatty fish like herring, mackerel, pilchards, sardines, sprats, tuna, salmon, trout and eels, may have very much more, between 5 and 20%, according to season of the year or stage of maturity of the fish when caught. In general, white fish are very similar to lean meat in composition. The protein is of similar high quality and the vitamins A and D are generally absent or present only in trace amounts. But fish muscle does contain adequate amounts of iodine and because bones are frequently consumed with the flesh of fish the calcium and phosphorus content is much better balanced. Filleted fish with bones removed is seriously deficient in calcium and phosphorus.

The flesh of the oily fish does contain vitamins A and D and the livers of fish like cod and halibut are particularly rich sources of these fat soluble vitamins.

Whole fish, including the bones (if made safe by cooking or grinding up), are better balanced sources of nutrients for dogs and cats than most meats.

Fish are usually less palatable than meats but nevertheless are mostly quite well accepted by these animals, but their smell and appearance may be less acceptable to some dog and cat owners.

Like meat, fish can contain parasites and should be cooked before being used as food. In addition, some fish muscle contains an enzyme, thiaminase, which breaks down the vitamin thiamin. This enzyme is destroyed or inactivated by heat and provides another reason for cooking fish prior to feeding it.

DAIRY PRODUCE

Cream, skimmed milk, whey, yoghurt, cheese and

butter are all milk products which usually contain in a more concentrated form some of the nutrients of the original milk. They are usually more palatable to dogs than cats but may be well liked by both species. A small number of cats and dogs may be unable to tolerate more than a minimum intake of milk sugar, lactose, which can result in diarrhoea in those animals which have insufficient lactase, the digestive enzyme which breaks down lactose into its component parts. These animals are easily identified and although they may be able to eat cheese and butter, should not be given milk or other dairy products.

Milk contains most of the nutrients needed by cats and dogs but is a poor source of iron and vitamin D. The riboflavin content is sensitive to sunlight and most of it will be destroyed together with the vitamin C (not a dietary essential for cats and dogs) if it is exposed to sunlight for more than an hour or two. It is also a poor source of iron and vitamin D. It is a good source of readily available energy, protein of high quality, fat, carbohydrate, calcium, phosphorus and several trace elements, vitamin A and B complex vitamins. It contains about 65 kcal/100 g with 3.4 g protein, 3.9 g fat, 4.7 g lactose, 0.12 g calcium and 0.1 g phosphorus.

Skimmed milk is milk from which most of the fat and fat soluble vitamins have been removed as cream. It therefore has almost no fat or vitamins A, E and D and a slightly higher concentration of protein and lactose. Dried whole milk or dried skimmed milk are more concentrated forms of their liquid counterparts.

Milk from Channel Island breeds of cow contains rather more fat and protein than the average and has an energy content of about 75 kcal/100 g. Otherwise it has similar properties. Goats' milk is very similar to cows' milk in composition and is of no extra value to cats and dogs.

Yoghurt is made by fermentation of whole or skimmed milk with lactic acid producing bacteria. It may have sugar added to it or some fruit pieces, or extra dried skimmed milk. Usually it contains the same nutrients as the milk or skimmed milk from which it is made but may have more energy if sugar has been added.

Cream is the fat from milk and is therefore rich in fat and fat soluble vitamins.

Cheese is made by the coagulation of milk protein using rennet in acid conditions. Most of the protein,

fat, calcium and vitamin A content are retained in the cheese while the milk sugar and B vitamins are removed in the whey. Most cheeses have similar amounts of protein and fat except for those like cottage cheese which are made from skimmed milk and so contain almost no fat. Cream cheeses contain most fat.

All dairy produce usually has high digestibility and the nutrient content is readily available to the animal. Apart from those individual animals with a poor tolerance for lactose, these foods are excellent sources of major nutrients and many minor ones.

EGGS

Eggs are good sources of iron, protein, riboflavin, folic acid, vitamin B_{12}, and vitamins A and D. They also contain appreciable amounts of most other nutrients except vitamin C and carbohydrates. Contrary to popular belief differences in nutritional value brought about by the system of egg production, i.e. battery, deep litter or free-range are very small. They may affect the folic acid content but very little else and the differences are probably not important in relation to total diet. Deep-coloured yolks and brown shells do not indicate rich supplies of vitamin A or its precursors because the orange pigment mainly responsible for yolk colour is not carotene.

Eggs are usually eaten without the shell and yet the shell provides a very good source of calcium being made mostly of calcium carbonate and protein. However, most dogs and cats are reluctant to eat egg shells and it may be difficult to get them to eat eggs with shell unless the shells have first been ground to a powder. Even without the shell they are excellent food. The white is almost all protein and water with trace minerals and some B vitamins. Most of the B vitamins and all of the fat soluble ones are found in the yolk which contains more fat and protein and much less water than the white. Eggs are a poor source of niacin.

Raw egg white contains avidin, a protein-rich material which makes biotin (a vitamin) unavailable to dogs and cats. It is therefore not good practice to feed raw egg whites as a frequent part of the diet. Cooking destroys the biotin binding effect and makes eggs safe. The dangers of feeding raw egg whites are often over-stated and it is unlikely that the feeding of one raw egg a day to the average dog will have any adverse effects. Cooked egg white is better digested and there is no advantage from feeding raw eggs, particularly as they are often associated with diarrhoea in some dogs.

CEREALS AND CEREAL BY-PRODUCTS

Cereals are the seeds of grasses. Generally they include grains like wheat, barley, oats, rice, rye, maize or corn and some sorghums. Cereal grains consist of the germ or embryo surrounded by a starchy endosperm whose function is to provide storage carbohydrate (starch) and some protein (gluten) to support the growth of the germ. This endosperm is itself surrounded by an aleurone layer, a thin layer of cells rich in protein and phosphorus and then comes the tough outer seed coat. Milling of cereals separates the various layers so that bran contains the tough outer coat rich in polysaccharides, cellulose and hemicelluloses (fibre), flour which is largely endosperm, and germ which is the embryo.

The whole grains of the common cereals wheat, oats, barley, rice, maize, contain about 12% moisture, from 7 to 14% protein, 2—5% fat and about 70—75% carbohydrate as starch. Wheat and oats and barley have higher protein content and less fat than maize and rice. Generally their value as foods for dogs and cats is as a source of energy with only minor contributions of protein to the total diet.

This depends on the amounts fed but there is little to choose between the cereals in the quality of the protein they provide. They do contain substantial amounts of other nutrients, particularly thiamin, calcium and niacin. The bran and offal portions obtained by separating the tough seed coat are good sources of dietary fibre and of phosphorus, but unless cooked before feeding, much of the phosphorus will be unavailable because it is present in a complex called phytate. Cooking makes this more available. The high fibre content makes bran useful as a bulking agent when diets of low nutrient content are required. Wheat germ or other cereal germs are rich in thiamin, protein, fat and vitamin E. Bran is also useful in that its inclusion in the diet tends to have a good effect on faeces consistency, reducing the likelihood of constipation or diarrhoea.

In the average household, cereal products are much more available than straight whole grains or meals. In the United Kingdom, flours made from wheat are required to be fortified with iron, thiamin and nicotinic acid or niacin, except for wholemeal flour which consists of the ground whole grain. They must also contain extra calcium and so foods like bread and biscuits baked mainly from flour are good sources of these nutrients. Bread has about 8 or 9% protein, 2% fat and 45% carbohydrate. It provides many minerals and some B vitamins.

Rice is often available as long grain rice or as 'pudding' rice. These are the whole grains minus their outer coats and so consist mainly of starch, about 85%, with low levels of vitamins, minerals, fat and protein (7%). Rice is not readily eaten by dogs or cats unless cooked and then is usually mixed with more appetizing foods before being fed. Because the gluten in rice is different from that in wheat, it is often used as a major energy source when investigating food allergies.

Breakfast cereals are usually made using a variety of processes from the whole grains of oats, wheat and maize, although rice and bran are also popular. The processing usually involves fairly extensive heat treatment in flaking or popping and this destroys most of their thiamin content. Many branded products now have additional thiamin and other B vitamins added after processing and may be treated as having similar nutritional values to the cereals from which they were derived. Digestibility is probably improved because of the cooking they receive. Sago or tapioca may be considered as a cereal by many people although in fact it is made from the starchy root of the cassava plant. It has much less protein than rice and is almost entirely 95% starch with small amounts of minerals and only traces of vitamins. For practical purposes it should be treated as contributing only energy. Cereals are not particularly palatable to cats and dogs even when moistened with water and usually need to be fed as part of the diet only. Their nutrient content is of lower digestibility than many other foods particularly if the cereals are not finely ground or cooked. Fine grinding or cooking markedly increases the digestible energy and dry matter values. This is mainly because of the effect in improving the digestion of starch.

FATS AND OILS

Fats and oils include obvious materials like butter, margarine, lard and dripping, the visible fat in meats and the invisible fats in substances like nuts, lean meats and other foods. Oils are distinguished from fats only by their melting point; they are liquid at room temperature, fats are solid. Fats and oils are made up of different fatty acids strung together with glycerol into triglycerides, three fatty acids plus one glycerol molecule. The differences between the various fats are basically because of the different fatty acids they contain.

Fats may be classified as containing largely saturated fatty acids or unsaturated ones. Most fats contain both kinds but the proportions differ. Some of the more unsaturated fatty acids — linoleic, linolenic and arachidonic acid (with 2, 3 and 4 double bonds respectively) — are known as essential fatty acids (EFA) because they are required in small quantities for normal health and cannot be synthesized in the animal body from other fats. Dogs like man, can convert linoleic acid into linolenic and into arachidonic acids by desaturation (addition of double bonds) and so need only to be fed sources of linoleic acid. Cats on the other hand appear to have some enzyme deficiencies which make the conversion from linoleic very slow or not possible. Linoleic acid is widely distributed in vegetable seed oils and occurs in small amounts in some animal fats, particularly pork fat and chicken fat. Arachidonic acid occurs only in small amounts in some animal tissue fats. It is not usually present in subcutaneous and storage fats and is easily destroyed by heat, so lard, dripping and rendered fats generally contain almost none.

All fats yield a similar amount of energy, about 2¼ times that obtained from protein or carbohydrate and their nutritional value in other respects depends largely on their origin and vitamin content. Vegetable fats are seed fats. Oil seeds contain 20–40% fat. This is almost pure fat with only traces of minerals and no vitamins apart from vitamin E. Wheatgerm oil is a good source of E activity followed by sunflower and cottonseed oils.

Vegetable fats are usually better sources of unsaturated fats like linoleic acid than animal fats, soya bean oil and corn or maize oil have about 50% of this fatty acid, sunflower seed oil contains even more — 65–70% — but coconut oil contains hardly any and olive oil only about 5–8%.

Milk fat and beef tallow contain hardly any, while lard and eggs contain similar low levels of 5–10%. Fish oils are a good source with over 20% of linoleic acid. They usually contain many other unsaturated fats as well.

None of the animal fats contains other than trace amounts of B vitamins but cod liver oil, butter and margarine are good sources of vitamin A. Margarine and cod liver oil, or other fish oils like halibut liver oil, are also good sources of vitamin D. Margarine has no inherent vitamins from its component vegetable fats but in the United Kingdom must be fortified with vitamins A and D. The very high levels in fish liver oil make this suitable for only limited inclusion in the total diet.

Fats, particularly animal fats, are greatly liked by cats and dogs. They add flavour and palatability to other foods. They also bind together dusty foods like cereal meals and are more than just a source of energy and vitamins A and D. They are highly digestible and slow down the rate of stomach emptying thus helping to give animals a feeling of satiety after meals.

Used cooking fat which has been used several times for deep fat frying should never be given as food. It is likely to contain peroxides and other toxic materials which can be harmful if fed to cats and dogs.

OTHER ANIMAL BY-PRODUCTS

Many kinds of by-product from the slaughtering industry are available as foods for cats and dogs.

Many are obtained fresh or frozen direct from the abattoir without processing and most of these have been mentioned previously. Others are first processed or are the result of processing of parts of the animal. Among these are dry meals such as blood meal, meat-meal, meat and bone meal, greaves (the dry remnants remaining after fat rendering), feather meals and poultry meals, which may contain heads and feet as well as other parts of the carcase.

These products form part of the animal feeding-stuffs trade and are usually produced to a specified level of protein, fat and ash content. The processes by which they are produced have variable control of the heat treatment given. Protein quality and availability can be very variable as can the ash or mineral content. They provide large amounts of protein from as little as 40% in some meat and bone meals up to 75 or 80% in a high protein meat meal. They can be very good value for money but require careful monitoring. Digestibility by dogs and cats is variable and protein digestibility may be as high as 90% or as low as 70%. They are often quite palatable and improve the acceptance of cereals when mixed with them. Their chief use is as part of dry manufactured foods.

The only product of this kind which finds much application in home-made foods is sterilized bone flour. It must be sterilized to reduce any risk of disease, particularly salmonellosis and foot and mouth disease. Bone flour contains about 36% calcium and 18 or 19% phosphorus and is a very good calcium−phosphorus supplement for meat, 15 g will adequately supplement 1 kg meat or meat by-product.

Fish meals are made by drying the whole bodies and offal of white fish or from the whole bodies of oily fish such as herring, mackerel or sprats when they are in over supply.

They are usually very good sources of good quality protein for use in foods for cats and dogs. The protein and fat content depends upon the fish used. White fish meal usually contains 62−66% protein with fat levels of about 6−8% and meal from oily fish may have up to 72% protein and 8−10% fat. Both kinds are rich in minerals as one would expect from the composition of whole fish. They are usually palatable, of good digestibility and a valuable protein source in the manufacture of prepared foods.

VEGETABLES

Vegetables can be classified into three kinds when considering their use as food. First, those where the whole plant or leaves and stem are used. These are the green vegetables like lettuce, cabbage, brussel sprouts, cauliflower, which may be eaten raw or cooked. They have high water content, a high fibre content and although they are important in the human diet are not of much value to cats and dogs. They are not usually very palatable to these species and their bulk and indigestible fibre content mean that they would

have to eat very large amounts to obtain a significant contribution to the nutrient intake. Some dogs and fewer cats may be given cooked vegetables but they do not usually make much contribution to the total diet. Dogs but not cats may obtain some vitamin A from this source. Vegetables are good sources of B vitamins but these may be destroyed in cooking or lost in cooking liquors if these are not also fed.

The second class is those consumed as roots or tubers where the main storage organ of the plants rich in starch are used as food. Examples are potatoes, carrots and turnips.

Root vegetables eaten raw are poorly digested by dogs and cats and not commonly given to them. Cooking gelatinizes the starch and makes it more digestible and most dogs will eat cooked potatoes or carrots. Their main nutritional value is as a source of energy although carrots would also provide some vitamin A for dogs. Cats do not commonly eat vegetables and their relative lack of palatability means they are only infrequently suitable. There is no risk in feeding these materials to cats and dogs.

The third class is those where the seed is eaten. This class includes peas and beans. They are relatively rich in protein and provide more energy than green or root vegetables, other than potatoes. They are a fairly good source of most B vitamins. Green peas, broad beans and runner beans are acceptable to most dogs when cooked but rarely form a major part of the diet.

Soya beans are a special case. They are a major source of protein and energy for humans in many parts of the world and are used world-wide for animal feeding either as whole beans or more commonly after processing to remove the oil. Soya beans have a tough outer seed coat or hull which is removed mechanically before extracting the oil by a combination of grinding and treating with solvents. The residue which is left contains the protein, carbo-hydrate and mineral portions of the seed with some small amounts of oil. It may be 'toasted' or heated to inactivate certain anti-nutritive factors (trypsin inhibitors and haemaglutinins) contained in the seed. These substances are sensitive to heat and the amount of heat treatment is controlled so that it does not at the same time denature the soya protein and reduce its nutritive value. The heat-treated or toasted de-fatted soya bean meal usually has a protein content of 48−50%, 30% carbohydrate, mainly as sugars not starch, 1—2% fat, about 5—6% minerals with 3—5% crude fibre.

The protein is of good quality and has high levels of essential amino acids. It is roughly equivalent to milk protein.

De-fatted soya bean meal may be used directly as a food ingredient or it may be further processed to make textured soya protein, often described as TVP. Most legumes contain complex carbohydrates and simpler sugars which are resistant to digestion by the digestive enzymes of animals like the dog, cat or man. They pass undigested into the large intestine where they may be fermented by bacteria with the consequent production of flatus or intestinal gas. This problem of flatulence is common with other legumes like green peas and beans discussed earlier. The degree to which flatulence occurs in animals fed soya products or peas and beans is unpredictable and seems to depend on the amounts fed and on the susceptibility of the animal which in turn may depend on the bacterial flora present in the gut. It should not be overlooked nor over-emphasized when considering the role of these materials as foods.

PREPARED FOODS

The manufacture of foods specially prepared for cats and dogs has developed into a large industry over the last 30 years or so. Most people who have a cat or a dog do not have much knowledge of nutrition, much experience of feeding animals, access to cheap supplies of traditional food items, the time or desire to pursue complicated preparation and cooking of food specially for their pet. They depend therefore on reliable prepared foods for a large part of the diet.

Seven out of ten people who own dogs say they feed canned pet food at least once a week and five say they feed it every day. The situation is similar with cat owners. Canned pet food then, makes a very important contribution to the diet of the Nation's pets, many of which are fed almost exclusively on such foods.

Prepared foods are available in several forms and may be considered in relation to their intended role in the diet or they can also be conveniently classified by their water content and method of preservation as indicated in Table 8.

Table 8. *Classification by water content and method of preservation*

Food type	% Water content	Preservation technology
Dry	5—12	Drying
Semi-moist	15—50	Reduced water activity by the use of humectants, mould inhibitors, low pH.
Canned	72—85	Heat sterilization
Frozen	60—75	Freezing

Whatever their form such foods may be formulated and sold as the whole diet for a dog or cat. *Complete* foods are capable of maintaining life and health of adults and may also be able to support growth, reproduction and work as well if fed without any other food except water.

Other *complementary* foods are more like the foods discussed earlier in this chapter and are not intended for use as the only food or to provide the total diet. They may be rich in some nutrients but inadequate in others as for example some dog biscuits high in energy and with adequate amounts of calcium and trace metals but with insufficient protein, some fats and vitamins to be fed as the only food.

Their major role in the diet is to provide a relatively cheap source of energy and as such they complement the relatively low energy, high protein canned meats.

CANNED FOODS

Canned pet foods have been available for many years as a variety of meat and fish-based products or meat, fish and cereal products. Their properties are well-known, they are a very reliable, safe and convenient way of providing moist attractive foods which are highly palatable to the cat or dog. The most important are those which contain little or no cereal or carbohydrate source and are presented as meaty or fishy chunks in gravy or jelly. The others are those which contain significant amounts of cereals and are best described as loaf products, meat and cereal or fish and cereal foods.

Because the nutritional needs of dogs and cats are different, manufacturers usually make foods specifically for dogs or for cats, very few are intended for both species. In practice it is probably quite safe to feed dogs on cat foods, but may not be safe to feed cats on dog foods and the practice is not recommended. There is adequate choice of brands and varieties to satisfy the needs of most pets within the species-specific range.

Most canned cat foods are formulated to supply a balanced diet, containing adequate amounts in relation to the energy content of all the minerals, vitamins, fats and amino acids known to be needed by the cat. So if the cat eats enough food to satisfy its energy needs, then it should at the same time obtain sufficient of all other nutrients. When energy needs are high as during growth or suckling of young, then specially-made high-energy foods may be more appropriate than ordinary foods which are principally intended for adult cat maintenance.

Digestibility values and so availability of nutrients from canned foods are high and because of the soft-moist, meaty or fishy nature palatability is good.

Canned dog foods too are usually formulated to provide a balanced diet with adequate amounts of all nutrients in relation to the energy content. It is possible to feed dogs satisfactorily on these only, but because the energy content is relatively low, large amounts are needed. This is rather wasteful of protein and also uneconomic. Most canned dog foods are not made with this in mind but are intended to be highly palatable sources of good quality proteins, vitamins and minerals to be fed in conjunction with cheaper biscuits or other mixers which primarily supply energy with some minerals and vitamins.

Feeding recommendations of canned foods which are expected to be fed in this manner usually indicate that the proportions of canned food to biscuit mixer can be varied quite widely to provide a more or less palatable and more or less energy-dense mixture to suit the needs of particular feeding situations. For most adult dogs an equal volume mixture of canned food and reputable mixer biscuit will provide a highly palatable, nutritious meal.

Canned foods are safe products with a very long storage life, not requiring special storage conditions. They are usually produced by chopping and mixing the main ingredients, adding gravy and processing in a sealed can. The processing involves combinations of time, temperature and pressure of steam which vary with can size and heat transfer characteristics

of the recipe, but which are sufficient to kill even the most harmful bacteria. There is little damage to or loss of nutrients from the food except for thiamin which is particularly sensitive to heat and so compensatory amounts are added to maintain adequate post-process levels.

The main ingredients of canned foods for both species are meat, meat by-products, other protein concentrates like vegetable protein, mineral and vitamin supplements and cereals. They provide a consistent and reliable form of feeding. Typical values for the nutrient content of canned foods and biscuit mixtures are shown in Table 9.

SEMI-MOIST FOODS

The preservation by reducing water activity, of meaty types of dog and cat foods with water contents between 15 and 30% or more and a shelf-life of several months, is a relatively new process. Water activity is a measure of the water which is available for bacterial or fungal growth in or on the surface of a food.

These organisms cannot grow and spoil food in dry products because there is not enough water present. Water activity (aW) is measured as relative humidity at equilibrium and most bacteria will not grow at levels below 0.83 and yeasts and moulds below 0.6. The low water activity in semi-moist foods is achieved by the inclusion in the recipes of humectants which tie-up the water such as sugars, salt, propylene glycol or glycerol. Further protection is provided by the use of preservatives such as sorbates to prevent yeast and mould growth or by the reduction of pH (increased acidity) with organic acids.

These foods can be made with a variety of ingredients including meat, meat by-products, soya or other vegetable-protein concentrates, cereals, fats and sugars. The technology allows the water content to vary over a wide range and so the product form may be as a fairly dry material (15% water) not dissimilar to a dry food; a soft-moist substance similar in appearance to mince or cubed meat (25—30% water) or as a much moister version with up to 50% water.

The most popular forms presently available in the United Kingdom contain about 25% water and so have a fairly high nutrient density. They are of average

Table 9. *Typical nutrient content of prepared foods for dogs and cats (means and ranges) g/100 g 'as is' basis*

Food type		Water	Protein	Fat	Ash	NFE*	Ca	P	Energy
Dry									
Complete for	from	6	21	5	7	61	1.8	1.3	350
dogs	to	6	28	8	6	52	2.0	1.5	380
Complete for cats		6	28	10	10	46	1.5	1.1	370
Mixer biscuits for dogs		8	12	5	5	70	1.2	0.6	355
Semi-moist									
Dog food		23	24	7	7	39	0.8	0.7	305
Cat food		25	25	15	6	29	0.7	0.7	340
Canned									
Meaty chunks in jelly — dogs		82	8	4	2	4	0.35	0.25	80
Meat and cereal — dogs		73	8	1	2	16	0.3	0.25	100
Meaty food for puppies		78	10	7	2	3	0.2	0.2	115
Meaty chunks — cats		84	9	4	1.5	2	0.2	0.2	75
Fish/meat/cereal — cats		75	9	2	2.5	12	0.6	0.5	100
Meaty food for kittens		76	12	8	2	2	0.3	0.3	125
Canned meaty dog food & biscuit mixture (3 : 1 by weight)		63	9	6	3	19	0.6	0.4	160

*NFE = nitrogen-free extract — a measure of carbohydrate content.

Note: There are many brands of foods available and their nutrient content varies widely. The tabulated values are indicative of the sort of values found. For information about particular branded foods contact the manufacturer at the address given on the label or packet.

or above average digestibility, 80–85% for most nutrients. They do not usually have a strong odour, do not dry up rapidly if exposed to the atmosphere and so can be left in the feeding bowl without becoming unattractive to pet and to owner. Cat products have not been so successful as dog products and this may be because the cat is more finicky in its choice of foods. Some cat products are available and it is likely that palatability problems will be overcome and they will constitute an alternative feeding form for cats in future. Typical nutrient contents of semi-moist foods are presented in Table 9.

DRY FOODS

Dry foods are available for both cats and dogs. Dog foods are sold as baked biscuits, extruded and expanded biscuits, extruded in solid cubes or cylinders like farm animal feeds or as mixtures of meals and flakes. They may be complete foods or formulated as mixers intended for feeding as part of the diet with protein-rich foods such as fresh meats, fish or canned dog foods.

Mixers are usually based on cereals and contain very little, if any protein concentrates. They may or may not be supplemented with minerals and vitamins to provide a complete balanced diet when fed in appropriate amounts with cooked or canned meats. Many of the cheaper kinds are not so supplemented and so would require other foods and supplements besides meat to provide an adequate diet. Such mixers are little more than cooked cereal with fat added sufficient for baking or extruding. Good quality mixers are supplemented with extra calcium, phosphorus, trace minerals and vitamins to balance their energy content. When mixed with good quality canned meats or cooked fresh meats they provide adequate amounts of all nutrients.

Dry complete foods for dogs come in similar physical forms but differ in their ingredient content. They are usually formulated to supply adequate amounts of all known nutrients for the stage of life for which they are intended. Loss of nutrients particularly of vitamins is limited because the baking or extrusion processes do not require excessive temperatures or time and sufficient supplements are added to counterbalance processing and storage losses.

Because they are dry and do not contain enough water for bacterial or fungal growth, they have a long shelf-life and will keep in dry, cool storage conditions for several months. They are usually made from cereals and cereal by-products; protein concentrates of animal or vegetable origin, like for example meat and bone meal, fish meal or soya bean meal; fats and mineral and vitamin supplements.

Dry cat foods are mostly available as extruded, expanded biscuits formulated to provide, with water, a complete diet for cats of all ages or for adult cat maintenance. Feeding recommendations often suggest that they are fed only as part of the diet with milk, fresh meat or canned cat food. We have seen that cats require a dietary source of arachidonic acid but the absolute level of intake is not well defined. This nutrient is only available from animal sources and so the inclusion of meaty foods in the diet is insurance against possible deficiencies of dry cat food. The ingredients of dry cat foods are similar to those of dry dog foods but more emphasis has to be given to the inclusion of proteins and fats of animal origin and some even include fresh meat rather than meat meals. Cats appear to have a need for greater levels of protein than dogs and so protein levels in dry cat foods are frequently higher than in dog foods. Typical analyses of the nutrient content of dry foods are given in Table 9.

Dry foods contain a greater concentration of nutrients and energy per unit weight than foods of higher moisture content and so relatively small amounts are needed to provide a particular quantity of nutrients.

Unless they contain large amounts of fibre the digestibility of dry foods is usually acceptable but lower than that of meats and canned foods and is similar to cereals.

They are considerably better digested by dogs than cats. Baked or extruded biscuits have been partially or wholly cooked and so are a good source of energy for both dogs and cats. They are easy to store and to dispense.

The main disadvantage of dry foods is that they are much less palatable than moister foods like meat or canned foods. There are considerable variations in palatability between brands of food because manufacturers take considerable trouble to enhance the acceptance of their own particular products. Cats seem prepared to accept the crunchy extruded biscuit forms very well but are not usually impressed by meals or flaked foods.

The mixer dog foods are meant to be fed with canned meat or meat and gravy and their low palatability is less of a drawback than it is with complete foods.

These foods provide a relatively cheap and useful source of energy which can add considerable flexibility to feeding programmes. If they are supplemented with minerals and vitamins it is easy to adjust the proportions of the diet to accommodate the nutrient needs of different animals.

BIBLIOGRAPHY

Anon. (1977) *Manual of Nutrition*, Eighth edition. Ministry of Agriculture, Fisheries & Food, HMSO, London.

Fonnsbeck, P. V., Harris, L. W. and Kearl, L. C. (Editors) (1976) First International Symposium 'Feed Composition, Animal Nutrient Requirements, and Computerisation of Diets'. Utah Agric. Exp. Sta., Utah State University, Logan, Utah.

Harris, R. S. and Karmas, E. (Editors) (1975) *Nutritional Evaluation of Food Processing*. Second edition. AVI Publishing, Connecticut, USA.

Kendall, P. T. (1981) Comparative evaluation of apparent digestibility in dogs and cats. *Proc. Nutr. Soc.* **40** (2), 45A (Abs.).

Liender, I. E. (Editor) (1980) *Toxic Constituents of Plant Foodstuffs*. Academic Press, New York.

Paul, A. A. and Southgate, D. A. T. (1978) *McCance and Widdowson's 'The Composition of Foods'*. Fourth edition. HMSO, London; Elsevier/North Holland Biomedical Press, Amsterdam, New York.

Proceedings World Soy Protein Conference (1974) *J. Am. Oil Chem. Soc.* **51**, 47A–208A.

CHAPTER 4

PRACTICAL USE OF PREPARED FOODS FOR DOGS AND CATS

D. W. Holme

Chapter 2 explained why cats and dogs need a regular supply of nutrients and that their needs are altered by the various demands of pregnancy, lactation, growth, exercise and environmental factors. Chapter 3 discussed the wide variety of foods which are available and the characteristics which make them more or less suitable for inclusion in the diet. This chapter aims to provide a practical, quantitative guide to the use of prepared or manufactured foods in the construction of feeding regimes for both species.

FACTORS TO BE CONSIDERED IN CHOOSING A FEEDING REGIME

The amount of food eaten must supply the animal's needs for energy and nutrients if it is to remain healthy. Most animals will eat sufficient of a palatable diet to meet their energy needs provided that it is within their physical capacity to do so. A satisfactory feeding regime is one which provides a balanced diet of sufficient concentration that a dog or cat can obtain its daily needs for energy and nutrients by eating an amount well within the limits set by appetite. Such a regime could consist of a single suitable food or a mixture of foods of differing energy and nutrient concentrations.

The daily needs are governed by the physiological status of the animal. For example young growing animals or lactating females require very much more in relation to their size than normal adults in the maintenance state. The more concentrated and more palatable foods are therefore most suitable for these stages of life where demands for nutrients are high,

and intakes may be limited by bulkiness of some foods.

In general it is not absolutely necessary that the daily intake of nutrients and energy should exactly match requirement because animals are resilient and able to store some surplus nutrients in body tissues when supply exceeds needs and to use these stores when food or nutrient supply is inadequate. Some nutrients cannot be stored except in very small amounts, examples are water soluble vitamins and amino acids. Storage and utilization both have costs and the most efficient use of food occurs when daily food supply more or less equals daily needs. Departure from this ideal is tolerated better by adult animals than by young growing ones or lactating females in which the consequences of under-nutrition or of an improperly balanced diet follow more quickly. Even with the adult we should aim to supply foods which on average meet daily needs each day, and certainly do so over a 7–10 day period.

FREQUENCY OF FEEDING

Most pet animals are adults which live mostly indoors in a temperate climate. They are not pregnant or lactating, not involved in regular heavy work or excessive exercise and not subjected to extreme environmental conditions.

Dogs in this situation will usually have a good enough appetite to eat all they require at one meal per day and it is quite satisfactory to adopt a once a day feeding regime. The advantages of a single meal are that it can usually be of sufficient size to satiate appetite; it is more controllable in that errors of dispensing occur only once a day so under- or over-feeding is less likely; it can easily be fitted into the household routine at whatever is the most convenient time. It is usually best to avoid late evening meals since dogs may need to excrete faeces or urine within a few hours of feeding and this can be inconvenient at 2 or 3 a.m.

There is no disadvantage in feeding more frequently than once a day provided that the total daily intake is limited to the dog's daily needs. Feeding two or three times a day at the same time as family meals is a common practice. The risk is that more food will be given and that over-eating and obesity will be the result. The correct number of meals for any dog is that which the owner finds most convenient. It is desirable to establish a routine and stick to it. Meal-times are the high spot of most days and dogs quickly become accustomed to being fed at the same time and place each day.

Dogs which are unwell or have poor appetites, or very old dogs, may benefit from being fed two or more times daily with smaller meals. Young growing dogs, working dogs and lactating females which require energy and nutrient intakes of 2 to 4 times as much as normal adults in relation to their size will also benefit from more frequent meals since this gives them a better opportunity to ingest the large amounts of food they need. Very young growing puppies may need 4 or 5 meals per day, but weaned puppies aged 7 weeks or more can be fed satisfactorily on two meals per day if sufficiently concentrated foods are given. There is no single optimum number of feeds per day except that which is convenient for the owner and which provides adequate opportunity for requirements to be met.

Cats are rather different. It is generally thought that cats which have gone wild, or genuine wild-cats must be opportunist feeders eating as and when they catch and kill prey. It might therefore be thought that they could be adapted to large meals at irregular intervals. However, it is likely that small rodents and birds which would constitute the major part of their diet are not big enough for one kill to provide for the animal's daily needs and more than one meal per day would be more usual.

Observations on domestic cats given completely free access to palatable foods have demonstrated that cats prefer to eat many small meals (12—20 meals per 24 hours) rather than one or two large ones. Most cats appear to be able to regulate intake so that they do not overeat and become obese when food is made available in this way. It therefore seems reasonable to feed cats several small meals rather than one or two large ones. This is quite satisfactory in practice and many pet cats are fed 'on demand' with food made available whenever the animal asks for it throughout the day. The average pet cat in the United Kingdom weighs almost 4 kg and needs about 350 kcal meta-bolizable energy per day. This would be provided in 90 g dry matter (100 g dry food) or rather more than one large can of a typical canned cat food. Very few cats are prepared to eat this amount of food in one meal and so at least two or more meals per day are necessary. It is therefore good husbandry to feed cats to appetite several times daily. Alternatively cats may be given free access to food which is renewed at least twice daily.

CATS AND DOGS ARE INDIVIDUALS

Most cats and dogs are kept in households in which they are the only cat or dog, or where there is not more than one other animal of the same species. Pet owners therefore tend to treat them as individuals and need to develop feeding practices suitable to their animal; taking account of the particular circumstances, likes and dislikes of the animal and of their own view of convenience, cost, variety and suitability of foods. They need to identify the particular needs of their animals and find a combination of food or foods to meet them.

It is not possible in a book of this kind to prescribe particular dietary regimes for each and every pet in every environment, therefore the feeding guides in this chapter are intended only as GUIDES to the use of prepared foods for average dogs and cats in the usual range of environments found in United Kingdom households. It is relatively simple for the individual owner to use these guides as a starting point to obtain an approximate estimate of their pet's needs, then by observation of the animal to decide whether to feed more or less, and by substitution of one food for another to arrive at a suitable regime.

The feeding guides found on the packets, cans or other packaging of manufactured foods are usually intended to apply to the average adult dog or cat living mostly indoors and given a moderate amount of exercise. They are based on meeting energy needs estimated as being between 130 and 140 kcal metabolizable energy per kg metabolic body size per day for dogs and 85 to 90 kcal per kg bodyweight per day for cats. The aim of using an estimate of metabolic body size (bodyweight in kg raised to the power ¾) is to make an allowance for the wide range of size in dogs and the fact that energy needs are not directly proportional to weight but to the weight of actively metabolizing tissue. The ¾ power function was shown by Brody to be a reasonable fit to the energy needs of a wide range of animals from mouse to elephant but is no more than an approximation. Having calculated approximate energy needs of adults in this way the amounts of food needed to meet these needs can be calculated from a knowledge of the energy value of the foods. These average amounts can then be rounded to a convenient unit for dispensing, which for canned foods may be ½ or ¼ can and for dry or semi-moist foods 10 or 20 g units. Since very few people actually weigh food for their pets but are more likely to dispense it by some form of volume measurement or by eye, it is common to find feeding recommendations given as cupfuls for dry and semi-moist foods. A cup is usually reckoned to contain about 80–100 g of such foods.

In order to allow for variability between dogs and for differences in environment, actual feeding recommendations are often quoted as a range which may cover from 20 or 25% below to 20 or 25% more than the estimated average. Although this may seem a very approximate method of arriving at feeding recommendations, it does in fact work out very well in practice. It should not however surprise owners to find that their particular dog or cat needs very much less than the amounts suggested. The best criterion for judging the adequacy of a feeding regime is the health and appearance of the dog or cat. If they are in good condition with good skin and coat, alert, active and neither too fat nor thin, they are on an adequate regime.

Prepared foods provide many alternative ways of feeding and range from highly palatable, moist canned foods to more concentrated dry foods. They cover a very wide range of flavours, textures and ingredients. They may be complete foods with appropriate amounts of all nutrients in relation to their energy content so that they can be fed as the sole diet. Or they may be complementary foods intended to supply only part of the total diet. Such foods may contain less than adequate amounts of some nutrients; for example, most dog biscuits do not contain enough protein to be fed as the only food and are meant to be fed with protein-rich materials like canned meats. Or they may be complementary foods because they are not so concentrated and animals would need to eat very large amounts to obtain all their needs from the one food.

Canned dog foods are complete foods in that they contain adequate amounts of all the nutrients needed by dogs but are nevertheless intended to be fed as complementary foods in conjunction with biscuits, because this is a more economical way of feeding and their high protein content and high palatability compensate for the inadequate protein content and poorer palatability of the biscuit. The high energy and carbohydrate content of the biscuit similarly complement or compensate for the lower energy content of moist foods.

Foods which have an adequate balance of nutrients in relation to their energy content (balanced diet) can be mixed together or fed in any proportion to constitute a satisfactory diet with the only limitation being that the total quantity given should provide adequate amounts of energy. It is therefore quite permissible and sensible to feed any combination of complete semi-moist, dry and canned foods to dogs.

Most commercially available cat foods — dry, semi-moist and canned — are formulated to provide at least sufficient nutrients for adult maintenance. Snacks and treats should not form a major part of the diet for any cat but most cats will benefit if given extras in the form of drinks of milk or meaty scraps and bacon rinds.

FEEDING CATS

The feeding of orphaned and very young cats is dealt with in Chapter 6 and will not be considered here. Kittens at birth usually weigh between 80 and 140 g with most weighing around 100 to 120 g. They are entirely dependent on the milk of the queen for about 4 weeks by which time they have probably trebled their birthweight and are beginning to explore their surroundings.

At this time, 4—5 weeks, the process of weaning or gradual replacement of the queen's milk by other foods, can begin. Weaning is a time of learning and is best done gradually to avoid upsets to the digestive system. The kitten has to become accustomed to new tastes and textures of foods and its digestive system has to learn to cope with new kinds of proteins, fats and carbohydrates. It is often suggested that the first new food should be milk-based and be offered from about 4 weeks of age. Although most kittens will drink such foods, their use is not essential and since most queens will continue to suckle until 7 or 8 weeks after parturition there is little advantage in beginning to wean kittens so early. By the fifth week they are usually beginning to eat the queen's food and will start to eat finely minced or chopped moist food if this is provided in a shallow dish for easy access. Because they will only eat small amounts to begin with, it is best to use highly palatable, moist, meaty canned foods. Some canned foods, like 'Whiskas Kitten Food' in the United Kingdom, are specifically made for kittens and contain higher levels of energy than most other products and these are the most suitable foods to use. Dry and semi-moist foods although more concentrated are much less suitable. They are less palatable and young kittens often refuse to eat enough to support proper growth. Digestibility of dry foods is usually lower than that of canned cat food and this makes them not so suitable for weanling kittens. By the time the kittens are 7—8 weeks old the proportion of their total nutrient intake coming from supplementary food should be at least 70—80% and they can be finally separated from their mother. Thereafter they are fed independently.

A weanling kitten at 7—8 weeks of age may weigh anything from 600 g to 1 kg. It will be very active and spend much of its waking time in play. The energy requirements of growing kittens are variable depending on size, activity and environment but are not usually less than 200 kcal metabolizable energy per kg liveweight. Kittens usually grow very rapidly if fed generously and will achieve a nearly adult weight of around 3.5 kg by 6 months of age. At this stage they are still very active and will usually eat enough food to supply 120—150 kcal/kg and it is not until they are about a year old that they settle down to the average adult intake of 85—90 kcal/kg. Table 10 is a guide to the estimated energy needs of growing kittens of various ages and weights. The

Table 10. *Estimated calorie needs of young growing cats in relation to their age and expected weight*

Age (weeks)	Expected weight kg	Estimated calorie need kcal/kg	kcal/day
4	0.3—0.4	> 200	70
6	0.4—0.7		120
8	0.6—1.0		160
10	0.8—1.2		200
12	1.0—1.4		240
14	1.1—1.6		260
16	1.2—1.9		300
18	1.3—2.1		340
20	1.4—2.4		350
24	1.6—2.8	150	350
28	1.8—3.2		360
32	2.0—3.5		380
36	2.2—3.8		400
40	2.4—4.0		400
44	2.6—4.2		400
48	2.8—4.4		400
52	2.8—4.6	90	400

weights for age are not extreme values but typical of what is encountered in practice. The estimates of calorie needs are based on the voluntary intake of growing kittens fed mainly on canned foods but include data from animals fed semi-moist and dry foods also.

Kittens very quickly reach intakes of 300—400 kcal per day and grow rapidly without increasing their daily intake to any degree. Intake is usually maintained at this level until maturity although growth gradually ceases and cats achieve a mature weight somewhere between 8 and 12 months of age. A small proportion of cats will continue to put on weight and become moderately obese, perhaps reaching weights of 6 or even 7 kg but few active cats weigh much more than 6 kg (males) and 4 kg (females). A survey has shown that the average weight of adult cats in the United Kingdom is about 4 kg.

Table 10 indicates the approximate energy need of growing cats. What amounts of food are needed to meet these requirements?

It has been said earlier that most cats will not overeat and become obese if given virtually free access to food unless they are confined indoors with little opportunity for exercise. Even then only a moderately small proportion is likely to become fat. Thus it is relatively easy to feed cats well by feeding them to appetite (giving them as much food as they want to eat) several times a day. Provided good quality prepared foods from a reputable manufacturer are used it does not matter which ones you feed. Cats can become very particular about their food and if fed only the one which they like, may refuse to eat anything else. This could lead to minor problems if the food became unavailable. It is a good idea to introduce a variety of different types of food, canned or dry and semi-moist and of different varieties of flavours while they are still growing. This will make it more likely that they will readily accept a variety of foods as adults.

There are no hard and fast rules about the quantities which cats should eat to maintain health. Table 11 indicates expected daily intakes of canned foods when these are fed as the only food. Corresponding figures for dry and semi-moist foods are also included although it is not common for cats to be fed exclusively on these products. It is more usual for them to be given as part of the diet either fed separately in small amounts, mixed in with canned food, given as tit-bits or they may be made available all the time with main meals of canned food given two or more times daily. In situations where free choice of canned and dry foods is allowed, most adult cats do not eat more than 25 g dry food, a quarter to one third of their total energy needs.

Remember there is no need to be concerned if cats eat considerably more or less than the amounts indicated in Table 11. Most cats with access outdoors will probably supplement their diet with small rodents and birds and many will be given small amounts of

Table 11. *Expected average daily intake of canned, dry and semi-moist foods by cats of differing weight and status*

Weight of cat (kg)	Expected daily intake					
	Canned food*				Dry food	Semi-moist food
	Av. quantity		WKF			
Young growing cats	g/day	cans	g/day	cans	g/day	g/day
1	265	2/3	165	½	60	70
1.5	400	1	250	2/3	90	100
2	470	1¼	300	¾	110	120
2.5	500	1¼	320	¾	115	125
3	535	1¼	350	¾	120	135
Adult cats						
2.5	300	¾			70	75
3	360	¾+			80	90
3.5	420	1			95	105
4	480	1+			110	120
4.5	540	1¼			120	135
5	600	1½			135	150
Lactating queen peak lactation						
3	1080	2½	680	1¾	245	270
3.5	1260	3	790	2	290	315
4	1450	3½	900	2¼	330	360

Note: *Canned cat foods usually contain 70–80 kcal metabolizable energy/100 g provided mostly as protein and fat, although some also contain cereal. Dry and semi-moist foods contain about 330 and 300 kcal/100 g respectively. 'Whiskas Kitten Food' (WKF) contains at least 120 kcal/100 g and is most suitable for growing kittens or lactating queens. Individual cats have different requirements and may eat considerably more or less than the amounts indicated. For example, energy intakes of more than 1500 kcal/day have been recorded at peak lactation.

human food such as milk, bacon rinds or other meaty or fatty scraps.

These 'extras' can account for 10–20% of a cat's daily needs. There is also no cause for concern if a cat does become fixed on one variety or brand of canned food, since foods manufactured by reputable companies are formulated to be nutritionally complete. Provided the cat is healthy and not obese and remains so for several months, the diet is satisfactory.

FEEDING CATS IN PREGNANCY AND LACTATION

There is usually no need to provide any special feeding for cats which are pregnant, particularly if a regime of feeding to appetite with a variety of foods is being followed. The extra nutritional needs of pregnancy are small and will be adequately catered for by normal prepared foods.

Once the kittens have been born the nutritional needs of the queen increase rapidly because she has to provide through her milk the nutrients and energy needed for the very rapid growth of her offspring until they begin to eat supplementary foods when about 5 weeks old. Depending on the number of kittens, this demand can easily reach three to four times her normal maintenance needs. In practice this does not present many problems. The queen should be encouraged to increase her nutrient intake by the provision of frequent meals and by offering more concentrated foods. It is good practice to offer milk as well as water at least twice a day, to provide free access to dry or semi-moist food and to give four or more meals of canned food daily. The use of foods specially made for growing kittens and lactating queens, like 'Whiskas Kitten Food' in the United Kingdom, which is a more concentrated but highly palatable canned food, is recommended.

FEEDING GROWING DOGS

Hand-rearing of orphaned pups is discussed elsewhere in Chapter 6. This chapter is concerned only with naturally-reared puppies and normal healthy adult dogs.

Feeding the puppy begins at weaning and although this can be started and is regularly done by some breeders by placing small amounts of food directly into the pups' mouths before they are up and walking, it is a laborious business and any practical advantages are minimal. Weaning will begin naturally when puppies are 3–4 weeks old and actively exploring their surroundings. At this age they will readily take to soft wet foods which are easy to ingest and although many people think that milk and milky feeds should figure prominently in a weaning regime, they are not essential. There are many equally suitable alternatives available. Canned and semi-moist complete foods or canned foods made specially for puppies are the most suitable, such as 'Pedigree Chum Puppy Food' in the United Kingdom.

In the early stages (3–4½ weeks) bitch's milk is still the most important source of nutrients and the puppies' digestive and immune systems are learning to handle new sources of nutrients. Thereafter the intake of other foods quickly increases and most litters can be completely weaned on to a varied diet or on to a single complete food by 6 weeks of age.

Once weaned, puppies grow at a rapid rate and need to ingest very large amounts of energy and nutrients relative to their size, like kittens they probably need two to three times as much as for adult maintenance. It is therefore sensible to think about using more concentrated foods than are required for adults. It is also more suitable to feed moderate amounts three or four times daily than to expect them to gorge themselves twice a day. On the other hand puppies usually have good appetites and given suitably concentrated food can eat enough on a twice-daily feeding regime. It is the total daily intake which matters, not the number of daily feeds. There is some debate about whether or not puppies should be fed to make the maximum possible weight gain of which they are capable or whether a more moderate rate of growth still compatible with development to the usual adult size for the breed is more desirable.

Our experience is that puppies of small and moderately sized breeds from Cairn Terriers to Labradors or Boxers will grow satisfactorily and develop to the usual adult size if fed about 335 kcal/kg metabolic bodyweight per day but that larger breeds like Newfoundlands and Great Danes need considerably greater intakes (up to 400 kcal) if they are to achieve satisfactory growth during the first 5 or 6 months of life. From 5 to 6 months the demand for energy and nutrients gradually reduces as rate of growth decreases until eventually at a year to 18 months it reaches the adult maintenance level. This is approximately 130–140 kcal/kg metabolic bodyweight for medium to large dogs with the giant breeds perhaps needing up to 200 kcal and small breeds about 110–120 kcal.

Table 12 presents estimates of the average calorie need of medium to large breeds and of giant breeds for the period of most rapid growth from weaning to 5 or 6 months of age.

Table 13 contains estimates of the amounts of various types of prepared food needed each day to supply the calories listed in Table 12.

Table 12. *Estimated energy needs of growing dogs in relation to their size (Weaning to 24 weeks of age)*

Size and weight of dog (kg)		Medium–large breeds 335 kcal/W¾	Giant breeds 400 kcal/W¾*
	1	335	
	1.5	455	
6 week old Beagle	2	565	
	2.5	665	
	3	765	
	3.5	855	
6 week old Labrador	4	950	
	4.5	1035	
	5	1120	1340
	5.5	1200	1430
	6	1285	1530
Adult Cairn	6.5	1365	1630
	7	1440	1720
	7.5	1520	1820
	8	1600	1910
	8.5	1670	1990
	9	1740	2080
	9.5	1810	2160
	10	1880	2245
	11	2020	2410
Adult Beagle or	12	2160	2580
Cocker Spaniel	13	2300	2750
	14	2400	2870
5 month old	15	2550	3050
Labrador	16	2680	3200
	17	2800	3350
	18	2920	3400
	19	3050	3500
	20	3170	3600
	22	need reduces as	3750
	24	animals mature to	3900
Adult Labrador	26	adult maintenance	4150
	28	needs of 130–140	4250
	30	kcal/W¾	4300
	32		4380
	34		4500
	36		4500
	38		4600
	40		4680

*Needs gradually reduce from 400 as dogs grow beyond 17 or 18 kg to about 300 kcal/W¾ at 40 kg.

Table 13. *Suggested amounts of various foods needed to meet the average energy needs of growing puppies and young dogs*

Weight of puppy (kg)	Type of food*: Canned meat for puppies plus mixer biscuit 3 : 2 by volume — mixture	Cans	+	g biscuit	Canned Puppy food only*	Canned food (cans)	+	Biscuit 1 : 1 by volume (g)	Semi-moist dog food (g)	Complete dry dog food (g)
1	210	½	+	40	⅔					
2	345	⅔	+	65	1				180	145
3	470	1	+	85	1½				245	195
4	590	1¼	+	100	2				305	245
5	690	1⅓	+	125	2¼				360	290
6	790	1½	+	145	2⅔				410	330
7	880	1¾	+	165	3				460	370
8	980	2	+	180	3¼				510	415
From 10 kg feed 1 : 1 by volume										
10	1060	2	+	270		2¼	+	320	610	490
12	1210	2¼	+	300		2½	+	365	700	560
14	1360	2½	+	350		3	+	410	780	630
16	1500	2¾	+	375		3¼	+	450	860	695
18	1650	3	+	400		3½	+	495	950	760
20	1800	3¼	+	450		3¾	+	530	1000	820

*Canned puppy food ('Pedigree Chum Puppy Food', United Kingdom) assumed to be 110–120 kcal/100 g. Biscuit 340/350 kcal/100 g.
Complete dry food = 380 kcal/100 g
Semi-moist dog food = 310 kcal/100 g

MINERAL AND VITAMIN SUPPLEMENTS

Contrary to many advertisements and popular beliefs, puppies do not require extra large amounts of minerals and vitamins. Provided that their needs as described in Chapter 2 are met, there is no advantage to be gained by over-dosing. This topic is also discussed in Chapter 7.

This is not to say that owners should exclude totally the use of mineral/vitamin supplements. Where an adequate balanced diet is fed they are unlikely to be of benefit and if given in excessive amounts can do harm. But given in moderate amounts they can have a small part to play. They help satisfy the needs of some people to give what they see as extra care and can act as an insurance for those individual animals who through some quirk need amounts outside the usual range. Basically they are unnecessary additions to prepared foods.

An important aspect of feeding growing dogs which is of concern to almost all who have ever owned a puppy but which does not receive much attention in literature is the effects of diet on the amount and consistency of faeces and the frequency of their deposition. It is a very difficult topic to discuss objectively. Faeces are not simply indigestible residues of food but also contain bacteria, mucus, the dead cells from the lining of the gut and materials positively excreted into the lumen of the large bowel. Faecal bulk or volume depends on several things including the amount of indigestible matter in the food, but also the fluid balance within the alimentary tract.

Owners usually have to gather and dispose of dog faeces and this job is more easily performed when faeces are well-formed, firm and not excessively fluid; more like sausages than scrambled eggs in consistency.

Food is only one of the factors influencing faeces bulk and consistency. In general foods of high digestibility result in smaller amounts of well-formed faeces but this is not always so. One of the factors influencing fluidity of faeces is the rate of passage of digesta through the tract.

The ingestion of very large amounts of food may speed up passage and give insufficient time for water reabsorption in the large bowel. Also bacterial fermentation of some food residues may produce gas and materials which irritate the gut and cause a decrease in transit time. Anything which upsets the water balance of the gut can result in very wet loose faeces.

Dietary factors have not been clearly identified so it would be unwise to suggest that the inclusion of some or omission of other ingredients will necessarily result in satisfactory faeces. Our experience suggests that puppies generally produce softer faeces than adults and that this is related to the large amount of food eaten relative to their size. Feeding several smaller meals of more digestible foods is usually helpful. Some puppies take longer to settle to diet changes, and high fat diets which usually slow down transit times and are highly digestible may at first result in greasy loose stools if introduced abruptly into the diet, despite usually being satisfactory once puppies have adapted to them. Observation over several days following a change of diet or feeding management is probably the best way of arriving at a suitable combination of food and management for the individual puppy. Dietary management is at least as important as the composition of the food fed.

FEEDING ADULT DOGS

A healthy adult dog can be fed totally on one food or with any number of combinations. It is not possible to cover more than a few but Table 14 provides a summary of the average energy needs of adult dogs and amounts of food (provided as canned food plus biscuit) needed to meet these needs.

The table can only serve as a starting point for a feeding regime, the actual amounts needed for the maintenance of any particular dog have to be obtained by trial and error and careful observation of the dog's health when the amounts given are varied. The suggested proportions of canned meat to biscuit are equal amounts by volume, approximately 3 : 1 meat: biscuit by weight. This ratio provides adequate amounts of all nutrients and is chosen to incorporate all the palatability benefits of the canned food. A 2 : 1 ratio would be perfectly satisfactory as a source of nutrients, but many small dogs or fussy eaters refuse to eat this amount of biscuit. Larger breeds or dogs with good appetites can easily manage this sort of mixture.

Table 15 provides the same information for typical semi-moist and dry foods.

Table 14. *Average energy needs of normal adult dogs and amounts of food needed to meet them.*
1. Canned food + biscuit

Weight of dog (kg)	Typical breed	Daily energy needed (kcal)	Food to provide this amount of energy — Canned meat and biscuit mixtures, equal volumes or 3 : 1 by weight, and 2 : 1 by weight					
			3 : 1			2 : 1		
			Total weight (g)	Cans +	Biscuit (g)	Total weight (g)	Cans +	Biscuit (g)
2	Yorkshire Terrier	240	155	¼	40			
6	Cairn	540	350	⅔	85	305	½	100
13	Beagle, Cocker	900	585	1	145	505	¾	170
20	Samoyed	1250	810	1½	200	702	1	235
25	Collie	1500	960	1¾	240	830	1¼	280
30	Boxer, Labrador	1700	1100	2	275	955	1½	320
35	German Shepherd Dog ♀	1900	1235	2¼	300	1070	1⅔	360
40	German Shepherd Dog ♂	2100	1365	2½	340	1180	2	400
50+	Great Dane, Newfoundland	3500	2270	4	570	2000	3¼	600

Note: 1. Energy needs increase by about 45 kcal for each kg increase in bodyweight from 20 to 40 kg.
2. Values are average estimates based on moderate exercise and reasonably warm housing. Individual dogs may need 25% more or less than the amounts suggested.
3. For large breeds with good appetites, the proportions of meat and biscuit may be altered from equal volume to 1 part meat to 2 parts biscuit, i.e. from 3 : 1 to 2 : 1 by weight.

Table 15. *Average energy needs of normal adult dogs and amounts of food needed to meet them.*
2. Semi-moist & dry foods

Weight of dog (kg)	Typical breed	Daily energy need (kcal)	Semi-moist food needed to provide this amount when fed as the only food (g)	Complete dry food needed (g)
2	Yorkshire Terrier	240	75	60
6	Cairn	540	170	140
13	Beagle, Cocker	900	280	230
20	Samoyed	1250	390	320
25	Collie	1500	460	380
30	Boxer, Labrador	1700	530	440
35	German Shepherd Dog ♀	1900	590	490
40	German Shepherd Dog ♂	2100	660	540
50*	Great Dane, Newfoundland	3500	1100	900

*Giant breeds appear to need almost 200 kcal/W¾ per day for maintenance or 50% more than dogs in the medium-sized range.

THE WORKING DOG

The working dog is also an adult but one which has more variable and much greater energy needs. The amount of extra energy required depends on the nature of the work. Sheepdogs covering many miles over rough terrain, often in inclement weather, may need considerably more than patrol or guard dogs. They can sometimes need 2–3 times normal maintenance amounts. Their feeding can usually be straight-forward. Simply give more of the same sort of food or, because the quantities needed are so large, use more of the concentrated semi-moist or dry foods. If there is a rest period during work it is sensible to give a small meal at that time but reserve the main meal until after work. All working dogs should only receive a small meal prior to working, since it is inconvenient for guard and patrol dogs to have to defaecate during a duty period. A full stomach is not conducive to efficient work.

The main meal should perhaps provide 2/3 of the daily needs and since dogs are often tired and have poor appetites, the more concentrated and palatable foods should be used. It is probably best not to include too much biscuit but to use complete foods and the more concentrated canned products like puppy foods. Working dogs should be given an opportunity to drink during the working period. The subject of feeding dogs under stressful conditions is covered in more detail in Chapter 5.

THE BREEDING BITCH

To plan a sensible feeding programme for the bitch, it is necessary to understand what are the extra nutritional and physical demands made by breeding.

A normal healthy bitch does not have any large increase in growth of new tissue during the early part of pregnancy. Most foetal growth takes place during the last 2 weeks and although there is considerable development of mammary and uterine tissues before this, the extra need for nutrients and energy over and above maintenance requirements are quite small. A bitch in good condition at mating will not require any special food during pregnancy and can continue to receive her usual diet. All that is necessary is that the amount is gradually increased during the second half of gestation. It has been found that increasing food allowance by 10% each week from the sixth week onwards, so that intake at birth is approximately 50% more than at mating, is a satisfactory regime for most dogs.

It may happen that a bitch with a large litter may have such an enlarged abdomen and such reduced activity that her appetite falls during the last week or 10 days.

In these cases it is sensible to feed more frequent smaller meals and perhaps introduce or increase the amounts of concentrated foods which will probably be used in lactation anyway. The objective is to have a bitch at parturition which is not overfat and which has maintained her appetite.

Lactation presents the biggest test of nutritional adequacy of any feeding regime. The bitch must eat, digest, absorb and use very large amounts of nutrients to produce sufficient milk of adequate composition to support the growth and development of several puppies. Experience and theory both indicate that the amounts needed are very large.

Consider a Labrador bitch of 28 kg with a litter of 8 puppies, total weight 12 kg at 3–4 weeks of age. At this stage the pups require about 200 kcal per kg per day, which they have to obtain as milk. The bitch therefore has to provide 2400 kcal as milk. Bitch's milk contains about 1300 kcal/l and so the amount of milk needed is at least $\frac{2400}{1300}$ = 1.85 l or 3¼ pints. This assumes that all the energy of the milk is available to the pups with 100% efficiency. There are obviously some losses of energy in the production of milk by the bitch but if we assume that the process has an efficiency of 75% then in order to produce 2400 kcal as milk, the bitch must obtain $\frac{2400}{0.75}$ or 3200 kcal from her food. In addition she will need to maintain herself and will need 1600 kcal for this. Her total food energy need is therefore at least 4800 kcal or 3 times the maintenance requirement.

Obviously bitches with greater milk production would need even more food. If the bitch is unable to produce enough milk or to eat the amounts of food she needs then earlier supplementary feeding of puppies may be necessary if they are to do as well as they should.

This calculation is based on estimates of the energy needs for satisfactory milk production but requirements for other nutrients are similarly increased. Protein quantity and quality will affect milk production. It is therefore necessary to ensure that the extra food supplied is of good quality and is not made up only of high fat or high carbohydrate foods. Because the amounts needed are very large, it is usually necessary to feed several meals per day or *ad libitum*. An example of the sort of regime needed to provide adequate intake in the bitch is presented in Fig. 12. This shows the weight changes of a Labrador bitch represented by the solid line, super-imposed on food intake data expressed as average weight of food consumed per day for each week of pregnancy and lactation. This dog had a litter of 8 puppies and at weaning, 6 weeks after parturition was in good con-

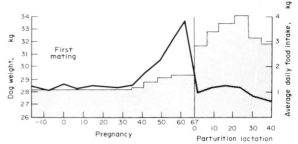

Fig. 12. Typical food intake and weight change of a breeding bitch during pregnancy and lactation.

dition but weighed some 1½ kg less than at mating when she had been rather fat. The food was an equal volume mixture (3 : 1 by weight) of a standard canned meat in jelly and mixer biscuit. At peak lactation during week 4 this dog ate her own weight of food, just over 28 kg, made up of 51 cans and 7 kg biscuit. This was a daily intake of 4 kg, 7¼ cans plus 1 kg biscuit.

This sort of intake is typical of a bitch which is fed to maintain adequate condition through lactation. It emphasizes the importance of proper nutrient balance at this critical phase of life. Deficiencies or imbalances are soon reflected in abnormal or reduced performance. In practice it means feeding frequently and making a lot of food and water available overnight.

The use of more concentrated foods like puppy food, semi-moist or complete dry foods is one way to achieve higher intakes. If the dog is willing to eat different kinds of foods this makes it easier, although it is quite satisfactory to stick to one or two foods if this is the normal regime. The important point is that it is necessary to encourage the bitch to eat at least two to three times her normal maintenance requirements. The breeding bitch does not require special vitamin/mineral supplements if good quality foods are used, merely enough of the right kinds of normal foods to meet the extra demands of the second half of pregnancy and lactation.

Feeding dogs and cats at various stages of their lives using prepared foods is really a straightforward affair. Most pet owners are untrained in nutrition and animal husbandry and require confidence that the feeding regime which they adopt will be nutritionally sound as well as satisfying their other expectations of palatability, convenience, price and suitability for their particular domestic arrangements. The range of types and varieties of prepared foods, most of which are nutritionally balanced (i.e. provide adequate amounts of vitamins, minerals and major nutrients in relation to their energy content) is such that they can provide this convenience and reassurance. The feeding guides provided by reputable manufacturers and the amounts suggested in Tables 10—15 give a good starting point from which to estimate the amounts needed by any particular dog or cat. Careful observation of the animal's appearance and behaviour will enable the owner to identify the correct level of feeding for his animal, its likes and dislikes and to arrive at a satisfactory feeding regime.

CHAPTER 5

FEEDING DOGS FOR HARD WORK AND STRESS

D. S. Kronfeld

INTRODUCTION

Hard work induces stress, so feeding for hard work should include consideration of nutritional requirements for stress as well as provision of fuels for muscular exercise. The preponderant fuels are fats and soluble carbohydrates, and provision of these nutrients has been the main aim of most previous diets designed to sustain or promote hard work. Our studies on racing sledge dogs have demonstrated a greater need for dietary protein than would be expected from a consideration of fuels, and that observed responses of red blood cells associate the protein demands of the hard working dog with stress. The proportions of protein, fat and carbohydrates thus become determined by stress as well as exercise.

A diet for hard work should be highly digestible, i.e. the proportion of food material that is absorbed as nutrients should be large, while the residue that is incorporated into faeces should be small. High digestibility is achieved by an abundance of fat, soluble carbohydrates, and relatively soluble proteins, and by low contents of insoluble proteins, ash and especially food fibre. In effect, high digestibility is inseparable from high energy density and low bulk.

The major staples or food energy sources for dogs are meat, meat by-products, cereal grains, and milling by-products. In this order, they decrease in expense and food value, in terms of digestibility, energy density and high quality protein. It follows that diets composed predominantly of grains and grain by-products should be fed when least expense is the predominant goal, and that diets which contain relatively more meat by-products and eventually meat itself should be fed as demands increase for hard work and stress.

Little is known in general and virtually nothing specifically about the dog's extra demands for hard work and stress on vitamins, minerals and electrolytes. In general, these should relate to the energy intake of the dog or the energy density of the diet. Stress may increase demands for potassium, calcium, magnesium, copper, iron and zinc, also vitamins A, C and E.

Hard work and stress tend to engender several clinical conditions that may be averted or mitigated by appropriate feeding programmes and diets. These conditions include the diarrhoea—dehydration—stress syndrome, exertional rhabdomyolysis ('tying-up'), bloat, lower bowel bleeding, stress anaemia, and metatarsal fractures. We are also currently studying the possibility that heat prostration may be influenced by diet.

SLEDGE DOG RACING

Much of the emphasis in this review derives from studies of racing sledge dogs. These weigh about 25 kg when fit for racing. The 'Alaskan Racing Huskie' is not a recognized breed, though it derives mainly from the same original Siberian stock as the current American Kennel Club Siberian Husky. Due to constraints in the breed standard, the AKC Siberian is no longer competitive in racing. Alaskans have variable infusions of several breeds, notably Irish Setter (the 'hound' type), German Shepherd Dog, Labrador, Airedale, Greyhound and Saluki.

The International Sled Dog Racing Association sponsors races limited to three, five or seven dogs, and unlimited races in which teams usually consist of ten to sixteen dogs. There are also weight-pulls and freight races.

One of my main collaborators is Harris Dunlap, MS, proprietor of Zero Kennel, Bakers Mills, New York. He has twice won the ISDRA Gold Medal for overall points in the unlimited class. He races about 10 times during January, February and March, starting in Minnesota, then the north east, finally Alaska. The early races consist of 2 heats of about 17 miles (27 km) on successive days. The North American Championship in Fairbanks consists of two 24-mile (38 km) heats then a third heat of 30 miles (48 km). Zero Kennel has averaged over 19 mph in several races. This may be compared to the 12 mph pace of the human marathon, the 15 mph pace of the 4-minute mile, and the 22 mph of the human sprint. A champion middle-distance team pulls sledge and driver in bursts up to 25 mph.

Another collaborator is Terry Adkins, DVM, MPH, a Lieutenant-Colonel in the United States Air Force. He was a veterinarian for the first Iditarod Trial Championship, then he went racing. He was placed tenth in 1981, running about 1,130 miles (1,800 km) in 13 days 8 h, averaging 85 miles per day from Anchorage to Nome. He aims for a sustained 10 mph trot.

My third collaborator is Robert Downey, BS, a graduate student who has conducted our treadmill studies. He is an intermediate racer who was placed thirteenth in the 1981 ISDRA seven-dog class. He is also an astute observer of a dog's condition and performance in relation to diet. His current main concern is that the heat exchanger at the base of the brain, the carotid rete, may determine stamina and race winning ability more than, say, heart size, hip–hock length or any other readily measurable item of conformation. The effectiveness of the rete is measured in terms of the temperature difference between the deep part of the ear and the rectum. This ear–rear difference is $0.25-0.5°C$ at rest and increases to $1.0-2.5°C$ during exhaustive exercise, when rectal temperature may reach $109°C$ while the rete keeps the brain below $107°C$. This procedure may influence selection of sledge dogs for racing in the future.

It is important for readers to recognize the practical experience of these collaborators, for much of the recommendations about feeding depend upon their observations in the field rather than controlled studies under laboratory conditions. One has a trade-off in relevance between controlled studies on Beagles on a treadmill or observations on world champion canine athletes racing under unconstrained, often severe, occasionally life-threatening trail conditions.

This review will begin with a practical description of diets and feeding that should be immediately useful for any feeder of dogs subjected to hard work and stress. This will be followed by a scientifically deeper discussion of digestibility, muscle metabolism and diseases.

IDEAL DIET FOR HARD WORK AND STRESS

Our studies of racing sledge dogs over the last decade have indicated that an ideal diet for hard work and stress should contain the maximum of fat consistent with optimal requirements of protein for stress and complex carbohydrates for 'feedability'. The latter term alludes to a characteristic of a diet that affects its flexibility in introduction and robustness during periods of duress. Our studies have confirmed that carbohydrates are not essential in the diet of dogs, but our drivers contend that a carbohydrate-free diet is difficult to introduce without digestive upsets and is more prone to render dogs susceptible to loose stools or diarrhoea during particularly gruelling periods of racing, for example on the Iditarod Trail, or during bouts of kennel cough or other viral-like epidemics that appear to pass from time to time through a sledge dog team. We are currently testing a series of four levels of carbohydrate fed to huskies running on a treadmill; meanwhile, 17% of available energy in the form of soluble carbohydrate was used in our two main teams in 1981 and was very satisfactory in regard to 'feedability'. In this practical sense, although our studies have shown that dietary carbohydrate is not essential for hard work, zero carbohydrate content appears to be sub-optimal for racing sledge dogs under extreme stress.

The protein content is much better established. A level of 28% of available energy in the form of high quality protein has been insufficient to sustain red blood cell indices through the middle-distance racing season or through the 1200-mile Iditarod Trail race. On the other hand, red blood cells have been sustained by 32 or 39% protein. This indicates that 32% is sufficient (Table 16). The fat content recommended, 51% of available energy, is the remainder

Table 16. *Comparison of adequate diet for maintenance with ideal diet for hard work and stress*

	Maintenance	Work & Stress	WR&S/M
Energy Density			
Kcal/g dry matter	3.5	5.3	1.5
Energy Proportions			
Protein %	16	32	2.0
Fat %	14	51	3.6
Carbohydrate %	80	17	0.21
Dry Matter Basis			
Protein %	13	42	3.2
Fat %	5	30	6.0
Carbohydrate %	66	22	0.33
Fibre %	10	2	0.20
Ash %	6	4	0.67
Digestibility %	70	90	1.3
Protein Quality %	55	85	1.5
Main Ingredients	Grain Grain by-products Soyabean meal	Meat Meat by-products Grain	

after needs for protein and carbohydrate have been met.

Our ideal racing diet, which we believe is probably in the optimal range for dogs subjected to all kinds of hard work and stress, may be compared to a minimal diet that is adequate for the maintenance of an average healthy adult dog which is relatively inactive in comfortable surroundings (Table 16). The ideal diet is much higher than the adequate maintenance diet in regard to digestibility, protein quantity and quality, energy density and fat. The dog at maintenance is more tolerant of bulk and carbohydrate. In effect the maintenance diet may contain more grain and grain by-products, while the ideal diet turns more to meat by-products and for extreme demands, more meat.

DIET BASED ON COMMERCIAL DOG FOODS

We have found no commercial product that approximates the proposed ideal diet for dogs subject to very hard work and stress (Table 16). The closest fit is achieved by some canned products that contain mainly meat and meat by-products, with very little grain or soy flour (Table 17). Such products are expensive relative to dry, grain-based dog foods

(Table 17). The ideal diet may be approached by a mixture of the two kinds of dog food. Using the typical values in Table 17, a mixture of canned : dry in the proportions of 3 : 1 on the basis of available energy would yield contents of 18% carbohydrate, enough for 'feedability', and 35% protein, enough for stress. This proportion on an available energy basis should be converted to a moist weight or 'as-fed' basis and, eventually for the feeder in the kennel, to an approximate volume basis (Table 18).

For economy, dogs are usually kept on dry food alone when not working. We prefer, however, to moisten the dry food and mix in a little canned meat because this establishes the mixing routine in the kennel management and because we doubt that the dry dog food is truly adequate for maintenance

Table 17. *Composition of canned 'meat dinner',
dry grain-based dog food, and mixtures*

Available energy %	Canned meat	Dry grain	Canned : Dry		
			3 : 1	1 : 1	1 : 3
Fat	˙55	24	47.0	39.5	31.7
Protein	40	20	35.3	30.0	25.0
Carbohydrate	5	56	17.7	30.5	43.3

Table 18. *Mixtures of canned 'meat dinner' and dry grain-based dog food on various bases*

Basis	Canned : Dry		
Available Energy[a]	1 : 3	1 : 1	3 : 1
Dry Matter[b]	31 : 69	42 : 58	73 : 27
As-Fed[c]	53 : 47	73 : 27	89 : 11
Volume[d]	45 : 55	66 : 34	85 : 15
Approximate Volume	1 : 1	2 : 1	6 : 1

[a]Proportions from Table 17 that correspond respectively to protein contents of 25, 30 or 35% of available energy.

[b]Conversion is based on energy densities of 6.0 and 4.4 kcal/g of dry matter in the canned and dry products shown in Table 17.

[c]Conversion is based on energy densities of 1.5 and 4.0 kcal/g moist or as fed of two products.

[d]A standard 420 g (14¾ oz) can holds about 300 g of the dry food shown in Table 17.

of a dog that will sooner or later be subjected to stress. So we move to something like a 1 : 1 mixture on a volume basis, i.e. one canful of the meat-based product to the same-size canful of the dry product at least 2 weeks before the first elective stress, i.e. a training run. Then as hard work and stress increase, the proportions change from 1 : 1 to 2 : 1 and so on. For racing sledge dogs fed commercial products, we work in the range of 1 : 1 to 6 : 1 of canned meat to dry dog food, varying the ratio with the demands of work and stress.

If the stress is due predominantly to physical exercise, then the amount of dry food may be held constant and the proportion changed by feeding more and more meat and meat by-products as required for energy. On the other hand, if the stress is more emotional than physical, e.g. guard dog training, then the amount of dry food is diminished as the amount of canned meat is increased as required for protein.

Mixing these two kinds of commercial products, both 'complete and balanced' according to nationally established standards, should ensure safety as well as flexibility with regard to economy and performance. When performance is paramount however, we add a little boiled rice to the canned food instead of using commercial dry food. Rice is much more digestible

than dry dog food, perhaps 95% compared to 75%. The rice is boiled for about 20 min with 2 volumes of water for 1 volume (e.g. a canful) of dry rice. To avoid nutritional deficiencies, we never use more boiled rice than a 5 : 1 mixture with canned 'complete and balanced' product, i.e. 5 canfuls of canned meat to 1 canful of boiled rice.

When economy is paramount, the predominant food must be dry and predominantly grain. This may be improved in nutritional value by a number of measures:

1. Moisten with about one-fifth volume of water. This increases voluntary food intake by an average about 10%. Water softens the texture and may bring out the aroma or flavour of dry food that is coated with fat and protein hydrolysates.

2. Moisten with about one-fifth milk, fresh, or diluted evaporated canned milk, or reconstituted dry milk. Milk improves the fat and protein contents of most dry dog foods. It greatly improves the protein quality, i.e. the overall amino acid profile. Rarely in my experience, (though commonplace in many articles about feeding dogs), wholesome milk may induce watery diarrhoea. This is attributed to poor hydrolytic digestion of lactose in the small intestine, followed by partial fermentation to lactic acid in the large bowel. Lactic acid would be poorly absorbed and retain water in the faeces. I have observed this phenomenon only once and believe that it is readily avoided by sound feeding management: introduce milk gradually, make sure that it is wholesome, and clean up any milk-moistened dry food that is left unconsumed for a few hours, depending on the ambient temperature.

3. Add protein supplements. Milk has been mentioned, other dairy products are also good, such as cottage cheese, dehydrated cottage cheese, or any other kind of cheese. One tablespoonful (about 15 g) of dehydrated cottage cheese per 450 g (1 lb) of dry dog food raises the protein contents by 3% and also improves protein quality. Two medium-sized eggs have the same effect on protein and supply a wide range of other essential nutrients.

Warnings against the feeding of raw eggs because of the avidin in the white fail to take into account the greater amount of biotin in the yolk, or the large number of separated whites that would be needed. I have not found estimates of this number for dogs, but about four egg whites per day are needed to induce biotin-deficiency in rats and about twenty a day for many days in humans.

4. Add fat supplements. Animal fats and vegetable oils may be added to dry dog foods. The risk is that increasing the energy density will lower the effective contents of essential nutrients through marginal zones towards deficiencies. Racing sledge dogs fed diets over-supplemented with fat simply lose their running ability and 'turn sour' long before any typical signs, such as poorer coats, become evident. Most dry dog foods contain abundant minerals, with the possible exceptions of iodine and zinc. However their vitamin contents are usually limited to 1.25 to 1.5 times 'adequate' standards on a dry matter basis that assume an energy density of 4.0 kcal per gram dry matter. Adding 60 g (2 oz) of animal fat to 450 g (1 lb) of dry dog food increases the energy density to 4.6 kcal/g, and we are reluctant to allow further dilution of essential nutrients.

The upper limit for daily use of vegetable oils to supplement dry dog foods is even lower, depending on the contents of polyunsaturated fatty acids. We usually recommend no more that 30 g (1 oz) of maize oil per 450 g (1 lb) of dry dog food. This will raise the polyunsaturate content to about 8% of available energy. More oil could threaten the balance between poly-unsaturates and vitamin E, which is a very complex matter.

HOME-COOKING FOR MAINTENANCE OR STRESS

My approach to home-cooking for dogs is based on the finding that equal volumes of dry rice and medium-fat ground meat contain about equal calories. Thus one may choose an appropriate total volume, e.g. one cup full for a 10 kg dog or two cupfuls for a 25 kg dog, then vary the proportions of rice to meat according to the desired proportions of carbohydrate, fat and protein. Two extremes are shown in Table 19.

Table 19. *Home-made diets for a 25 kg dog at maintenance or under stress*

Ingredients	Maintenance	Work & Stress
Rice, dry, cupfuls[a]	4/3	1/3
Meat, fatty, cupfuls	2/3	5/3
Water, cupfuls	4	4
Maize oil, tablespoonful[b]	1	1
Bone meal, dessertspoonful	1	1
Iodized salt, teaspoonful	1	1
Available Energy %		
Protein	18	32
Fat	15	51
Carbohydrate	60	17

[a]One standard breakfast cupful holds about 240 ml of water or 8 fluid ounces and about 200 g of dry rice or ground meat (mince or hamburger).

[b]One teaspoonful contains about 5 g of water, about the same of salt, a little less oil, and a little more powdered bone meal. One dessertspoon is equivalent to 2 teaspoons, and 1 tablespoon to 3 teaspoons.

Rice comprises two-thirds of the staple diet for maintenance, but one-sixth for the most serious stress. The latter extreme is seldom needed, but it does approach the ideal we have proposed for stress and hard work. The amount of food shown in Table 19 is for a dog under stress but not greatly increased energy demand. During hard training and racing, 25 kg sledge dogs will consume 6 to 8 cupfuls, i.e. three to four-times maintenance.

A second feature of this approach to home-cooking is the realization that a single supplement package can be devised for use with any mixture of rice or other cereal grain and meat, provided meat constitutes at least one-third to provide fat and protein. Both grains and meat are deficient in calcium, hence both need bone meal (or some other supplement, such as dicalcium phosphate). Both grains and meat have variable and usually low contents of iodine, which may be provided conveniently as iodized salt. Also in doubt are vitamin E and, in beef or mutton, poly-unsaturated fatty acids; these nutrients are supplied by corn oil. The rest of the vitamins and trace minerals are abundant in liver.

For use in home-cooking for dogs, human-grade liver can be chopped into 5 mm cubes. These are packed into plastic ice-cube trays, most of which have spaces that hold about 15 g (1 oz) of liver.

The third feature of this approach is the ease of cooking. The water is brought to boil with the oil, bone meal and salt. The rice is added and stirred then allowed to simmer for 10 min. The ground or chopped meat and liver is added, and the lot allowed to simmer for another 10 min. Do not overcook. Cool before feeding. One may cook every day or else cook larger batches and refrigerate or freeze for convenience.

DIGESTIBILITY

The importance of digestibility was first emphasized in reports of the performance of sledge dogs in the Antarctic (Orr, 1966). Dogs fed a diet of seal meat and fat, that contained 70% fat on a dry matter basis, retained body weight and vigour. Other dogs fed a high-protein, low-carbohydrate diet had persistent diarrhoea and failed to maintain body weight or vigour. A third group was fed a 'balanced' mixture of beef and grain, 45% fat and 22% protein on a dry matter basis, ostensibly the best diet. These dogs produced well-formed stools but lost their vigour. Digestibility studies showed that poor performance was associated with poor efficiencies of digestion of dry matter and especially protein. These observations led to two main conclusions: high-fat content is valuable, and poor digestibility is undesirable. Two other points were evinced, though less surely, namely that carbohydrate is not necessary and probably not helpful, and that dietary content of protein should not exceed that of fat when carbohydrate is low.

The importance of digestibility in regard to stamina was demonstrated more directly by observations of our own Beagles (Downey, Kronfeld and Banta, 1980). Eight young males were selected from sixteen for their willingness to run in a team of four on a treadmill. It was inclined at 7° and run at 14.4 km/h (9 mph). The dogs were fed four diets for four periods of 14 days in a change-over design. New diets were introduced progressively over 4 days, then exhaustion tests were conducted 3 and 10 days later. Mean exhaustion times for the four diets were found to correlate positively with their energy densities, fat contents and digestibilities but negatively with carbohydrate contents. Daily amounts of food consumed

were recorded, so sixty-four sets of data were available for multiple regression analysis of exhaustion time (T min) and intakes of digestible carbohydrate (C g/day), fat (F g/day), protein (P g/day) and dry matter (D g/day).

$$T = 60 + 3.3F + 2.6C + 2.4\,P - 1.9D \text{ min}$$

The amount of variation in exhaustion time that could be accounted for in terms of variation in diet was 30%. Also the difference between mean exhaustion time in dogs fed the worst diet (the best-selling dry dog food), and the best experimental diet was 30%, was 15 miles v 20. The common value of 30% was fortuitous but both parameters showed a powerful influence of diet upon stamina.

In the above equation, the negative influence of dry matter as such counterposed against the positive influence of energy yielding nutrients may be construed to show the disadvantage of bulk and the advantage of a high digestible energy density. These features of a diet intended to promote stamina had often been assumed previously but never demonstrated.

More generally, digestibility in dogs has been shown to be improved by animal fat and protein, and to be depressed by food fibre and carbohydrate. Substitution of one-third of vegetable protein by animal protein improved digestibility from 79 to 91% in dogs but only 89 to 90% in humans (Hegsted et al., 1974). Fat digestibility in a canned meat product was 96% but only 90% in a dry grain-based dog food. Increments of 3, 6 and 9% alpha-cellulose were found to progressively depress digestibility of dry matter and protein in Beagles. Following comparisons of responses of Beagles to nine diets, digestible energy and nitrogen were stated to tend to decrease as dietary carbohydrate increased in the first four diets (Rosmos et al., 1976). Simple regression applied to all nine diets showed highly significant negative correlations between dietary carbohydrate and digestibility of both energy and nitrogen.

Signs of deficiencies of iodine and copper or zinc have been observed in dogs fed diets heavily supplemented with calcium. This may occur when soyabean meal is supplied as a protein supplement for cereal grains, such as ground corn. Soyabeans are rich in phytin which binds calcium, so with grain deficient in calcium and with soy binding calcium, supplementation with calcium must be heavy. Phytin also binds zinc and iron. Absorption of iron is also depressed by starch. Absorption of calcium, magnesium, zinc and phosphorus is depressed by wheat. In sum, diets based on cereal grains are abundant in fibre, starch, phytin and, after supplementation, calcium, and these components combine to depress the efficiency of absorption of food energy, fat, protein and several minerals.

The weight of bulk

In addition to their effects on the availability and absorption of nutrients, bulky foods handicap an animal by their retained weight. In our studies of Beagles on a treadmill for example, the extra faecal bulk resulting from the dry dog food amounted to about 150 g per day. This is equivalent to about 7 kg handicap for a race-horse.

SOURCES OF ENERGY FOR MUSCLE

Several sources of chemical energy are used for contraction of muscle. These sources are called upon in an orchestrated manner. The immediate source is a specific compound, adenosine triphosphate (ATP), which has two high-energy phosphate bonds. Each muscle fibre contains enough ATP to contract for less than 1 s. It is replenished immediately by high-energy phosphates from creatine phosphate, sufficient for a few more contractions. Something less than a 10 s sprint may be sustained by these phosphate bonds. We do not know how to influence their availability by training or diet.

High energy phosphate bonds are generated within the muscle fibres by the breakdown of glycogen, a carbohydrate stored in the cells, and glucose, taken up by the cells from the blood, to lactic acid. This process, glycolysis, does not use oxygen; it is anaerobic. It is less efficient than aerobic metabolism or oxidation. Lactic acid that accumulates during anaerobic metabolism eventually has to be oxidized, and during the period of its accumulation, the body is said to have an oxygen debt.

Besides glucose, the other main blood-borne fuels are fatty acids, principally those mobilized from fat depots. Fatty acid metabolism in the muscle cells is entirely aerobic. In animals running at half maximal speed, increased blood flow is thought to carry more than enough oxygen, glucose and free fatty acids to the working muscles, so that the limit of aerobic metabolism is the activity of the small intracellular vesicles in which oxidation occurs, the mitochondria (Table 20). The number of mitochondria increases with training only in those muscles that are worked.

Metabolic regulation

In healthy working muscles, balances between aerobic and anaerobic processes, between utilization of intra- and extra-muscular fuels, and between carbohydrate and fat, are exquisitely controlled. The controls are multiple, overlapping, redundant and changing in predominance with the intensity and duration of work. Brief intense work demands glycolysis. A greyhound sprinting for 30 s at 38 mph probably replenishes most of its ATP by anaerobic breakdown of muscle glycogen. Longer and lighter work relies mainly on the oxidation of glucose and fatty acids carried by blood to muscle. The huskies of Zero Kennel running for 55 min at 19.2 mph at Kalkaska in 1978 were replenishing ATP by oxidation, mainly that of fat.

The oxidation of fatty acids automatically retards the utilization of glucose and glycogen. Acyl-CoA

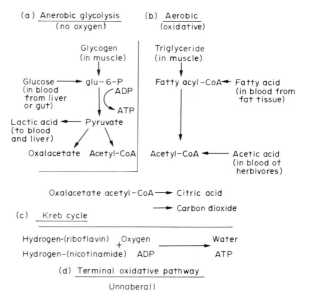

derivatives of fatty acids inhibit 3 key enzymes in glycolysis. Citric acid powerfully inhibits the one which converts glucose-6-phosphate (glu-6-P) to fructose-6-phosphate. Accumulation of glu-6-P inhibits its formation from glucose or glycogen. Training or feeding more fat have been shown to increase fat oxidation by working muscles. This automatically reduces or spares the utilization of carbohydrate.

The interplay of metabolic controls is complex in the extreme and this allows the possibility that at some intermediate level of work where fat oxidation may reach its zenith, its inhibitory influence on glucose utilization may abate slightly so that peak oxidative activity uses both fuels freely. This situation may occur for example, in a sledge dog or bird dog near 20 mph.

Hormonal responses

During intense exercise, release of epinephrine from the adrenal glands promotes rapid breakdown of glycogen in muscle and liver. Liver muscle glycogen breakdown is also promoted by the secretion of glucagon from the pancreas; these processes promote the utilization of carbohydrate.

Norepinephrine release from nerve endings in adipose tissue is a major factor in mobilization of fat in the form of free fatty acids which are used by muscles and glycerol, this is taken up by the liver and converted to glucose.

Insulin secretion subsides during exercise. It remains above a minimal level needed to permit glucose uptake by working muscles but does not tend to promote excessive glucose uptake. This conserves glucose in the blood for vital support of the brain. (Nervous tissue does not need insulin to facilitate glucose uptake.)

Energy used in racing dogs

I estimate that Zero Kennel sledge dogs running 17.6 miles at 19.2 mph for 55 min expend 15.32 kcal/min or 838 kcal for the race. The 20 kg dog at 19.2 mph and the 60 kg human athlete at 11.1 mph are both expending 15.32 kcal/min. This consumes 3.2 l of oxygen, about 13 or 29 times the resting levels for man or dog respectively. The dog is a super-athlete.

The best estimates of utilization of blood-borne fuels during prolonged running involved the use of radioactive tracers in glucose and free fatty acids (Paul and Issekutz, 1967). The dogs were running on a treadmill, wearing masks to measure oxygen consumption and to trap radioactive carbon dioxide for analysis. The dogs were mongrels averaging about 13 kg bodyweight. Estimates of fuel consumption are given in Table 20.

Most people think about muscles burning glucose, but this fuel accounts for only 16% of oxidation at rest, relatively less during prolonged running at a fairly slow speed. Oxygen consumption increased 6-fold, but glucose oxidation only 4-fold. Oxidation of free fatty acids increased 13-times however, so that it eventually accounted for 71% of oxygen consumption.

Even more fascinating is the large fraction of oxygen consumption not accounted for in terms of the two fuels, glucose and fatty acids, which receive nearly all of the attention of exercise physiologists. Some of this fraction must represent oxidation of ketone bodies, especially as exercise becomes prolonged. But what about that 54% unaccounted for oxygen consumption at zero hours (before exercise)? Does this carnivore burn more amino acids than is usually recognized?

Table 20. *Oxygen consumption and relative contributions of glucose and fatty acids during running on a treadmill inclined at 15° at about 4 mph for 4 h*

	0	1	4
Duration of exercise, h	0	1	4
Oxygen consumption, ml/min	85	500	500
Percent of oxygen consumption accounted for by oxidation of:			
Glucose	16	11	11
Fatty acids	30	49	71
Percent of oxygen consumption *not* accounted for:	54	40	18

NUTRITIONAL STRATEGIES FOR PROMOTING STAMINA

Studies on humans riding bicycle ergometers have

shown that muscle glycogen content is an important determinant of stamina (Bergström *et al.*, 1967). Two alternative strategies focus on the muscle content of glycogen (Kronfeld and Downey, 1982).

The better known strategy, 'carbohydrate-loading', aims to maximize muscle glycogen before exercise through a regimen of dietary changes with a training sequence that induces first depletion then over-compensatory repletion of muscle glycogen. Typically, a human athlete is trained on a 'mixed diet'. About 7 days before an event, the athlete is subjected to exhaustive exercise. This is followed for 3 days by light training on a low-carbohydrate diet. Repletion occurs during the next 3 days of light training on a high-carbohydrate diet. Overcompensation leads to muscle glycogen contents of up to 60 g/kg in humans, horses and probably dogs.

'Carbohydrate-loading' is essentially the same process that leads to classical 'Monday morning disease' of draught horses. It has led to 'tying-up' in racing sledge dogs, which was alleviated by lowering dietary carbohydrate from 40% to 30% then 20% and eventually to zero (Kronfeld, 1973). It has also been associated with myoglobinuria in humans, both mild or severe, and with focal myocardial necrosis. The benefits and risks of 'carbohydrate-loading' should be assessed carefully in humans. The procedure appears at the moment to be unjustifiable for horses and dogs.

An alternative strategy is to spare muscle glycogen utilization by adapting the muscle to oxidize fat. As mentioned above, fatty acid derivatives inhibit utilization of glycogen and glucose. This was shown first in heart muscle then skeletal muscle. Adaptive increases in oxidation of free fatty acids occur during training.

This adaptation is associated with the number of mitochondria increasing during training, and a con-comitant decline in utilization of muscle glycogen and blood glucose. The ability to mobilize body fat reserves and thus make more fatty acids and ketone bodies available for working muscles is enhanced by training, by bouts of exercise on successive days, and by food deprivation in dogs fed a cereal-based diet.

Studies on racing sledge dogs have indicated accommodation to the level of fat in the diet (Hammel, Kronfeld, Ganjam and Dunlap, 1977). Three matched groups were fed three diets that contained 61, 45 and 34% of available energy in the form of fat during 6 months of training and racing. Blood samples were taken before and after an exhaus-tive run. Increases in plasma-free fatty acids and betahydroxybutyrate during exercise were signifi-cantly greater in the dogs fed 61% fat. Moreover, two performance groups were selected, the two best and two worst dogs in each of the three dietary groups. Increases in plasma-free fatty acids during exercise were twice as high in the best group than in the worst group. Thus, fat mobilization during exhaustive exercise was related to performance and to dietary level of fat during training.

Uses of protein

Oxidation of amino acids by working muscles during exercise is usually regarded as undesirable in terms of energetic efficiency, especially if atten-tion is focused on the muscle alone. If one views the whole body, and the potential for the amino group to be transferred in the form of alanine to the liver, a more balanced perspective may be obtained. The amino group does not have to be wasted as urea, it might be synthesized into other substances in the liver. The metabolism of protein in the whole body deserves further investigation on a comparative basis — herbivores and omnivores vs carnivores.

A second use of dietary protein is for the build up of body proteins, notably muscle. During growth, the optimal range of protein intake is usually 2- or 3-times the minimum requirement for protein. This generali-zation appears to apply well in dogs. One might expect that superior muscle development in an adult during training would be favoured by a protein intake in the optimal range for growth. This expectation has not been demonstrated convincingly, even when athletes are given anabolic steroids. Coaches and athletes aiming for muscle hypertrophy continue to use relatively high protein diets, but those aiming for stamina are less inclined.

The third use of dietary protein is to promote the generation of red blood cells. 'Sports anaemia' is receiving an increasing attention in human athletes; even though its relationship to performance is uncertain (Dressendorfer *et al.*, 1981). Responses of red blood cells are very consistent in canine athletes, and appear to relate to performance, stress and dietary protein.

Oxygen transport

Perfusion of working muscle with oxygen is a function of blood flow rate and the volume of oxygen carried per unit volume of blood. This does not seem to be the limiting factor in a human running at 60% of maximal oxygen uptake.

Indeed the oxidative capacity of mitochondria in working muscles probably sets the limit. There is more of a chance in the dog than in the human athlete, however, for blood transport of oxygen to become limiting, for the dog is capable of relatively much higher increases in oxygen consumption, up to 30 times the resting level when running at 20 mph.

Red blood cells, training and racing

Two responses are important. The first is an increase in the number of red blood cells during training. At Zero Kennel, while dogs were undergoing progressively more strenuous training from October to December, their red blood cell counts increased from an average of 6.3×10^6 cells per cubic millimetre to 7.0, 7.1 and 7.2×10^6 cells/mm^3 in dogs fed 31, 40 and 52% protein on a dry matter basis (Kronfeld et al., 1977).

The red cells became slightly larger in dogs fed more protein, so that packed cell volumes (haematocrit readings) were 49, 51 and 53%. These differences were slight but statistically significant; whether they would make an appreciable difference in stamina would depend on how close oxygen perfusion of working muscle would be to the ultimate limit. These values are below the point at which increasing viscosity of blood becomes a disadvantage during exercise; practical experience in Greyhounds suggests that this point is represented by a haematocrit in the 60–62% range.

The second response is a decrease in red blood cells during a period of maximal stress. We have observed this in Zero Kennel dogs through the January to March racing season, and in Iditarod dogs during 16 days of racing.

The Zero Kennel dogs competed in nine events, each two or three heats of 15 to 30 miles, run on successive days. Red blood cells were sustained on the 40 and 53% protein diets, but fell 10% in dogs fed only 31% protein.

Another stern test was conducted with an Iditarod team. The dogs were matched into pairs, then one from each pair was assigned by coin flip to the only commercial product for stressed dogs or to a canned chicken–pork lung diet like the highest protein diet fed to Zero Kennel in the preceding study. With the Alaskan mountains and weather in mind, we further fortified this diet with chicken fat, freezing the contents of three 690 g cans with an extra 120 g of fat. Final protein contents of the stress diet and the frozen fat–fortified chicken–pork diet were 30 and 38% respectively. Before the race, red blood cell counts were the same in both groups of dogs. After 16 days, averaging 80 miles a day in sub-zero weather, red blood cell counts fell 27% in dogs fed 30% protein and 15% in those fed 38% protein.

These two studies combine to show that the protein requirement for stress and hard work is more than 38% but not 40% on a dry matter basis. In terms of available energy, at least 28% should be provided in the form of protein which has a quality (efficiency of utilization) of about 70%. Comparable figures are about 25% protein (energy basis) for growth, gestation and lactation, and 9% protein as a minimum for maintenance (if dogs will eat such a low protein diet).

Red blood cells and stress

Stress depresses red blood cell indices in dogs. Stress, 'a syndrome produced by diverse nocuous agents' (Selye, 1936) involves release of adrenal corticoids that inhibit anabolism in general and especially the production of red blood cells. Exhaustive exercise in our huskies trebles plasma glucocorticoid concentration.

Stress associated anaemia, together with anaemia induced by haemorrhage, is affected by tissue protein reserves, hence by dietary protein prior to stress as well as the repletion period. Repletion of liver and muscle protein reserves (ratio of protein to DNA) requires 3- to 4-times the protein intake needed for zero nitrogen balance under maintenance conditions. The margin of dietary protein needed for the extreme stress of racing may be even larger.

Performance and red blood cells

Red blood cell depression may reflect excessive stress in an animal. Steel (1963) suggested that the haemogram is useful in identifying racehorses that have passed the peak of fitness before other observable signs. In 1981, our dogs were fed a diet composed of whole chicken, pork lung and rice. The day after winning the ALPO International race at Saranac Lake, three 15-mile heats at an average speed of 19.25 mph, resting blood samples were taken. The driver, Harris Dunlap, was asked to rank the dogs from 1 (low) to 5 (high). There was a linear correlation between performance rank and each red blood cell index, the best being packed cell volume, $R^2 = 0.57$. Similarly, Terry Adkins ranked his dogs after the 1981 Iditarod Trail race, 1,130 miles in 13.3 days. Resting samples were taken, and again performance ranks were highly correlated with red blood cell indices, the best being red blood cell counts, $R^2 = 0.71$.

In summary, our findings suggest that red blood cells may be a useful index of fitness for aerobic work, tolerance of stress, and adequacy of dietary protein in the dog.

THE DEHYDRATION–DIARRHOEA–STRESS SYNDROME

Prolonged exhaustive exercise leads to stress and dehydration in dogs (Adkins and Morris, 1975). Paradoxically, they are often reluctant to drink, and must be enticed by adding a preferred flavour to the water, e.g. meat juice or milk. We have tried adding salt or sodium acetate, which would alleviate a suspected hyponatraemic hypovolaemia, but most dogs do not drink this solution. The stressed dog seems more susceptible to digestive upsets. A common proximal cause is an abrupt change in diet. Signs range from mild to severe. Stools may be loose, abundant, pale, foamy, accompanied by little flatus. Worse are profuse water explosive diarrhoea with foul smelling flatus and signs of pain and cramps. Diarrhoea

contributes further to dehydration and stress, establishing a vicious cycle. Control involves rest and rehydration. The diarrhoea may be treated symptomatically or specifically. Frequency of this syndrome may be diminished by avoiding abrupt food changes and perhaps, by using a food that has optimal proportions of protein, fat and carbohydrate, such as the proposed 'ideal diet' (Table 16).

EXERTIONAL RHABDOMYOLYSIS

Our only experience of this disease in the field has been associated with 'carbohydrate loading', as described above. Obviously, this procedure should be avoided. Hypoglycaemic seizures observed in hunting dogs also appear to follow the feeding of a meal rich in carbohydrate.

Experimental studies have shown that dogs depleted of potassium or phosphorus may develop rhabdomyolysis, these conditions may not occur commonly in dogs because their diets contain abundant potassium and phosphorus. The experiments were intended to simulate exertional rhabdomyolysis in humans subjected to heat stress. For this reason, electrolyte mixtures including potassium phosphate have been given to Greyhounds to prevent 'cramps'. Tests of the efficacy of this intervention would be interesting.

ACUTE GASTRIC DILATION ('BLOAT')

Acute gastric dilation is not uncommon in large dogs. We have encountered it in fox hounds fed free choice, dry dog food all day. We recommend that the food should be removed at least 9 h before strenuous exercise. A dog hot after exercise should be allowed to cool and be given at least two small drinks, 15 min apart, before a small feed. Only after this period of accommodation should it be returned to the enclosure that presents food free choice. See also Chapter 8.

BLEEDING

Occasionally sledge dogs bleed through the anus during a strenuous run. The amount of blood is usually small, perhaps 100 ml, though this may be startling on a white coat or snow. The blood is bright red, indicating that it is arteriolar or capillary blood released in the lower bowel. We find that this condition is eliminated when meat and meat by-products comprise half or more of the diet. Two features of dry, grain-based dog food are suspect. One is vegetable fibre or bulk that may place a physical strain on the lower bowel. The dogs release faeces while running, and the effort is marked when typical grain-fed faeces must be eliminated. The other feature is the high iron content of most commercial dry foods. This reaches the therapeutic range at maintenance intakes, and levels at which gastrointestinal irritation may be expected when the dog is at 3-times maintenance.

ANAEMIA

The discussion above emphasized the role of stress in inhibiting formation of red blood cells, and the influence of dietary protein on accommodation to stress and sustain red blood cell indices. Iron is always abundant in commercial dog foods or our home-made recipes. We remain concerned about vitamin E and selenium, because many highly stressed dogs appear to have fragile red blood cells. We have not studied this directly, but notice haemolysis in blood samples handled carefully. Thus if there is any doubt about the vitamin E and selenium contents of the diet, we administer capsules to highly stressed dogs about once a week.

METACARPAL FRACTURES

One of the most common problems in racing sledge dogs is lameness associated with no obvious proximal cause (Stoliker, Dunlap and Kronfeld, 1976). Pain may be elicited by pressure on metacarpal bones, usually the middle second. If the dog is run hard, under the excitement of a race, this lameness may turn into a frank fracture. Careful radiography has revealed small spiral partial fractures in dogs with this kind of lameness. We suspect that running such a dog may lead to extension of the fracture. This condition bears some resemblance to

'bucked shins' in horses or marching fractures in humans, involving torsion of the bone.

Metacarpal fractures have occurred too commonly in teams fed diets deficient in calcium. Adding bone meal does not make the dogs run faster, so it tends to be left out of the diet. The relationship to fractures, via secondary nutritional hyperparathyroidism, is clear to us but not easy to explain to drivers.

BIBLIOGRAPHY

Adkins, T. O. and Kronfeld, D. S. (1982) Diet affects erythrocyte depression in dogs during a 1200 mile race (in press).

Adkins, T. O. and Morris, J. C. (1975) The Iditarod — sledge dogs and DVMs. *Mod. Vet. Pract.* **56(7)**, 456—461.

Astrand, P. (1967) Diet and athletic performance. *Fedn. Proc. Fedn. Am. Soc. exp. Biol.* **26**, 1772—1777.

Bank, W. J. (1977) Myoglobinuria in marathon runners: possible relationship to carbohydrate and lipid metabolism. *Ann. N.Y. Acad. Sci.* **301**, 942.

Bergström, J., Hermanssen, L., Hultman, E. and Saltin, B. (1967) Diet, Muscle Glycogen and Physical Performance. *Acta Physiol. Scand.* **71**, 140—150.

Burrows, C. F., Kronfeld, D. S., Banta, C. A. and Merritt, A. M. (1982) Fibre affects digestibility and transit time in dogs (in press).

Downey, R. L., Kronfeld, D. S. and Banta, C. A. (1980) Diet of Beagles affects stamina. *J. Am. Anim. Hosp. Assoc.* **16**, 273—277.

Dressendorfer, R. H., Wade, C. E., and Amsterdam, E. A. (1981) Development of pseudoanemia in marathon runners during a 20-day road race. *J. Am. Med. Assoc.* **246**, 1215—1218.

Hammel, E. P., Kronfeld, D. S., Ganjam, V. K. and Dunlap, H. L. (1977) Metabolic responses to exhaustive exercise in racing sledge dogs fed diets containing medium, low and zero carbohydrate. *Am. J. Clin. Nutrit.* **30**, 409—418.

Hartley, W. J., Kater, J. C. and Mackay, A. (1963) Goitre and low copper status in a litter of meat-fed pups. *N.Z. Vet. J.* **11**, 1—5.

Hegsted, D. M., Kent, V., Tsongas, A. G. and Stare, F. J. (1974) A comparison of the nutritive value of the proteins in mixed diets for dogs, rats and human beings. *J. Lab. Clin. Med.* **32**, 403—409.

Hermansen, L., Hultman, E., and Saltin, B. (1967) Muscle glycogen during prolonged severe exercise. *Acta Physiol. Scand.* **71**, 129—139.

Karlsson, J. and Saltin, B. (1971) Diet, muscle glycogen and endurance performance. *J. Appl.*

Physiol. **31**, 203–206.

Knochel, J. P., Barcenas, B., Cotton, J. R., Fuller, T. J., Haller, R. and Carter, N. W. (1978) Hypophosphatemia and rhabdomyolysis. *J. Clin. Invest.* **62**, 1240–1246.

Knochel, J. P. and Schlein, E. M. (1972) On the mechanism of rhabdomyolysis in potassium depletion. *J. Clin. Invest.* **51**, 1750–1758.

Kronfeld, D. S. (1973) Diet and the performance of racing sledge dogs. *J. Am. Vet. Med. Assoc.* **162**, 470–473.

Kronfeld, D. S. and Downey, R. L. (1981) Nutritional strategies for stamina in dogs and horses. *Proc. Nutrit. Soc. Aust.* **6**, 21–29.

Kronfeld, D. S., Dunlap, H. L. and Adkins, T. O. (1981) The red blood cell connection. *Team & Trail* **18(9)**, 4.

Kronfeld, D. S., Hammel, E. P., Ramberg, C. F., and Dunlap, H. L. (1977) Hematological and metabolic responses to training in racing sledge dogs fed diets containing medium, low or zero carbohydrate. *Am. J. Clin. Nutrit.* **30**, 419–430.

Merritt, A. M., Burrows, C. F., Cowgill, L. D. and Street, W. (1979) *J. Am. Vet. Med. Assoc.* **174**, 59–61.

Mirkin, G. (1973) Carbohydrate loading: a dangerous practice. *J. Am. Med. Assoc.* **223**, 1511–1512.

Orr, N. T. M. (1966) The feeding of sledge dogs on Antarctic expeditions. *Br. J. Nutrit.* **20**, 1–11.

Paul, P. and Issekutz, B. (1967) Role of extramuscular energy sources in the metabolism of the exercising dog. *J. Appl. Physiol.* **22**, 615–622.

Randle, P. J., Garland, P. B., Hales, C. N. and Newsholme, E. A. (1963) The glucose fatty acid cycle. *Lancet* **i**, 785–789.

Rennie, M. J., Winder, W. W. and Holloszy, J. O. (1976) A Sparing Effect of Increased Plasma Fatty Acids on Muscle and Liver Glycogen Content in the Exercising Rat. *Biochem. J.* **156**, 647–655.

Reinhold, J. G., Faradji, B., Abadi, P. and Ismail-Beigi, F. (1976) Decreased absorption of calcium, magnesium, zinc and phosphorus by humans due to increased fibre and phosphorus consumption as wheat bread. *J. Nutrit.* **106**, 493–503.

Robertson, B. T. and Burns, M. J. (1963) Zinc metabolism and the zinc-deficiency syndrome in the dog. *Am. J. Vet. Res.* **24**, 997–1002.

Romsos, D. R., Belo, P. S., Rennink, M. R., Bergen, W. G. and Leveille, G. A. (1976) Effects of dietary carbohydrate, fat and protein on growth, body composition and blood metabolite levels in the dog. *J. Nutrit.* **106**, 1452–1464.

Ryan, A. J. (1981) Anabolic steroids are fool's gold. *Fedn. Proc. Fedn. Am. Soc. exp. Biol.* **40**, 2682–2688.

Selye, H. (1936) A syndrome produced by diverse nocuous agents. *Nature* **138**, 32.

Sheehan, G. (1975) Blood urine: don't panic, collect a specimen. *Physician's Sportsmedicine* **3**, 29.

Steel, J. D. (1963) Hematology and its relationship to track performance. In *Equine Medicine and Surgery*, Editor J. F. Bone. First edition, p. 402, American Veterinary Publications, Wheaton, IL.

Stoliker, H. E., Dunlap, H. L. and Kronfeld, D. S. (1976) Bone mineral measurement by photon densitometry in racing sledge dogs, and its relationship to bodyweight, sex and bone fractures. *Vet. Med. Small Anim. Clin.* **71**, 1545–1550.

Wannemacher, R. W. and McCoy, J. R. (1966) Determination of optimal dietary protein requirements of young and old dogs. *J. Nutrit.* **88**, 66–74.

CHAPTER 6

REARING MOTHERLESS PUPPIES

A. T. B. Edney

The loss of the mother of puppies at any time is a catastrophe. It can however be successfully overcome if all the needs of each puppy are met by other means. The task is a demanding one. A great deal of dedicated application is needed to achieve a satisfactory outcome. Nevertheless, successful rearing of orphaned puppies is very rewarding and engenders a strong sense of achievement. It also forges very strong bonds between those doing the work and the puppies which are entirely dependent upon them.

A puppy's mother does not have to die to deprive it of vital nourishment. Life support is removed by loss of milk or by simple rejection of a puppy by its mother. In either of these situations further investigation is needed to try to discover why the bitch has no milk or if there is any abnormality of the puppy which might cause its rejection. If there is some obvious deformity present, it would be wiser not to attempt to rear such individuals.

The most obvious alternative to a bitch rearing her puppies is for another individual to do so, that is for another bitch to act as a foster mother. Although this is a very much more satisfactory arrangement than trying to hand rear puppies, the chances of a bitch at the right stage of lactation, and with sufficient resources to rear a litter being available at just the right time are poor. It can however be done and communications within a breed fancy obviously improve the chances of finding a foster mother.

Motherless puppies have vital requirements in two main areas — nutrition and provision of a suitable environment. There are two very important aspects of husbandry which are literally vital. These concern the ambient temperature around the puppies, and providing the stimulus which provokes urination and defaecation of each puppy.

Newborn puppies are unable to control their body temperature effectively. They gradually change from being largely poikilothermic to being homeothermic during the first week of life. That is, for 5 days or so their body temperature is directly related to the environmental temperature. Because of this, a steady ambient temperature of around $30°-32°C$ is needed. Over the first 4 weeks of life the ambient temperature can be gradually lowered to $24°C$ (at 1 month). It is equally important that sudden changes of environmental conditions are avoided and disturbances are minimized outside socialization, exercise and hygiene activities.

Ideally the environment would be controlled by means of an incubator. Otherwise a heating pad with adequate insulation of the pen is probably better than an infra-red heating lamp. There is considerable danger of overhead lamps drying puppies out excessively. A little baby oil can be rubbed into each puppy every 2–3 days to help prevent drying out.

Some authors (Sheffy, 1978; Kirk, 1968) advise that puppies should be kept in separate compartments for two reasons. Firstly, to avoid puppies suckling each other. Secondly, so that the faecal consistency of each puppy can be readily seen. There are, however, advantages of a high level of socialization with litter mates. From about 5–6 weeks it is just as important to begin socializing puppies with people. This should not be excessive, but brief periods of gentle additional handling will make the adjustment to human behavioural patterns easier later on. From weaning to about 4 months is a crucial period for proper integration as a pet animal.

Newborn puppies are normally either eating or sleeping. After puppies have fed, a vital aspect of tending motherless puppies is to simulate the mother's tongue action on the ano-genital area which provokes reflex defaecation and urination. The application of this stimulus has to be taken over by the person tending the puppies. The necessary result can be achieved by applying a piece of damp cotton wool at the ano-genital area. It is sometimes possible to effect the same response simply by running a dampened forefinger along the abdominal wall.

This stimulation should be a routine carried out after each feed. After this procedure each puppy needs to be carefully cleaned up. Most puppies benefit from gentle handling before feeds to allow some exercise and promote muscular and circulatory development.

After about 2½–3 weeks, puppies begin to explore their surroundings. A larger area is needed for their increasing activities. Great care must still be taken to avoid chilling, excessive disturbance or exposure to hazards outside the puppy pen.

As the puppy develops, active periods become more evident between sleeping and feeding. At about the age of 3 weeks, puppies are able to relieve themselves without their mother's stimulation or the simulated equivalent. They will begin to wander away from their bed to relieve themselves, but do not do so in particular places until they are fully weaned at about 7–8 weeks. They will then favour particular areas and will usually pass urine or faeces at roughly hourly intervals. Puppies usually indicate clearly that they are seeking a place to relieve themselves and can be taken to an appropriate place outside or on a newspaper.

Anti-worming is advisable from the age of 3 weeks. As the common roundworm of dogs is the most likely endoparasite to be present, appropriate anti-worming compounds are normally administered at this age, the treatment being repeated every 2 weeks up to the age of 6 months.

FEEDING

Puppies grow at a rapid rate. They can double their birth weight in a matter of days. Within 3 weeks an average sized puppy can have increased its birth-weight 4 times. An increase of 5–10% in bodyweight can occur each day. Because of this puppies require quite large quantities of their mother's milk or a food comparable to it. To be analogous this food has to be a concentrated source of nutrients based on the composition of normal bitches' milk. Accurate determination of the composition of bitches' milk presents practical difficulties. The subject has been extensively reviewed by Baines (1981). The practical difficulties of collecting milk samples which accurately represent what is actually ingested by puppies are obvious. It is clear that the composition of bitches' milk differs markedly as lactation progresses and may well vary during any one day. The milk at the beginning, middle or end of any one feed may also be quite different. It must also be remembered that puppies normally take very small amounts of milk at frequent intervals during the day. That is, they don't take all the milk which can be expressed from the bitch's teats at one time. Obviously it is necessary to formulate a milk substitute based on the best information available regarding the normal composition of bitches' milk, but it is always something of a compromise.

Even with the constraints about analysis interpretation already cited, it is clear that cow's milk is grossly inadequate as a substitute for rearing puppies. The protein, fat and calcium levels are much lower and the energy concentration is only about half that required. The level of lactose present is probably higher than puppies can tolerate for any length of time.

Average analysis of milk as % (in brackets % dry matter), (Baines, 1981)

	Bitch	Cow	Goat	Cat
Moisture	77.2	87.6	87.0	81.5
Dry matter	22.8	12.4	13.0	18.5
Protein	8.1 (35.8)	3.3 (26.6)	3.3 (25.3)	8.1 (41.3)
Fat	9.8 (43.2)	3.8 (30.6)	4.5 (34.6)	5.1 (25.6)
Ash	4.9	5.3	6.2	3.5
Lactose	3.5 (15.2)	4.7 (37.9)	4.0 (30.8)	6.9 (26.7)
Calcium	0.28 (1.24)	0.12 (0.96)	0.13 (1.00)	0.035 (0.2)
Phosphorus	0.22 (1.01)	0.095 (0.76)	0.11 (0.84)	0.07 (0.4)
kcal/100 g	120	65	71	142

The situation cannot be rectified by simply giving more because of the limitations of the volume puppies can accommodate. Concentration of the nutrients present by evaporation simply increases the problem of excess lactose.

The popular belief that goat's milk more nearly approximates that of bitches is not borne out by examination of analyses. There is in fact very little analytical difference between the milk from goats and cows.

Cow's milk can however be fortified in a relatively simple manner to produce an effective, if imperfect, replacement for bitches' milk.

A modified version of the formulation used by Björck *et al.* (1957) can be used successfully to rear puppies.

Artificial milk for puppies (after Björck et al., 1957)

Ingredient	Amount
Fresh cow's milk	570 ml (1 pint)
Single cream (18% fat)	200 ml
Egg yolk	1 (15 g)
Cod liver oil	2-3 drops (0.03 g)
Sterilized bonemeal	4 g
Citric acid	2 g

Puppies can only accommodate a maximum of 10–20 ml at any one feed, and it is likely that they take very much less than this when feeding normally. They tend to feed on a 'little and often' basis. Puppies require nutrients at the rate of about twice that of an adult on a unit bodyweight basis.

Morris (1974) suggests the following as the caloric needs of average sized puppies.

Approximate calorie needs of growing puppies (Morris, 1974)

Week	kcal/kg/day
1	120
2	140
3	160
4	180*
to weaning	

*240 in our experience

Björck *et al.* advise feeding puppies 6 feeds daily up to 3 weeks, but this can only be a rough guide.

Comparison of analysis of bitches' milk with modified Björck formulation as % (with % dry matter in brackets)

	Modified Björck formula %	Bitches' milk %
Moisture	82.5	77.2
Dry matter	17.5	22.8
Protein	3.4 (19.4)	8.1 (35.8)
Fat	8.5 (48.5)	9.8 (43.2)
Lactose	4.2 (24.0)	3.5 (15.2)
Calcium	0.27 (1.54)	0.28 (1.24)
Phosphorus	0.16 (0.91)	0.22 (1.01)
kcal/100 g	105	120

Feeds at 3 days would be of the order of 2–4 ml for a puppy weighing around 200 g, and for a puppy weighing 800 g at 3 weeks, feeds would be of the order of 50 ml each. Sheffy (1978) recommends calorie intakes which are very similar but suggests feeding at 8-hour intervals is all that is needed for most puppies. Our figures are somewhat higher being nearer 240 kcals/kg/day at 4 weeks.

Whatever regime is adopted, feeding by hand is a very demanding procedure. Foods can be administered by means of a small syringe, a toy doll's bottle or an intra-gastric tube. Fresh foods should be made up daily and fed warm, (38°C). Food must be given slowly and must not be forced into the puppy. The temptation to project fluid down the throat with a syringe must be resisted as inhalation pneumonia is a very real risk.

Intubation is relatively easy. A number 8 French human intra-gastric feeding tube is normally suitable for puppies weighing around 200–500 g. The distance from the last rib to the tip of the nose can be measured and marked off on the tube as a guide. If the puppy is held upright, the tube can be introduced over the tongue and the milk substitute injected slowly into the puppy.

When feeding from a miniature bottle, the hole in the teat may need to be enlarged so the flow is improved and the puppy does not suck in air.

When puppies begin to start exploring their surroundings at about 2½ and 3 weeks, the milk substitute can be made available to them in shallow dishes. From 3 weeks good quality prepared foods (canned) may be introduced in the same way. This can be mixed with the milk substitute to begin with and then offered separately. In this way the change-over to solid food can be made over 3 to 4 weeks. Small amounts of crushed biscuit meal can be introduced during this process so that puppies are slowly changed from being entirely dependent on a milk substitute at 3 weeks to being fully weaned onto prepared foods at about 6–8 weeks. It is useful to get puppies used to variety.

Feeding frequency will depend on the breed of dog and type of food given, particularly with regard to energy density. Generally speaking puppies may be fed to appetite four times daily at weaning. The feeding frequency can be reduced to three meals daily at 3½–4 months and thence to 2 meals at 6 months. This may be retained as the adult regime or reduced to one main meal once the dog is mature at around 1 year.

BIBLIOGRAPHY

Björck, G., Olssen, N. B. and Dyrendahl, S. (1957) Artificiell Uppfödning av Hundvalpar. *Nord. Vet. Med.* **9**, 285.

Kirk, R. W. (1968) In *Canine Medicine* Ed. by E. T. Catcott, pp. 809–813, A. V. P., Illinois.

Mapletoft, R. J., Schutte, A. P., Coubrough, R. I. and Kuhne, R. J. (1974) The perinatal period of dogs, nutrition and management in the hand rearing of puppies. *J. S. Afr. Vet. Ass.* **45**, 183.

Morris, L. S. (1974) Cited by Mapletoft *et al.* (1974), *op. cit.*

Sheffy, B. E. (1978) Symposium on Canine Paediatrics, pp. 7–29. 'Nutrition and Nutritional Disorders'. *Vet Clin. N. Am.* **8**, No. 1.

Baines, F. M. (1981) Milk substitutes and the hand rearing of orphaned puppies and kittens. *J. Small Anim. Pract.* **22**, 555–578.

CHAPTER 7

FEEDING GROWING DOGS WITH SPECIAL REFERENCE TO SKELETAL DISEASE

Å. A. Hedhammar

INTRODUCTION

Dog breeders are usually very concerned about skeletal development and also aware that feeding is of prime importance to achieve optimal skeletal characteristics. Knowledge of requirements, products available and how they should be used are essential when discussing nutrition as it relates to skeletal disease, (see Chapters 2, 3 and 4).

With the exception of lactating bitches, there is never a greater demand for proper nutrition than during growth. During the period of most rapid growth especially in puppies of the fastest growing breeds, it is most important to feed an optimal diet in an optimal way. It is now known that 'proper' and 'optimal' in this respect does not mean the maximum content of nutrients in a diet and the maximal amount of such a diet. Puppies not only need sufficient amounts of energy, protein, minerals and vitamins to allow optimal skeletal characteristics, they also need it in balanced proportions, neither too little nor too much. Before weaning has started the bitch will supply a complete and balanced diet for her puppies. As weaning progresses more and more of the bitch's milk will have to be replaced by something which can also guarantee proper nutrition for her offspring.

ENERGY AND ITS EFFECT ON RATE OF GROWTH

In early life puppies double their weight several times in a very short period. There are great differ-ences between breeds as can be seen from the graphs in Fig. 13. Especially, puppies of the fastest growing breeds need a lot of food to fully realize their growth capacity. During the period of their most rapid increase in size and weight, food consumption may be more than double that of an adult dog of comparable weight and size.

In this respect it should be remembered that total food consumption, within genetically determined limits, does regulate the rate at which an individual dog gains weight and size.

Growth is stunted by lack of energy intake caused either by too little food or decreased food consumption due to disease. The final size of the dog is however very little affected by the rate of growth. Final size may be permanently stunted only if energy intake is severely decreased during a critical period of life. If deprivation is only temporary, compensatory increase in the rate of growth and the length of the growth period finally enables the dog to attain full size. Maximum growth rate within growth capacity can be achieved by a generous supply of palatable diets.

The total amount of energy needed daily by a growing dog increases as long as it is still growing. At the same time the amount of energy per kg bodyweight decreases. To adjust food consumption to an increasing size neither giving too much nor too little is sometimes a difficult matter of judgement. It is nevertheless of prime importance for optimal skeletal development.

In affluent societies, it is rare to find healthy dogs which are underfed. Awareness of the need for a lot of food and pride in their dog's size, rather make owners of large-sized dogs prone to feed them as much as possible.

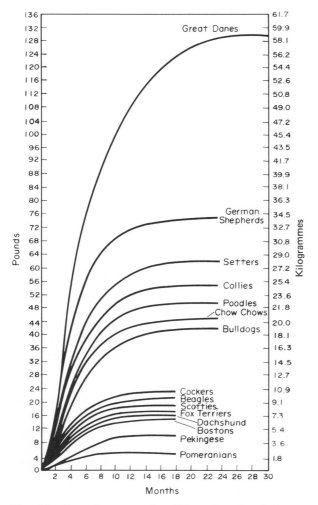

Fig. 13. Growth curves for fifteen breeds of dogs. Courtesy of R. W. Kirk, Cornell University, Ithaca, New York. Adapted from *Current Veterinary Therapy III*, 1966, W. B. Saunders & Co., Philadelphia, p. 716.

Economic reasons seldom restrict owner's ambitions to have their dogs grow very rapidly. Striving for sheer size in show dogs at an early age invites more problems. As feeding too much even of a correctly balanced diet may contribute to skeletal disease it is important to supply food in adequate amounts.

It is impossible to give advice on the exact amount of food, and thereby energy, which should be fed at each occasion to an individual dog. Besides differences in breed and stages of life there are also differences in activity and environmental temperature. Unfortun-

ately established standards of size and weight for growing dogs of many breeds are not available. Ideally they should also be divided according to sex.

A careful physical evaluation including an assessment of the state of nutrition is helpful but is not a guarantee of proper nutrition. An obese dog can be lacking specific nutrients and a lean puppy can be growing at a rate which is not compatible with optimal skeletal development. Ideally a puppy should put on weight and grow at a rate which is neither too slow or too fast. The weight, size and state of nutrition should be compared to littermates or other dogs of the same age and breed.

THE AMOUNTS OF SPECIFIC NUTRIENTS NEEDED DURING GROWTH

As with energy, the requirements of specific nutrients are also greatest during early life and the period of most rapid growth. Protein, fat, minerals and vitamins are needed to promote healthy development including optimal skeletal characteristics.

As total food consumption is quite high due to a simultaneous need for a lot of energy, puppies will usually get large amounts of the specific nutrients, that is if they are fed well composed diets. If the diet is lacking in specific nutrients there is a risk that even a generous supply will create a state of deficiency. In fact, signs of deficiency are easily brought about during growth by generous feeding of diets lacking in specific nutrients; rickets in dogs being one of the classical examples.

The composition of bitches' milk indicates the proper composition of a diet to be fed for optimal development during the very first period in a dog's life, Fig. 14. Never in a dog's life will there be a demand for a higher level of any nutrient than during that period. Bitches' milk is a complete and balanced diet composed by nature itself. As for all species, the need of the growing puppy progressively diminishes and after weaning, a diet less dense in specific nutrients will supply the puppy with all nutrients needed.

In Chapter 4 recommendations on dietary composition have been discussed. In Table 3, cited from the publication *Nutrient Requirements of Dogs*, the requirements are expressed as a percentage or units per kg of diet dry matter. With reference to skeletal

Figure 14. *Comparison of bitches' milk and the NRC recommendations*

	Bitches' milk Dry matter 25%	Bitches' milk Dry basis 100%	NRC recommendations Dry basis 100%
Protein (%)	8	32	22
Fat (%)	9	36	5
Linoleic acid (%)	1.1	4.4	1
Calcium (%)	0.3	1.2	1.1
Phosphorus (%)	0.25	1.0	0.9

disease it can be of great value to stress once again that these figures are designed to provide the nutrients required for the entire life-cycle of all breeds of dog (including support of normal growth) and that the figures presented are not minimum requirements but rather recommended allowances.

Protein

Protein is essential for growth. An adequate amount of good quality protein is needed to build bones. Recommended levels of protein according to the NRC (1974) (22% protein on a dry matter basis) will promote normal skeletal development in puppies of all breeds at all stages of growth. In normal circumstances (see also Chapter 5) there are no beneficial effects of a higher level of protein, although for practical reasons the level of protein in diets for growing dogs may vary considerably. Due to enhanced palatability of a diet containing very high levels of protein, the risk of overnutrition increases, which can eventually prevent optimal skeletal development in large sized breeds.

Calcium, phosphorus, vitamins A and D

Calcium and phosphorus, the main constituents of bone, are of particular interest with reference to skeletal development. Vitamins A and D are essential for absorption and handling of calcium within the body. In dogs, deficiency in calcium is uncommon today. Contrary to a common belief, levels of calcium according to the NRC standards give even growing dogs of fast growing breeds a wide margin of safety.

Many dog breeders continue to recommend supplementation with extra calcium even when complete and balanced diets are fed to growing dogs of rapidly growing breeds such as Great Danes and St Bernards. However, balance studies in German Shepherd Dogs as well as Great Danes at various stages of growth from weaning onwards have not indicated any need for a higher level of calcium in the diet than that recommended by NRC. Even on a high calcium diet the true absorption of calcium in Great Danes never exceeded 50% of the recommended intake according to the NRC.

In fact, too much calcium in a diet interferes with the absorption of zinc and magnesium and may create deficiencies of these nutrients although they are adequate for normal conditions.

Diets for growing dogs should also contain sufficient amounts of phosphorus in balanced proportions to calcium. The recommended amount being 0.9% phosphorus on a dry ·matter basis and the optimal ratio between calcium and phosphorus about 1.3 : 1.0.

Sufficient and balanced amounts of calcium and phosphorus in the diet are most important when feeding puppies of large and fast growing breeds.

The soluble vitamins A and D promote normal skeletal development (see Chapter 2). The amount recommended by NRC in diets for growing dogs should neither be exceeded nor gone below to any greater extent as too much vitamin A or D may create disturbed skeletal development as well as deficiencies of these nutrients.

CHOICE OF DIET

Whether correctly balanced diets for growing dogs should be home-made or supplied by the manufacturers of dog food is mostly a question of time, interest and knowledge. If the diet is correctly composed, according to internationally accepted norms (NRC) it makes little difference whether the ingredients are blended at home or by well known manufacturers of dog food.

A mixture of 3 parts of vegetable products such as

bread, rice and corn and 1 part of animal products as meat, fish and eggs, will make up a diet containing about 25% good quality protein on a dry matter basis.

That is equal to the level of protein in most dry type dog food intended to be used in growing dogs. Such a home-made diet is usually lacking in minerals and fat-soluble vitamins and will have to be supplemented in this respect (see below).

Special diets for puppies

Not only diets especially designed for puppies but also many other commercially available diets contain all nutrients needed in sufficient and balanced amounts and can therefore be used as the only source of nutrient. These diets often referred to as complete and balanced for all stages of life can be used for growing puppies of all breeds. In diets to be used for puppies there is no need to exceed the levels which have been recommended by NRC. Too high levels of some nutrients may create problems due to over-nutrition.

SUPPLEMENTATION

Diets low in minerals and vitamins need to be supplemented when fed to growing dogs, otherwise signs of deficiency will be seen especially in giant breeds. If calcium or vitamin D is lacking in the diet, rickets will be seen in puppies which are not getting any supplements.

The amount of minerals and vitamins which should be given as supplement depends on levels already present in the diet.

Complete and balanced diets need no supplementation at all. Home-made mixtures of meat and cereals, which are lacking calcium and vitamin D, need to be supplemented with large amounts of these constituents to attain the status of complete and balanced diets for growing dogs.

As composition of the diet is more important than the amount of each nutrient fed per kg bodyweight, supplementation should aim at correction of the balance of what is actually eaten by the dog.

Bone meal is essentially a calcium and phosphorus supplement. Most bone meal preparations contain about 30% calcium and 15% phosphorus. Their main value is to supply calcium and phosphorus to home-made meat based diets which would otherwise be severely deficient. Meat such as lungs, liver, heart and lean muscle meat contain only about 0.005–0.01% calcium and 0.07–0.04% phosphorus. The ratio between calcium and phosphorus is also imbalanced at 1 : 20 or higher.

Examples of the amount of supplements to be given to reach the levels recommended by NRC (1.1% calcium, 0.9% phosphorus and 500 International Units vitamin D per kg dry matter): (a) If the diet is composed solely of ingredients poor in calcium and vitamin D, a good rule of thumb is to give 5 g bone meal and 150 IU vitamin D per 100 g dry matter. That is 2–3 g bone meal and 400 IU vitamin D per kg of a fresh diet (25% dry matter).

(b) If the diet is composed partly of a complete and balanced dog food and partly of ingredients which are poor in minerals and vitamins, supplementation should be adjusted to balance what is lacking in the unbalanced ingredients. That means that if the diet is composed partly of a complete and balanced dog food and partly of 500 g fresh products poor in calcium and vitamin D (i.e. meat and rice) 1–1.5 g bone meal and 200 IU vitamin D should be added to balance what is actually lacking in that part of the diet.

NUTRITION AS IT RELATES TO SKELETAL DISEASES

Food consumption and the rate of growth have for a long time been two of the more objective measurements for testing the adequacy of a diet. However, maximal rate of growth is not always compatible with optimal skeletal characteristics in animals with a genetic capacity for rapid growth and a predisposition for various skeletal diseases.

Dogs of giant breeds have a genetic capacity for a very rapid increase in weight and size. The growth rate is comparable to that in fattening pigs and broiler chickens, developed and raised by man because of their ability to convert feed into meat very rapidly. In giant breeds of dogs as in pigs and broilers, rapid growth is accompanied by a high prevalence of various disturbances in skeletal development. The individuals with the most rapid growth are the ones most prone to disturbance in their skeletal development. Several skeletal diseases occur, and among the most frequent are hip dysplasia, osteochondrosis, hypertrophic osteodystrophy and other rickets-like conditions. The effect is more serious in dogs as they live out their life span and are not killed as food animals at a comparatively early age.

Rickets is no longer a common problem

Before dog breeders became aware of the need for vitamin D and of calcium and phosphorus in balanced proportions, enlargement of the metaphyseal regions and the costo-chondral junctions due to rickets and nutritional secondary hyperparathyroidism were the most commonly occurring disturbances in skeletal development in dogs.

More than 100 years ago it was known that puppies fed a mixture of meat, starch, sugar and oil developed rickets, but if calcium in some form was added to the diet the dogs remained normal. Much later it was shown that vitamin D, a substance in cod-liver oil, could prevent rickets from developing by enhancing absorption of calcium from the gut. Nowadays the necessity of vitamin D and calcium in diets of growing dogs is greatly appreciated by dog breeders and therefore true rickets is rare in veterinary practice today.

Dog breeders are still very concerned about any signs related to rickets, especially broadening of metaphyseal regions of long bones and bulging costo-chondral junctions. These changes could be called rickets-like as they resemble rickets in its clinical appearance but without defective mineralization of developing cartilage and newly formed bones as made evident by radiographs and histological sections.

Compared to all established standards, these dogs are often on a diet containing an excess of both vitamin D and calcium and the conditions are neither cured nor prevented by adding vitamin D or calcium.

Broadening of the metaphyseal regions of long bones is, to some extent a physiological event during development, necessary to allow longitudinal growth.

During periods of rapid growth, especially in giant breeds, it is sometimes so pronounced that it is difficult to distinguish it from pathological processes, including rickets. Physiological broadening of the metaphyses will regress and there are no signs of impaired skeletal development when the animal is mature.

Pathological processes that resemble rickets are, for example, retained cartilage and hypertrophic osteodystrophy. Retained cartilage is due to a serious disturbance in the maturing process of growth cartilage very similar to that seen in osteochondrosis of the joint cartilage. The aetiology is not yet fully established but it is shown that the frequency and severity of the changes are affected by both genetic and nutritional factors. As with other metaphyseal osteopathies it is more common at an increased rate of growth. Total food consumption as it affects rate of growth is therefore a nutritional factor of importance.

Hypertrophic osteodystrophy is not caused by vitamin C (ascorbic acid) deficiency

The clinical features of what is known as hypertrophic osteodystrophy (HOD) resemble scurvy in infants to such an extent that it is understandable that for a long time it was recognized as skeletal scurvy in dogs. Histological sections from affected dogs clearly demonstrate that they do not exhibit changes typical of vitamin C deficiency as described in man, monkeys and guinea pigs. HOD is a hypertrophic condition caused by enhanced deposition and decreased resorption of bone, while bone lesions seen in vitamin C deficiency of affected species are osteoporotic.

It is now also known that plasma levels of vitamin C vary greatly and can be influenced by, for example stress and pain. This explains how such determinations could be misinterpreted as proof of vitamin C deficiency in the aetiology of HOD. Great variations occur in the clinical course of HOD, even without any treatment, this could explain why the clinical effects of vitamin C therapy could also be claimed. It has been shown that the clinical course of this disease is more or less unaffected by any treatment, including treatment with megadoses of vitamin C.

Hip dysplasia is affected by rate of growth

Hip dysplasia is a developmental condition in dogs and recently estimated to have a heritability of almost 50%. It has been shown that the incidence and severity of hip dysplasia can be affected by energy intake during growth, before as well as after weaning. Incidence and severity of hip dysplasia increases with elevated food consumption and thereby increased rate of growth.

It has been proposed that megadoses of vitamin C during pregnancy reduce the incidence of hip dysplasia, provided the puppies are kept on a similar regimen until they reach young adulthood. However no data have ever been presented to back up this statement. The vitamin content was not determined in plasma or in tissues of treated or untreated dogs, nor in dogs with or without hip dysplasia. Neither was there any attempt made to verify by histological and chemical means, the hypothesis that dogs with hip dysplasia have a connective tissue of a quality typical of that seen in vitamin C deficient animals. Since 1976 no report in support of the vitamin C theory has been presented. For practical purposes the treatment and prevention of hip dysplasia with vitamin C can be discarded.

SUMMARY

Nutrient interactions are just as important as absolute nutrient levels and no single item in the diet should be considered in isolation. The careless use of supplements may create a direct problem via toxicity or upset the balance of nutrients in the diet and indirectly create signs of deficiency.

Dogs of those breeds which are most liable to develop skeletal disease, should be reared under optimal environmental conditions with reference to skeletal development. Regarding nutrition this means that they should be fed a balanced diet according to the recommendations by NRC. Excessive supplementation should be avoided. Not even a balanced diet should be fed unrestricted to puppies of fast growing breeds. Controlled feeding of a balanced diet facilitates optimal skeletal characteristics rather than maximal rate of growth.

CHAPTER 8

FEEDING ANIMALS WHICH ARE ILL

J. Leibetseder

INTRODUCTION

One of the most important pre-conditions for health and well being is adequate and appropriate nutrition. A healthy organism is endowed with the capacity to take in adequate amounts of food, digest and absorb the nutrients, to carry them off by way of blood and lymphatic vessels and to transform these nutrients into specific substances the organism needs or to oxidize them to provide energy.

The metabolites which result from this process must be detoxicated and excreted. Many control mechanisms keep the composition of the blood and extracellular fluids, as well as the individual's body-weight within fairly narrow limits. All these processes have a load capacity to cope with varying food intakes and changing amounts of various nutrients so as to avoid noxious side effects.

The extreme feeding habits of working dogs in the Arctic where very high intakes of fat and protein are fed and dogs in China which are fed high levels of carbohydrates as rice, illustrate the flexibility of canine digestive processes. This remarkable adaptation of healthy organisms to varying amounts and types of nutrient without detrimental effect is often reduced in cases of disease.

On the other hand disease states are usually accompanied by higher demands for some essential nutrients as well as an increased requirement for energy. Some articles about the nutrition of sick animals and many dietetic prescriptions contain guidance which is no longer tenable at the present level of knowledge. All established dietetic measures need to be looked at critically to assess their therapeutic validity if they are to be acceptable to modern medicine.

The relationship between nutrition and disease is in two main areas:

1. Diseases caused by nutritional errors. These can be put into four categories.
   (a) Under-feeding, resulting in a lack of available energy.
   (b) Over-feeding, resulting in an excess of available energy.
   (c) Deficiency disease resulting from a net lack of essential nutrients, e.g. hypo- or avitaminosis.
   (d) Nutrient intoxication, resulting from contamination of food by toxic substances or an excess of essential nutrients where too much is harmful, e.g. an excess of fat soluble vitamins or trace elements such as copper or fluorine.

2. Diseases which can be influenced by dietetic measures but not actually caused by faults in feeding. These conditions can be further classified as:
   (a) Illness where other measures besides dietary adjustment are crucial to successful treatment, e.g. trauma resulting from an accident.
   (b) Distinct metabolic diseases or functional disorders of particular organs which require specific dietary treatment, e.g. diabetes mellitus resulting from endocrine pancreatic failure.

In a few cases there are inter-relations between categories 1 and 2, e.g. in cases of diabetes mellitus where it is associated with obesity. In such cases there may well be several factors which influence dietary therapy, in the case of obese animals with diabetes mellitus calorie restriction may be needed to control obesity and the elimination of simple sugars from the diet to avoid sudden high peaks of circulating blood sugar.

NUTRITION AND DISEASE IN GENERAL

Diseases usually manifest themselves by specific pathological lesions accompanied by physiological changes, the result often has profound nutritional consequences. During a fever for example, the general level of metabolism is increased by about 10% by a 1°C rise in body temperature. A 10°C rise in body temperature would double the metabolic rate. This high level of metabolism means that more enzymes are used and the requirement for the nutrients which go to make enzymes, that is protein, B vitamins and some trace elements is increased accordingly.

In infectious disease the metabolism of the immune-system is intensified for immuno-globulin synthesis. A sufficient supply of protein is required for the increased synthesis necessary as well as an adequate intake of essential nutrients to deal with these nutrients especially vitamins and trace minerals for the enhanced level of metabolism.

It has been shown recently that the first signs of infectious disease can be observed as variations in the plasma levels of certain trace elements (Beisel et al. 1974). It has been found that in many cases the plasma copper concentration increased whereas iron and zinc levels decreased. It is believed that micro-organisms are more sensitive to copper than the host and bacteria need the iron and zinc for their growth and reproduction. The first protective reaction of the body is to try to damage the micro-organisms by increasing circulating copper levels and to withdraw the availability of essential growth promoters iron and zinc.

Research is under way to examine the extent to which this first protective reaction of the body can be supported by dietetic measures.

It is generally accepted that every disease implies a stress situation associated with strains on certain metabolic functions which make it desirable to supply all nutrients needed for the increased rate of synthesis of the enzymes and hormones regulating metabolic processes.

The requirements of sick animals are in most cases higher than those of healthy ones. This situation is frequently aggravated by the fact that in most cases food intake is reduced or even ceases altogether. The composition of the feed, its nutrient content, digestibility, acceptance and the mode of feeding is of crucial importance for sick animals.

If pet owners prepare the food for diseased dogs and cats themselves they need to take particular care to use components of high digestibility (for example all cereals used must be well cooked as raw starch is poorly digested by carnivores) and proteins of high biological value (for example cooked eggs or meat with a low content of connective tissue such as tendons or cartilage, cottage cheese, and no glandular organs apart from liver).

In general animal protein is better digested and biologically more valuable than plant protein and is usually more palatable for carnivores. Dietary components with high levels of crude fibre need to be reduced or omitted as they tend to reduce the digestibility of the whole ration. In any case 'home-made' diets need to be supplemented with vitamins, minerals and trace elements because commonly used ingredients are naturally insufficient and may show considerable variation in 'made-up' diets.

When feeding commercially available pet food, 'complete diets' only should be used. That is food which contains all essential nutrients and energy sources in concentrations at least sufficient for adult animals. It is recommended that additional vitamins and trace elements are provided where the food intake is reduced in sick animals and where there are no contra-indications. Commercially produced complete foods are more suitable than self prepared foods as they are better balanced and the pet owner can rely on the declared essential nutrients.

Besides the composition and the content of nutrients, the acceptance of food is decisively important. The 'best' food is useless if it is not eaten by the animal. Because taste perception is reduced in most illnesses (especially those attended with fever) any low palatability is severely aggravated by inappetence. Pet owners usually know the type of food preferred by their animals. Specially flavoured foods can be used qualitatively, rich sources of energy (as glucose or fat), protein of high biological value (as cooked egg, meat or cottage cheese), vitamins and trace elements can all be added to make the food nutritionally more effective.

In general sick animals meet their water needs

well enough, even though they may be increased. Food with a high water content (such as canned food) is normally better accepted than dry food. This also has a good deal to do with the fact that flavours are best appreciated in dissolved form and because salivation is usually diminished in sick animals, especially when there is a fever. As a result canned and semi-moist foods are perceived more intensively by animals which are ill. The addition of fat may also increase the acceptance of some foods to some individuals.

If patients completely refuse to eat any food voluntarily, it is necessary to start to administer essential micro-nutrients such as vitamins and trace elements in tablet form or dissolved in drinking fluids, preferably combined with glucose.

In well established illnesses with anorexia it may be necessary to feed formula diets by means of a syringe or stomach tube.

The temperature of the food may also improve food intake. The influence of temperature on palatability is well established. Food immediately taken out of a refrigerator should not be given to animals. Acceptance is best when food is fed at body temperature. Cold food should be at least allowed to reach room temperature. It is even better to warm food to around 37–38°C, but not beyond, before it is offered.

Sick animals with reduced appetites should be fed small frequent meals, that is between 4–6 times daily. Any food presented should be removed after 15 min if not eaten. Fresh food subsequently offered is much more likely to stimulate the patient than if large quantities of uneaten food are allowed to remain before the animal.

These considerations are also valid for other convalescent animals such as those cases being prepared for, or recovering from, surgical procedures.

Gastro-intestinal disease therapy

As a general principle of treatment, noxious substances and toxic bacterial metabolites need to be removed promptly from the gastro-intestinal tract. The stomach and intestine need to stabilize and the further intake of injurious material be stopped. This can usually be achieved by withholding solid food for 1 or 2 days. If water and electrolyte balance can be maintained by parenteral administration of fluids so that there is no risk of dehydration, patients can be prevented from drinking as well for short periods.

At the beginning of treatment the gut may be evacuated by the use of laxatives. During the fasting period patients may be allowed to take small amounts of astringent or spasmolytic fluids (such as tea sweetened with small amounts of glucose).

In cases of chronic enteritis efforts can be made to modify the gut flora by use of antiseptic compounds, enzymes or bacterial preparations such as live yoghurt. Chemotherapy such as the use of non-absorbed antibiotics is indicated where there is specific bacterial infection present. Supportive use of Vitamins A and B (possibly C as well in some cases) may help by increasing epithelial protection and improving capillary permeability.

The nutritional consequences of intestinal tract disease can be grouped together under the heading of malassimilation. This can result from either maldigestion, malabsorption or both. Any pathological change in the gut mucosa results in both impaired absorption but inadequate digestion particularly in the final breakdown of peptides and oligo-saccharides, changes which take place in mucosa cells.

Malassimilation eventually results in a failure to meet the requirements of essential nutrients and signs of deficiency disease result. To reduce the chances of this happening patients should be fed a bland, easily digestible, well absorbed ration at small meals several times a day. The most useful diet in most cases would contain no more than 2% crude fibre, and only small amounts of lactose containing nutrients (i.e. milk and milk by-products). Only cooked starch and small amounts of any plant protein or connective tissue such as tendon, fascia or cartilage. Cooked eggs, meat and cottage cheese should be the main protein sources of good digestibility and biological value. Where the digestion and absorption of fat is disturbed, medium chain triglycerides as coconut oil for example, may be given to improve fat absorption and utilization.

Predigested carbohydrates containing oligo-saccharides are more easily digested than the dextrinized starch of cooked cereals. Animals which have lost a considerable amount of fluid by way of emesis and diarrhoea soon deplete themselves of B vitamins. To avoid deficiencies occurring any food provided should have double the concentration of B vitamins present in normal rations.

Most animals with gastro-intestinal disturbances experience some degree of dehydration usually with a loss of skin elasticity and depletion of electrolytes, particularly chloride ions where vomiting is persistent. Acidosis is likely to occur with profuse diarrhoea and alkalosis when vomiting predominates. In moderate dehydration the patient may correct the deficit by drinking. If the animal is vomiting so much that even water is not tolerated by mouth, then intravenous restoration of fluid balance is needed.

SPECIAL DIETETICS

Special diets are available and are an essential part of the treatment of many disturbances of organic function. In several diseases appropriate dietary control is an important and sometimes vital part of the treatment. Unfortunately records of experimental investigation and critical clinical observations to evaluate the value of dietary measures are lacking in the case of many diseases. The efficacy of some frequently prescribed diets is sometimes questionable. In such cases it is more reasonable to feed the patient on a correctly balanced normal ration without any dietary restriction because an unsuitable diet or a profound dietary change can be an unnecessary additional stress on the animal and often the owner as well. On the other hand proven effective diets are indispensable for therapeutic purposes. The efficacy and safety of such dietetic measures need to be tested as critically as any other type of therapy.

Some diets must be fed for a very long time, sometimes for the rest of the animal's life. Any dietary regime prescribed by a veterinarian must be complied with by the animal's owner as strictly as any other kind of treatment.

If a suitable diet is not eaten and assimilated, this results not only in deficiency diseases but can also increase the amount of non-absorbed nutrients reaching the large intestine. This can cause further upsets because of changes in the make-up of the bacterial flora in the lower gut. The influence of feed composition on rectal flora is quite marked even in normal animals. Figure 15 illustrates how changes in the type of food fed can alter a number of parameters in the gut and the blood.

GASTRIC DILATION AND TORSION

The accumulation of large amounts of gas in a dog's stomach is a life threatening situation and a real emergency. Most cases occur in large, deep-chested dogs such as Bloodhounds, Borzois and Great Danes. German Shepherd Dogs (Alsatians), Irish Wolfhounds and St. Bernards are also very prone to the condition.

Analysis of the contents of the stomachs of affected dogs suggests that swallowed air is the main contributor to the gas present. Van Kruiningen et al. (1974) in an extensive review of the subject concluded that a number of factors usually come together to precipitate a crisis:

1. Aerophagia related to greedy feeding
2. A readily fermentable substrate in the stomach
3. Appropriate fermentative bacteria present
4. Intercurrent gastric disease

These help to indicate the action which is needed to prevent the condition in susceptible breeds.

A number of suggestions have been made to attempt to reduce the likelihood of gastric dilation and torsion in dogs:

1. Avoid all unnecessary excitement at feeding time
2. Feed the daily allowance in 2–3 or even more separate meals
3. Keep exercise periods as far away from feeding times as possible
4. Give food to the dog so that it eats with its head up in an elevated position
5. Feed wet foods

Pearson (1975) recommends pre-soaking any biscuit fed to susceptible dogs.

PANCREATIC INSUFFICIENCY

Exocrine pancreatic disease is seen most frequently in German Shepherd Dogs (Alsatians). Subclinical disease is probably present long before symptoms of pancreatic insufficiency appear. By the time disease is evident pathological processes such as atrophy or cirrhosis are usually well advanced. Pancreatic disease may be associated with infectious disease such as canine distemper. Faulty nutrition does not seem to

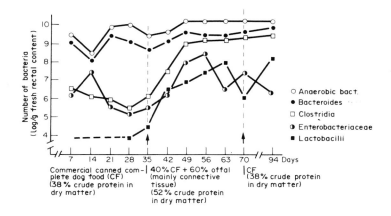

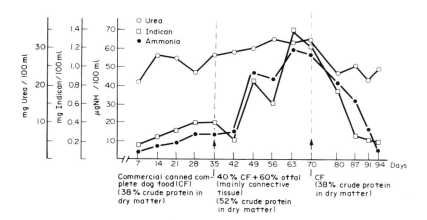

Fig. 15. Influence of the feed-composition on rectal flora and blood-parameters.

be a cause of pancreatic disease but recent studies indicate a partial correlation between pancreatitis and obesity. Dogs with pancreatic insufficiency usually have a ravenous appetite, lose bodyweight and pass large amounts of putty coloured, foamy faeces with a putrid rancid odour.

Specific treatment is only possible by substituting the deficient digestive enzymes. The dosage is related to the amounts of protein, carbohydrate and fat in the gut rather than the size of the animal. Enzymes are normally administered as tablets or as a powder which is mixed in with the food. Animals with pancreatic insufficiency need special dietary consideration. Because there is a net lack of trypsin, chymotrypsin, amylase and lipase there is maldigestion of protein, polysaccharides and fat in most cases. The diet should have a restricted fat level, the energy mostly supplied by easily digested carbohydrates (as oligo-saccharides and cooked cereals containing dextrinized starch) as well as protein of high biological value (as cooked eggs, finely ground meat with the minimum of connective tissue, cottage cheese and very little plant protein). Such diets need a vitamin and mineral supplement.

Where the dietary treatment and enzyme replacement are successful, improvement in the consistency and reduction in the volume of faeces are accompanied by a steady gain in bodyweight. Treatment has to continue for the rest of the animal's life.

DIABETES MELLITUS

Diabetes mellitus is a metabolic disorder characterized by a relative lack of available insulin. The main symptoms are hyperglycaemia and glucosuria. These characteristic signs are accompanied by excessive thirst and urination. There is general body wastage if effective treatment is not instituted promptly.

Animals with diabetes mellitus require very close supervision of their diet. A balance must be struck between the quantity and type of food eaten, the level of activity allowed and the dosage of insulin administered. Where the intake and output of energy is kept fairly constant the dosage of insulin can be adjusted to keep the plasma glucose level within reasonable tolerance limits. Hospitalization may be necessary at the outset to establish the most suitable dose of insulin for the animal's food intake and level of activity.

The most important aspect of dietary treatment is to standardize energy intake and output as far as it is practicable. Contrary to a widely held belief, carbohydrate does not increase the need for insulin (unless it is in the form of simple sugars when it can produce hyperglycaemic peaks), provided it does not increase the total energy intake. In humans the recommended maximum percentage of energy derived from carbohydrate is of the order of 40–45% of the total energy. A dog fed on a canned meat and biscuit diet on a 50 : 50, volume to volume basis would receive about 35–45% of its energy as carbohydrate, which is not an excessive amount.

The most important points to remember when feeding diabetic dogs are that prepared foods subjected to quality control procedures have a distinct advantage over more improvised diets as the objective is to keep the dietary intake as unchanging as possible. The food allowed needs to be divided into several meals to spread the load on the endocrine system. This can be achieved by feeding half the total energy allowed in the middle of the day and the remainder divided up into meals in the morning and evening. Energy output must be controlled as well, compatible with a reasonably normal life. As oestrus in diabetic bitches frequently results in setbacks, spaying is often advisable if this is the case. Diabetes mellitus is usually a progressive disease in dogs so continual surveillance of cases is needed if the animal is to lead a reasonable life for a number of years. Everything depends on the dog having a sensible, co-operative owner.

FOOD-INDUCED ALLERGY

The commonest manifestations of food-induced allergy in dogs are as skin changes. To a lesser extent digestive disturbances are seen. Usually the most difficult aspect of the management of food induced allergy is to convince the owner that the fault lies with the animal and not with the food. There is some evidence to suggest that German Shepherd Dogs (Alsatians) are specially susceptible to food-induced allergies.

The main feature of dietary managment is the identification and subsequent avoidance of the allergen concerned. As the resolution of clinical signs is the only indicator of the absence of a particular allergen, treatment of lesions is usually straightforward and palliative unless there are secondary complications such as super-imposed infection. Unlike man, multiple sensitivity to a number of related proteins is not usual in dogs. That is allergy, is usually to one specific component of the diet. The detection of allergens is made easier by this although there are many other practical difficulties. If complete owner co-operation is not possible in the home, then hospitalization is recommended for the determination of the allergen. This has the additional advantage of taking the dog away from any possible airborne allergens in its home environment.

A test diet which includes proteins not normally available to the dog needs to be fed to the exclusion of all other foods for a period of at least 5 days. A diet of mutton and rice is the traditional one used but if a single source of protein is fed such as boiled fish or chicken, this would probably serve as well to begin with. Baker (1974) suggests that tap water should be replaced by bottled spring water during any tests to eliminate the possibility of water-borne allergens.

The proteins which are the commonest allergens for dogs are from beef, wheat (gluten), and milk (casein). It would be sensible to carefully introduce each one into the diet which should then remain unchanged for 5 days and observe any signs of an allergic reaction.

Once the allergen has been identified it must be excluded from the dog's diet permanently as there is very little evidence that food induced allergy in dogs decreases with age.

CARDIAC DISEASE

Most cardiac disease leads to functional cardiac insufficiency. As far as nutrition is concerned only chronic cardiac failure is of relevance. For the most part cardiac insufficiency is a consequence of valvular or muscular disease of the heart. The effects develop slowly and eventually involve every organ of the body. Cats with cardiac failure tend to take less rigorous exercise than dogs and so are less affected by the condition.

The dietary aspects of heart disease in dogs and cats can be grouped into two main areas:

1. The intake of large amounts of food can lead to excessive filling of the stomach and intestine. As a result the diaphragm is kept in a forward position. Cardiac function, already impaired, is further hampered mechanically. The volume of any one meal needs to be restricted to avoid unnecessary gastric pressures and to reduce the amount of gas in the intestine. Obese animals need to be fed a calorie restricted regime to reduce adiposity.

2. The kidneys of animals with cardiac insufficiency tend to retain sodium and water. This gives rise to the clinical picture of ascites (dropsy) and local oedema. The basis of this effect is believed to be, either the reduction in sodium and water filtration or an increase in reabsorption of sodium which brings water back into the tubules of the kidney.

The reversal of this process can be brought about by desalination. This is achieved by restricting further sodium intake and by diuresis. The more extra-cellular fluid which is lost the more sodium is removed with it.

Attempts to treat canine cardiac failure only by feeding low salt diets are not very rewarding as it takes a very long time to effectively desalinate dogs. In addition, dogs enjoy as we do, fairly salt diets and do not usually find low salt regimes very palatable.

Salt restriction may however, be an effective adjunct to other cardiac treatment such as diuresis. A diet may be made up using muscle meat (without added salt), pasta with potatoes and rice as an energy source, with dicalcium phosphate and a salt-free supplement to make up for any mineral and vitamin shortfall.

An example of a simple formula (Table 22) shows that sodium restriction can be achieved with such a diet.

Although low sodium diets are not usually very palatable for dogs and cats, it is possible to improve them by adding flavours, by roasting or even frying. If meat and meat by-products are cooked in plenty of water and the liquor is subsequently discarded the total sodium content of the food can be reduced. If this is done a 50 : 50, volume : volume mixture of meat and cereal will still provide approximately the level of sodium needed.

Dietary measures must be supported by proper nursing. Exercise needs to be reduced particularly where the climate is hot and humid. Dogs should be walked only as far as they can safely tolerate without signs of distress and all excitement must be avoided. Adequate ventilation of the housing and cutting the hair on long coated dogs in hot weather are all measures which can be combined with conventional diuretic therapy in cardiac cases.

In addition to dietary management, medical therapy is indicated in most cases both to improve cardiac function and to control oedema with the use of diuretics.

KIDNEY DISEASE

Dysfunctions of the kidney are frequent in aged animals, particularly dogs. Treatment of kidney disease and the minimalization of their consequences become essential for the prolongation of life in most cases.

Kidney disease is usually the result of noxious influences such as pathogenic micro-organisms, bacterial toxins, allergic reactions, toxic contamination or auto-immune disease. Kidney disease is not normally the result of faulty nutrition. The objectives of dietary measures in cases of kidney failure are to adjust the intake of protein, electrolytes and water to the optimum level the kidney is able to deal with.

Table 22. *Sodium levels in a 'cardiac' diet*

	mg Na/kg body weight	% Na in dry matter of food
Requirement of healthy animals	130	0.4
Recommended Na-intake of patients with cardiac insufficiency	13—20	0.04—0.06

Average Na-content of
    meat and meat byproducts,
    most cereals
		0.2
		0.02

Diet consisting of:
    1/3 meat (30% dry matter)
    + 2/3 cereals (90% dry matter)
		0.03
		0.017

contains on average		0.05

Table 23 summarizes the diet needed and the rationale of treatment.

Adequate water intake

Patients with insufficient kidney function always show polyuria and polydipsia (increased water output and intake). Because of this drinking water must always be available *ad libitum.*

Adequate sodium supply

Oedema is not normally a feature of renal failure in dogs and cats. Limitation of sodium intake is not usually necessary. The situation is usually one of considerable sodium loss by way of the damaged kidney. Where this is the case about 100 mg/sodium per kg body weight is recommended as a supplement for normal foods. One half may be given as sodium chloride and one half sodium bicarbonate to help

Table 23. *Diet in kidney failure*

Dietetic Measures	Intention
1. Adequate water intake	Optimum hydration
2. Adequate sodium supply	Compensation of sodium loss via the damaged kidney
3. Controlled potassium intake	Prophylaxis against hyperkalaemia
4. Adequate energy supplied in the form of carbohydrates and fat (up to one third of the total dietary energy as fat)	Prevention of protein being used as an energy source and thus contributing to uraemia
5. Control of protein intake	
(a) restriction where indicated	Reduction of protein break-down products in tissues (e.g. urea, hydrogen ions)
(b) by providing good quality protein supplements	To compensate for heavy protein losses via the damaged kidney

prevent acidosis. This is the equivalent of about 0.1 g NaCl and 0.2 g $NaHCO_3$ per kg bodyweight.

If sodium loss is not compensated the patient will eventually become sodium depleted. As a result the blood supply to the kidneys is affected sufficiently to reduce kidney function.

Controlled potassium supply

In cases of renal insufficiency potassium retention often occurs where the kidney is unable to eliminate potassium. Dietary potassium restriction is made easier where protein restricted diets are used as high protein foods are usually the ones rich in potassium.

Non-protein sources of energy

Adequate supply of energy as carbohydrate and fat minimizes the oxidation of amino acids absorbed or liberated from the catabolism of body protein. Easily digested carbohydrates as cooked cereals, dextrinized starch or glucose fed plus fat or oil up to 10—20% of the dry matter of the diet depending on individual tolerances. Kidney diets should normally have digestible energy levels of between 3500—4300 kcals per kg dry matter.

Protein intake

It is necessary to differentiate between kidney insufficiency with uraemia and other kidney disease with high losses of protein via the urine. In uraemic cases the metabolites normally excreted by the kidney, particularly urea, are retained because of reduced blood clearance. Protein intake must be adapted to the decreased kidney function if an increase in circulating urea and related substances is to be avoided.

In order to meet minimum protein needs, two criteria must be considered. The absolute amount of protein required and secondly the biological value of the proteins available. The normal recommendation (NRC 1974) is for 1.6 g per kg metabolic body weight, (see Chapter 1) if the biological value is 100, that is the biological value of egg protein. This is tabulated as Table 24 where the minimum requirement of

protein is given for various sizes of dogs.

Corresponding to the biological value the amount of protein has to be increased in order to administer the required amounts of essential amino-acids (Table 25).

Consider the average content and biological value of protein. Table 26 shows the required amounts of protein sources to balance minimum protein metabolism in adult dogs.

Healthy dogs are usually fed more protein than they actually need, normally for reasons of palatability as dogs tend not to find protein-restricted regimes very palatable. The levels of reduction recommended may seem severe but if proteins of high biological value are used the amounts should be sufficient and the palatability acceptable.

With these dietary considerations uraemia can usually be prevented or at least reduced for a long period as most patients are able to excrete some urea and related metabolites, provided they have about 25% of their functional glomerular capacity left.

In kidney disease with well established or severe

Table 24. *Minimum protein requirement of adult dogs*

Body weight kg	Egg protein g/day
5	5.3
10	9.0
15	12.2
20	15.1
30	20.5
40	25.5
50	30.0

Table 25. *Biological value of some proteins*

Protein source	Biological value	Factor, egg protein has to be multiplied by to supply the limiting amino-acids
Egg	100	1.00
Beef	76	1.30
Casein	71	1.40
Soybean protein	64	1.55
Gluten	40	2.48

Table 26. *Minimum amount of protein sources for adult dogs*

Body weight kg	Egg number/day	Beef g/day	Cottage cheese (20% fat in dry matter) g/day
5	0.75	30	60
10	1.50	55	100
15	1.75	75	135
20	2.25	90	170
30	3.00	125	230
40	3.70	155	285
50	4.30	180	330

proteinuria the renal protein loss must be replaced by adequate amounts of biologically active protein. As a general rule about twice the amount lost by way of the kidney should be added to the basic requirement by the addition of one hard-boiled egg for every 100 g of the usual diet or an equivalent amount of other valuable protein sources such as ground muscle meat or cottage cheese.

Animals with kidney disease, particularly where uraemia is well established suffer from inappetence often with vomiting. Food given to nephritic animals must therefore be palatable and with the highest quality components. Patients should be fed several times daily. Animals with renal insufficiency need additional water soluble vitamins. Vitamins of the B group are 'washed out' by the polyuria which is always present. There may also be a failure of re-absorption where kidney tubules are damaged. In severe cases therapeutic levels of up to ten times the normal amount given may be needed. These may be administered orally or where there is persistent vomiting, parenterally.

OBESITY

Obesity is the commonest form of malnutrition in man and dogs in the western world. Between 28% and 34% of dogs are said to be overtly obese in the United Kingdom. A survey in Austria reported 44% of dogs to be obese. The only figure available for cats is one survey where 9% of cats were found to be obese. Obesity is an excessive accumulation of fat in the body, it is not just being overweight. The condition is 1/3 more common in females than males and twice as common in neutered animals. Lewis found that obesity in dogs was twice as common in dogs owned by obviously obese owners. Mason found that obesity was more common in dogs fed 'do-it-yourself' diets than those fed prepared foods. Lewis also found that only 5% of dogs were judged as being underweight.

About 1/4 of obese dogs have orthopaedic complications. Many other complications are associated with obesity, including reduced lifespan, congestive heart failure, and a reduced resistance to infectious disease.

Obese animals do not necessarily eat very much as it does not take a large energy intake to maintain fat animals. But obesity can only result from an energy intake greater than output, *at some time* in the animal's life. That is the animal has been in positive energy balance and the excess energy is stored as fat. Few cases in dogs are the result of endocrine disorders, the only estimate available is 5% of cases seen.

The treatment of obesity should, on the face of it be very simple. Everyone who has spent any time at all in small animal practice knows that it is not easy to get good results any more than it is in man. It is a problem of case management. It is usually useless simply to tell an owner to feed less or even just to suggest a diet. There has to be a concerted plan of attacking the problem. The first need is to convince the owner that there is a problem. Usually the animal is presented because of one or more of the complications of obesity, hardly ever because of the obesity itself. Obesity is not a joke, it can cause quite serious problems and it is certainly something which should be taken seriously.

It is necessary to have the co-operation of everyone who comes into contact with the animal. Anything less is a waste of time.

The objective is to put the animal into negative energy balance by decreasing energy intake or increasing energy output, or both. Increasing exercise alone can be hazardous, particularly if there is congestive heart disease, or joint lesions. Far better to let the animal become more active, which it usually does of its own accord as fat is lost.

There are two degrees of reducing energy intake — restricted calorie intake and total calorie restriction, i.e. starvation. Whatever regime is adopted, it is important for the clinician to write down instructions to owners, preferably on a pre-printed form. If the owner can keep a simple graph it can be an effective motivator. In any case, a graph should be kept with the animal's records.

After initial consultation and counselling, the dog should be weighed carefully and a target weight estimated from the normal bodyweight of dogs of the type presented. The target weight should not be too ambitious. A bodyweight loss of 15% or so in 10 weeks is a reasonable achievement.

If 60% of the calorie requirements for a dog of the target weight is prescribed , that is a good starting point. The NRC tables for energy requirements can be taken at 100%.

A diet can be prescribed based on the calorie density of food. Most canned foods have a calorie density of about 80—100 kcal/100 g, whereas biscuit is normally about 350 kcal/100 g, it is therefore not too difficult to work out a suitable diet.

Allow no other food at all. The only supplement allowed is drinking water which should be given *ad libitum.* If the total amount allowed is given in several meals it may help, but care must be taken as the owner may feed the day's allowance at each meal. What owners rarely realize is that one or two biscuits which may only weigh 30—40 g, may make all the difference between success and failure as this may represent 100 or so calories.

The habit of giving a little treat at a particular time of day is hard for an owner to abandon. Unfortunately this is usually something calorie dense and may well spoil everything. It is better if pieces of meat or meat-based canned food are cut up and fed as treats at the usual time. The dog should be weighed every week. The body weight carefully recorded on a graph. This should be compared with the owner's records if there are any. The total amount of calories allowed should be reduced by *20%* every time the weekly weighing shows no reduction. This method allows the highest food intake compatible with a steady weight loss. It usually surprises the owner how much food the dog is allowed. It may *seem* more than it was getting. If smaller reductions than 20% are prescribed, the same result will be achieved, it will simply take longer.

Once a drop in body weight occurs, weight loss is usually steady in dogs (unlike man). This is important as the owner sees very little difference in the dog's appearance, even though good progress is being made. The simple graph becomes all the more important at about 3 weeks. It can be drawn forward to a point (say) 6—8 weeks and usually be shown to be on line for the target weight.

A change in the dog's demeanour is often the first sign to be noted. A happier, more active dog usually begins to exercise itself more. It is helpful to get the owner to keep a diary of the dog's every activity. Very often the owner will volunteer information such as 'the dog went up the stairs unaided or played with a ball for the first time for many months'. The interest created can be a strong motivational power at a time when it is really needed. Although the energy output from such activity will not account for very many calories, it all helps to keep the animal in negative balance. The frequency which the dog is seen has a direct relationship to success and the maintenance of an optimum state afterwards. If there are no signs of success after about 6 weeks, in spite of regular surveillance and consultations, the animal will probably need to be hospitalized. It is better if a veterinarian can examine the dog at each weekly weighing, although this can be quite costly in professional time.

Weighing, counselling and allocating dietary amounts can usually be left to a well-trained nurse as long as results are reported promptly to the clinician in charge of the case. Once a reasonable target weight has been achieved, a maintenance ration needs to be prescribed as further weight reduction is not needed, and bodyweight will increase rapidly once control is removed. De Bruinje (1979) showed that even dogs which had lost 25% of their body weight could be back to 90% of their initial weight within 10 days of re-feeding. The amount of food for maintenance should not be more than 10% of the calories allowed in the reducing regime unless weight loss still occurs at follow-up weighings. Regular weighings are still needed and a follow-up at 3 and 6 months will help prevent a return to the obese state which so often happens in human patients.

The alternative to calorie restriction is withholding food altogether. Such a regime requires even more care in surveillance, and hospitalization is necessary. The proponents of starvation as a regime for treating canine obesity claim that there are no adverse physiological changes of any significance and no problems of re-feeding have been reported. A vitamin/mineral supplement and drinking water is all that is allowed.

Lewis reports weight losses of 7, 12, 16, 20 and 23% at the 2nd, 3rd, 4th, 5th and 6th week. A higher proportion will be lean body mass than with calorie controlled regimes. Ketosis does not seem to occur. However the greatest care is needed embarking on this procedure. If anything goes wrong, such as the animal failing to eat once the desired body weight is reached, it will certainly be difficult explaining it to the owner. Deaths have been reported in humans treated for gross obesity by starvation. As a sensible calorie controlled regime is effective, there seems little need to use a more potentially hazardous method.

CONCLUSIONS

Attention to the proper nutrition of medical and surgical patients is vital. Optimal nutrition in general and specific dietetic measures are essential aids to other medical treatment. Although nutritional therapy and dietetics are an indispensable part of medical care the subject is not as yet very well developed in dog and cat nutrition. Experience is however gradually being accumulated by veterinarians enabling guidance to be given to owners of dogs and cats. The food industry has made some diets commercially available to greatly facilitate the dietary treatment of common conditions such as chronic nephritis, obesity and general convalescence.*

The success of all dietary measures is ultimately dependent on the animal's owner. Much depends on a good understanding of the need to apply and persevere with dietary control, sometimes for the remainder of

the animal's life and time spent counselling owners on appropriate feeding is always well worthwhile.

BIBLIOGRAPHY

Baker, E. (1974) Food Allergy. *Vet. Clin. N. Amer.* **4**, 79.

Beisel, W. R., Pekarek, R. S. and Wannemacher, R. W. (1974) The impact of infectious disease on trace element metabolism of the host. In *Trace Element Metabolism in Animals,* 2nd Ed. Edited by Hoekstra, W. G., Suttie, J. W., Ganther, H. E. and Mertz, W. University Park Press, Baltimore.

Cremer, H. D., Heilmeyer, L., Holtmeier, H. J., Hotzel, D., Kuhn, H. A., Kuhnau, J. and Zoller, N. (1972–1980), *Ernährungslehre und Diätetik.* Vols 1–3, Georg Thieme Verlag, Stuttgart.

De Bruinjie, J. J. (1980) Biochemical observations during total starvation in dogs. *Chem. Abs.* **92**, 556.

Edney, A. T. B. (1978) Dietary management in small animal practice. *Vet. Rec.* **102**, 543.

Edney, A. T. B. (1981) Ernährung und Krankheit. *Wien. Tierärtzl. Mschr.* **68**, 115.

Gaines Dog Research Centre (1977) *Basic Guide to Canine Nutrition,* 4th Ed. White Plains, New York.

Leibetseder, J. and Jaksch, W. (1978) Nutrition related disease of the gastro-intestinal tract, heart and kidneys in dogs and cats. *Die praktische Tierarzt.* **59**, 101.

Lewis, L. (1977) Obesity in the dog. 1st Kal Kan Symposium Proceedings, Ohio State University, p. 19.

Mason, E. (1970) Obesity in Pet Dogs. *Vet. Rec.* **86**, 612.

NRC (1974) *Nutrient Requirement of Dogs,* Report No. 8, National Academy of Sciences, Washington.

NRC (1978) *Nutrient Requirements of Cats,* Report No. 13. National Academy of Sciences, Washington.

Pearson, H. (1975) Gastric dilation and torsion. *Pedigree Digest* **2**, 6.

Van Kruininingen, H. J., Gregoire, K. and Menton, D. J. (1974) Acute gastric dilation: a review of comparative aspects by species and a study in dogs and monkeys. *J. Am. Anim. Hosp. Assoc.* **10**, 294.

Weinberg, E. D. (1974) *Roles of Temperature and Trace Element Metabolism in Host–Pathogen Relations; in Trace Element Metabolism in Animals,* 2nd Ed., *op. cit.*

Nephritis, Obesity and Convalescent Diets in the United Kingdom.

CHAPTER 9

FLUID THERAPY AND INTRAVENOUS NUTRITION

L. W. Hall

Fluid therapy in dogs and cats has been the subject of many publications but the nutritional requirements of animals unable to eat or retain food have received little attention. The length of time impaired intake can be allowed to persist before treatment becomes essential has been debated and some veterinarians consider it is unnecessary to provide nourishment for small animal patients deprived of food for only a few days. However, before this view can be accepted some evidence is needed that even short periods of starvation or malnutrition are harmless. Various investigations and clinical experience in man show that malnutrition results in impaired wound healing, loss of body tissue and eventually, of course, death. General appearance and observed weight loss suggest that many sick animals receive insufficient protein and calories to meet their needs. Indeed it seems highly probable that inadequate protein and calorie intake contributes significantly to morbidity and mortality, some animals dying from the effects of starvation rather than the primary disease.

Published nutritional requirements of dogs and cats are derived from observations on normal healthy subjects. Less is known of the requirements of cats than of dogs and almost nothing is known of the metabolic needs of sick animals. Only a few introductory studies have been carried out in surgically or accidentally traumatized animals but they do indicate that fit normal animals and animal patients may have quite different nutritional needs.

RESPONSE TO STARVATION

In normal healthy animals starvation results in a predictable metabolic response which depends on the ability of the animal to metabolize fat from its adipose tissues and to use the free fatty acids and ketone bodies produced as its primary energy source. It is known that the brain and heart muscle can utilize ketone bodies in addition to glucose and that both heart muscle and the liver can utilize free fatty acids. According to Cahill (1970) insulin is the chief hormonal factor in this response and it is interesting that by raising plasma levels of free fatty acids, starvation lessened rather than enhanced the anaesthetic depression of heart and liver function in experimental animals.

In ill subjects the body becomes unable to utilize fat stores as an energy source and liver glycogen stores become exhausted after about 24 h of starvation. Protein breakdown to amino acids and subsequently to carbohydrate residues then becomes the main source of carbohydrate intermediates. The combination of catabolism with starvation results in the breakdown of large quantities of protein, the extent of this breakdown is directly related to the severity of the disease or injury and the nutritional status of the patient. Moore (1959) had observed this post-injury catabolic phase and concluded that it must be obligatory so that attempts to reverse it by the infusion of amino acids would only lead to increased urinary nitrogen losses but more recently it has been shown that the administration of amino acids and carbohydrates in combination does reduce and may abolish post-operative nitrogen losses (Johnston *et al.*, 1966).

In man the increasing use of total parenteral nutrition has inevitably led to complications such as the hyperglycaemic, non-ketotic coma syndrome; dangerous hypoglycaemia may follow unplanned discontinuation of high concentrations of intravenous glucose. There is much to learn from all this experience because it would seem that all these problems can be avoided by good management based on an understanding of the metabolic background of starvation in diseased states. This understanding however, can only be attained when the effects of starvation in canine and feline disease have been determined by controlled investigation. Until this time any recommendations such as those in this chapter can only be regarded as guidelines which may well need revision as knowledge grows.

SPECIAL PROBLEMS OF INTRAVENOUS NUTRITION

To be adequate any diet must contain all the materials necessary for synthesis of body tissues and their metabolism and must therefore, include carbohydrates, fat, protein, mineral salts, vitamins and water. It is unusual to make a separate assessment of water and electrolytes for incorporation in the diet because once water balance has been obtained it is likely that the volume of water which an adult animal can utilize safely under most conditions is limited to about 80 ml/kg/day and the other materials must be contained in this volume. Another limitation encountered in intravenous nutrition is the inherently low calorie content of nutrients; 4 kcal/g for carbohydrate and protein, 7 kcal/g for ethyl alcohol and 9 kcal/g for fat (see Chapter 10). A third limitation is the concentration of the fluid which is to be infused which can be given without causing thrombophlebitis.

At one time the intravenous administration of glucose constituted the standard way of attempting to provide calories but 1 l of 5% glucose (isotonic water) yields only 200 kcal and this is quite insufficient for any dog or cat to meet its needs from the infused fluid alone. When 10% glucose is used the total available for the provision of energy may be reduced by spillage of up to 30% of the administered glucose in the urine. The urinary loss is reduced by slow infusion because the blood concentration of glucose remains lower but the incidence of chemically induced thrombophlebitis is increased as the duration of infusion is prolonged. The utilization of glucose is dependent upon insulin and this together with the

other limitations restrict its use to a source of calories in parenteral nutrition.

Fructose (laevulose) is metabolized in the liver to glycogen and its metabolism is independent of insulin. It is more rapidly utilized than glucose and its administration results in the more rapid clearance of ethyl alcohol from the bloodstream when they are given together.

The alcoholic sugar sorbitol, is oxidized via sorbitol dehydrogenase to fructose in the liver and its metabolism is thus, like fructose, independent of insulin, making it particularly useful in stress situations. It is antiketogenic and liver protective so that it is probably the sugar of choice in the presence of severe liver damage.

The marked anabolic effect of ethyl alcohol has been known for a long time and it is a useful source of calories (7 kcal/g) although it may have a very soporific effect on dogs and cats if it is infused too rapidly. It is usually administered in combination with amino acids and carbohydrate (fructose) to accelerate its clearance from the blood. Although it is rapidly metabolized, too fast infusion leads to urinary loss.

There is no doubt that fats as emulsions, provide the richest source of calories for intravenous diets (9 kcal/g) and available emulsions consist of oil particles 0.5 to 1.0 μm in diameter in water, in combination with an emulsifying agent, with glucose, glycerin or sorbitol added to make the preparation isotonic. Cotton-seed oil emulsions should not be used in dogs because on their path to the liver they accumulate chylomicrons, developing a particle diameter of more than 1 μm and being destroyed by the Kupffer cells. Dogs given cotton-seed oil emulsions die within a few days from gastro-intestinal disturbances, liver necrosis and acute anaemia. Dogs given soya bean oil emulsions under similar conditions do not suffer this fate but like all fat emulsions those of soya bean oil tend to be associated with fatty infiltration of the liver, anaemia and coagulation defects when used over long periods. This and their relatively short shelf-life greatly restricts the use of soya bean oil emulsions in dogs and cats.

In the body, injected or synthesized amino acids form a biochemical pool from which the cells synthesize protein and there is a continuous exchange of amino acids in the pool with those in existing protein. Because new protein is constructed via the amino acid pool blood, plasma and albumin administered to maintain the blood volume and plasma protein levels will not promote protein synthesis. The physiological way of supplementing the supply to and replacing losses from the pool is the administration of amino acids in the correct ratio. Chemically the amino acids exist in two isomeric forms (dextro- and laevo-rotatory). The laevorotatory (*l*) forms are, with few exceptions, the only ones found naturally and apart from methionine and phenylalanine the body is unable to utilize dextrorotatory (*d*) forms of amino acids. If *d*-isomers are infused they are excreted unchanged in the urine and if present in large quantities, may promote an osmotic diuresis.

The ideal composition of amino acid mixtures for intravenous nutrition has been the source of much debate and the mixtures available for infusion fall into two main groups, (i) synthetic amino acids and (ii) protein digests or casein hydrolysates. The casein hydrolysates contain a mixture of *l*-amino acids and simple polypeptides and usually have a low pH. Amino acids are available both as mixtures of the active *l*-forms and inactive *d*-forms or as pure synthetic *l*-preparations. The pure laevo- preparations are expensive but are probably the solutions of choice for dogs and cats.

The major complication of intravenous feeding is thrombophlebitis at the site of infusion but osmotic diuresis and dehydration result from too rapid infusion of substances which have a renal threshold for excretion. Measurement of haemoglobin, cholesterol, proteins, bilirubin and electrolytes in the blood may be affected by the intravenous infusion of fat emulsions and when such measurements are requested the laboratory must be informed that the animal is receiving these emulsions. It must be stressed that whenever adequate gastrointestinal feeding is possible, be it orally, by nasogastric tube or pharyngostomy tube, it should be adopted as the procedure of choice. It is only when gastrointestinal feeding is proving impossible that intravenous feeding is indicated and it must be remembered that intravenous regimes are both expensive and time-consuming. It is always sound practice to reduce catabolic responses by raising the environmental temperature and moreover, the diet prescribed must be balanced according to age and species requirements.

INDICATIONS FOR INTRAVENOUS NUTRITION

Intravenous feeding may be indicated pre-operatively in animals whose condition has made adequate oral intake impossible for some weeks prior to presentation for treatment, as may be the case in young animals suffering from achalasia or pyloric stenosis. It may also be necessary when the disease has been associated with severe diarrhoea or malabsorption. Intravenous feeding may be necessary to supplement oral feeding in cases where there has been a steady weight loss in spite of efforts to maintain adequate gastrointestinal intake. Another indication may be a consistently low blood glucose level, in the absence of excess insulin, which reveals inadequate calorie intake.

The plasma protein level can be misleading. A normal level does not necessarily mean satisfactory protein balance, and a low level may result from failure of anabolism, loss of plasma proteins from raw surfaces or replacement of blood loss with fluids other than blood and plasma. When plasma protein production is not occurring in the liver even adequate intravenous feeding will not raise a low plasma protein level and in these circumstances, the level should be raised by plasma infusion for the sake of the physical properties of the proteins themselves.

Intravenous nutrition is probably most often contemplated for animals undergoing operations on the gastrointestinal tract. In fact most of these are well able to tolerate the 2 to 3 days of imposed starvation which most surgeons demand. The administration of adequate water and electrolytes in the immediate post-operative period will tide them over until they are capable of resuming normal feeding. Although the administration of intravenous amino acids and fat would probably be of benefit to most of these animals it is not necessary and therefore scarcely justifiable in view of the difficulties and high costs involved. If however the animal is still unable to take a normal diet by the third post-operative day due to paralytic ileus or any other cause, full intravenous feeding should be started without delay. Even obese animals need intravenous feeding from this time, for the breakdown of amino acids to provide carbohydrate residues still occurs even in the presence of excessive fat stores. Pyrexia or unconsciousness of more than 3 days' duration may be another indication for instituting parenteral nutrition.

PREDICTION OF ANIMAL'S REQUIREMENTS

Adult cats are all about the same size (3—5 kg) and need between 200 and 400 kcal/day for maintenance, while a lactating queen may need up to 600 kcal/day. Dogs vary enormously in size and smaller dogs have a relatively greater energy turnover. For example a Chihuahua may need about 120 kcal/kg whereas a St. Bernard's needs may amount to no more than 42 kcal/kg for maintenance (Table 24). These requirements may need to be doubled for fast-growing puppies and even trebled for lactating bitches.

No exact practical assessment can be made for nitrogen requirements of sick animals. It seems logical to administer a basal nitrogen allowance to prevent nitrogen depletion in the catabolic stage of illness but in the anabolic phase this must be increased. Growing puppies and kittens may be regarded as being in an anabolic state, the protein or amino acid nitrogen allowances for growth may provide a guide to needs for body repair. It is generally accepted that cats have a protein need nearly twice that of dogs. In the catabolic phase a dog may thus be allowed about 1 g/kg of protein and a cat 2 g/kg per day; in the anabolic phase these allowances may be doubled.

In all cases of parenteral feeding it is necessary to give vitamin supplements and it has been suggested that these should include:

Ascorbic acid	250 mg
Thiamin	1 mg
Riboflavin	3 mg
Nicotinic acid	8 mg
Pyridoxine	2 mg
Pantothenic acid	4 mg
Cobalamin	10 μg

Numerous mixtures of this nature are available for addition to intravenous solutions.

All these figures cannot be regarded as more than general guides to therapy and they must not be accepted for more than they are — that is the minimum requirements to cover resting metabolism, the specific dynamic effect and some physical activity. The problem is to know what any individual animal requires and any fixed regime, even if tailored to take account of the species, age, sex and size, will mean that some animals are likely to be undertreated. Those most likely to be undertreated are those with the most severe metabolic problems and whose need for adequate nutrition is greatest.

PRACTICAL GUIDE TO INTRAVENOUS FEEDING

In view of the as yet unresolved uncertainties there is little point in trying to formulate detailed prescriptions for use in small animal practice for the inaccuracy will be so great that the nursing work-load involved in their administration cannot be justified. In general two types of regime have proved both reasonably satisfactory and relatively simple to carry out in practice. The first involves the use of concentrated sugar solutions which must be given into the vena cava; the second utilizes fat emulsions which may be given into a peripheral vein.

Many solutions designed for intravenous nutrition are now available but detailed studies of their suitability for use in dogs and cats have not been carried out. However experience has shown that one or two can be used to prevent weight loss over periods of up to 10 days.

Table 24.

	Weight (kg)	kcal/kg.
Chihuahua	2.3	120
Pekingese	4.5	100
Boston Terrier	9	80
Kerry Blue Terrier	18	66
Boxer	27	60
German Shepherd Dog	36	54
Deerhound	45	52
Newfoundland	68	46
St. Bernard	91	42

Data derived from J. T. Abrams, *Feeding of Dogs* (1962)

(a) Fat free regime

The best available solution appears to be Aminoplex 5* the composition of which is given in Table 25. The solution contains pure 1-amino-acids in a balanced ratio of the eight essential amino acids and of the non-essential which should provide for maximum utilization; *l*-ornithine-*l*-aspartate which effects the detoxication of ammonia within the urea cycle and is of particular value in hepatic disorders, and *l*-malic acid which it is claimed promotes the generation of adenosine triphosphate (ATP) within the tricarboxylic

Table 25. *Composition of Aminoplex 5**

Constituent	Content per litre
Nitrogen	5 g
Calories	1000 (4.2 MJ)
L-Isoleucine	1.20 g
L-Leucine	1.65 g
L-Lysine HCl	3.19 g
L-Methionine	2.40 g
L-Phenylalanine	1.65 g
L-Threonine	1.20 g
L-Tryptophan	0.60 g
L-Valine	1.95 g
L-Arginine	3.95 g
L-Histidine	1.05 g
L-Alanine	5.55 g
Glycine	4.50 g
L-Proline	1.50 g
L-Ornithine-L-Aspartate	0.75 g
Nicotinamide	0.05 g
Vitamin B6 HCl	0.03 g
L-Malic acid	2.01 g
Sorbitol	125 g
Ethanol	50 g
Potassium	15 mMol
Sodium	35 mMol
Chloride	62 mMol

*Geistlich Sons Limited, Newton Bank, Long Lane, Chester, United Kingdom

acid cycle, releasing a phosphate radicle to provide a rapid and powerful source of energy. Calories are provided from sorbitol and ethanol.

For dogs it would appear to approach the presumed ideal solution — e.g. a 10 kg Terrier estimated as needing about 800 kcal and 3.2 g N_2 per day given 800 ml of Aminoplex 5 over a 24 h period will receive 800 kcal, 4 g of N_2 and most of its other requirements. Similarly, a 30 kg Labrador needing about 1800 kcal and 10 g N_2 per day can be maintained on 2 l per day of Aminoplex 5 because it will receive 2000 kcal and 10 g of N_2 from this volume of solution. Overloading with water is unlikely to be a problem in either case because the Terrier will receive 80 ml/kg/day and the Labrador 66 ml/kg/day on this regime.

Aminoplex 5 is reasonably satisfactory for cats although to provide the estimated calorie and N_2 requirements may necessitate the administration of excessive quantities of water. An average cat needing 500 kcal per day together with 2.5 g N_2 can be fed by the infusion of 500 ml of solution (which will provide precisely these amounts) but at the expense of a water load of about 100 ml/kg per day. It may therefore be necessary to administer a diuretic to prevent water intoxication or to reduce the calorie and N_2 intake to below presumed optimal levels.

Aminoplex 5 must always be administered through a catheter into the vena cava and because of its alcohol content it should, for optimal results, be given at a constant low rate of infusion (not more than about 120 ml/h).

(b) Fat emulsion regime

Although fat emulsions may be given into a peripheral vein, regimes incorporating their use are not so easy to employ in veterinary practice because the need to provide nitrogen in the form of amino acids complicates prescription of the fluids and places a heavy burden on nursing staff. For example, the use of fat in 'Intralipid'* 10% at the rate of 4 g/kg for 4 h followed by 500 ml of 8% amino acid solution and 500 ml of 5% glucose solution over the remaining 20 h provided 1895 kcal/day for a 34 kg Doberman.

*'Intralipid', Paines & Byrne, Greenford, Middlesex, United Kingdom.

Teeter (1974) suggests that a 10 kg dog can be fed by 350 ml of 10% 'Intralipid' plus 100 ml of an 8.5% amino acid solution and 100 ml of 10% glucose solution giving a total of 550 ml, or 55 ml/kg, of water per day.

In addition to the problem of prescription and administration, fat emulsions have other characteristics which make them rather unattractive for veterinary use. Their shelf-life is short, they need to be stored in a refrigerator and they are expensive. Their intravenous infusion to dogs has given rise to lipaemia, necessitating frequent blood counts, pyrexia and vomiting. Moreover the advantage of infusion into a peripheral vein is offset by the difficulties encountered in most dogs and cats of keeping the infusion running smoothly and slowly for more than a few hours.

TECHNIQUE AND ADMINISTRATION

For long term administration fluids need to be given through a catheter inserted into the jugular vein and advanced until its tip lies in the anterior vena cava. It is most important that these catheters are introduced aseptically (and preferably by percutaneous puncture rather than by cut-down techniques). The dressing around the catheter entry site should be renewed if it becomes wet or dirty and all catheters should be removed as soon as possible since the most important factor influencing the development of catheter-related infections is the time the catheter is in the vein. There is no evidence that antibiotic therapy will reduce the incidence of intravenous catheter infection.

Accurate delivery of prescribed fluid volumes over 24 h can be a problem if expensive infusion pumps are not available. Motor driven syringes need frequent re-filling and drip infusions can run most erratically. Calculation of infusion rates from delivery sets is usually simple since the number of drops/ml of an intravenous delivery set is normally specified by its manufacturers and the number of drops/min to achieve the desired vol/day is a simple calculation. If the volume requirements per hour are calculated and marked on the infusion bottle a visual check can be made to ensure that fluids are being given at the correct rates.

Serious complications attributable to venous cannulation such as air embolism, pneumothorax, haemothorax and penetration of a major blood vessel or the heart leading to haemothorax or cardiac tamponade can almost invariably be traced to avoidable errors — usually the use of excessive force during catheterization. With catheter-through-needle designs no attempt must be made to withdraw the catheter whilst the needle is still in the vein or guillotine severance of the catheter may result.

UNDESIRABLE EFFECTS OF INTRAVENOUS NUTRITION

It has recently been shown that the blood—brain barrier, long thought to isolate the brain from the rest of the body, does not protect it from dietary influence. Variations in concentrations of choline and amino acids in the plasma can be correlated with fluctuations in the brain's content. A diet high in carbohydrates and low in protein, such as is often fed to animals suffering from chronic renal disease, stimulates the synthesis of serotonin (an inhibitory neurotransmitter) because its precursor, tryptophan, can enter the brain without competition from other amino acids which are mostly taken up by muscle. Thus the implications of intravenous infusions of amino acids must always be considered. For example, their infusion in acutely ill animals suffering from incipient renal or hepatic failure may lead to alterations in consciousness due to changes in central neurotransmitter levels.

Even more recently, it has been shown that the increased carbon dioxide production resulting from the metabolism of large quantities of glucose in human patients with injury or sepsis may result in the need to initiate artificial ventilation of the lungs. There is no reason to suppose that this response does not occur in dogs and cats and hence if large quantities of glucose are infused respiratory failure may well result.

BIBLIOGRAPHY

Askanazi, J., Nordenstrom, J., Rosenbaum, S. H., Elwyn, D. H., Hyman, A. I., Carpentier, Y. A. and

Kinney, J. M. (1981) Nutrition for the patient with respiratory failure. *Anesthesiology*, **54**, 373.

Biebuyck, J. F., Lund, P. and Krebs, P. A. (1972) The protective effect of oleate on metabolic changes produced by halothane in rat liver. *Biochem. J.* **128**, 721.

Biebuyck, J. F. (1981) Total parenteral nutrition in the peri-operative period — a time for caution? *Anesthesiology*, **54**, 360.

Blackburn, G. L., Maini, B. S. and Pierce, E. C. (1977) Nutrition in the critically ill patient. *Anesthesiology*, **47**, 181.

Burrows, C. F., Kolata, R. J. and Soma, L. R. (1977) Shock: pathophysiology and management. In, *Current Veterinary Therapy* VI (Edited by R. Kirk) p. 26. Saunders, Philadelphia.

Cahill, G. F. (1970) Starvation in man. *New Engl. J. Med.* **282**, 668.

Clowes, G. H. A., O'Donnell, T. F., Ryan, N. T. and Blackburn, G. L. (1974) Energy metabolism in sepsis. *Ann. Surg.* **179**, 684.

Cornelius, L. M. (1980) Fluid therapy in small animal practice. *J. Am. Vet. Med. Assoc.* **176**, 110.

Daly, J. M., Vare, H. M. and Dudrick, S. J. (1970) Correlation of protein depletion with colonic anastomotic strength in rats. *Surg. Forum* **21**, 77.

Edgren, B., Hallberg, D., Hakansse, I., Meng, H. C. and Wretlind, K. A. J. (1964) Long term tolerance study of two fat emulsions for intravenous nutrition in dogs. *Am. J. Clin. Nutrit.* **14**, 28.

Finco, D. R. (1972) General guidelines for fluid therapy. *J. Am. Anim. Hosp. Assoc.* **8**, 166.

Foster, S. J. (1970) Some aspects of fluid therapy in practice, *J. Small Anim. Pract.* **11**, 337.

Garnett, E. S., Bernard, D. C., Ford, J. (1969) Gross fragmentation of cardiac myofibrils after therapeutic starvation for obesity. *Lancet*, i, 914.

Hall, L. W. (1967) *Fluid Balance in Canine Surgery*. Baillière, Tindall & Cassell, London.

Hall, L. W. (1980) Preliminary investigations of the effects of injury on the body fluids of cats and dogs. *J. Small Anim. Pract.* **21**, 679.

Haskins, S. C. (1976) Blood volume support. *Vet. Clin. N. Am.* **6**, 265.

Hawkins, R. A. and Biebuyck, J. F. (1979) Ketone bodies are selectively used by individual brain regions. *Science,* **205**, 325.

Irving, M. H. and Rushman, G. B. (1971) Parenteral nutrition for the surgical patient. *Anaesthesia,* **26**, 450.

Jeejeebhoy, K. N. (1963) Metabolism of intravenously infused albumin. *Nutritiodieta,* **5**, 356.

Johnson, I. D. A., Marion, J. D. and Stevens, J. Z. (1966) The effect of intravenous feeding on the balances of nitrogen, sodium and potassium after operation. *Bri. J. Surg.* **53**, 885.

Ko, K. C. and Paradise, R. R. (1971) The effect of halothane on the contractility of atria from starved rats. *Anesthesiology,* **34**, 557.

Kronfeld, D. S. (1976) Canine and feline nutrition. *Mod. Vet. Pract.* **57**, (1) 23.

Michell, A. R. (1979) The pathophysiological basis of fluid therapy in small animals. *Vet. Rec.* **104**, 542.

Mons, A. M., Biebuyck, J. F., Saunders, S. J. (1979) Tryptophan transport across the blood—brain barrier during acute hepatic failure. *J. Neurochem.* **33**, 409.

Moore, F. D., (1959) *Metabolic Care of the Surgical Patient.* Saunders, Philadelphia.

Morris, M. L. (1975) Feline dietetics. *Feline Pract.* **1**, 39.

Owen, O. E., Morgan, A. P., Kemp, H. G. (1967) Brain metabolism during fasting. *J. Clin. Invest.* **46**, 1589.

Renegar, W. R., Stoll, S. G., Bojrab, M. J. and Simpson, S. T. (1979) Parenteral hyperalimentation — the use of lipid as the prime calorie source. *J. Am. Anim. Hosp. Assoc.* **15**, 411.

Schuberth, O. and Wretlind, A. (1961) Intravenous infusion of fat emulsions, phosphatides and emulsifying agents. *Acta Chir. Scand.* **278**, 1.

Seeberg, V. P., McQuarrie, E. B. and Secar, C. C. (1955) Metabolism of intravenously infused sorbitol. *Proc. Soc. Exp. Biol. Med.* **89**, 303.

Spencer, I. O. B. (1968) Death after therapeutic starvation for obesity. *Lancet,* i, 1288.

Teeter, S. M. (1974) in *Current Veterinary Therapy* (Edited by Kirk, R. W.). Saunders, Philadelphia, pp. 88—90.

Wurtman, R. J. and Fernstrom, J. D. (1974) Nutrition and the brain. In, *The Neurosciences.* Ed. by Schmitt, F. O. and Worden, F. G., pp. 685-693. M.I.T. Press, Boston.

CHAPTER 10

EVALUATION AND VALIDATION OF PREPARED FOODS

P. T. Kendall

The evaluation of foods used for the nutrition of domestic animals is a matter of great importance. Prepared foods for dogs and cats are no exception and the petfood industry aims to provide safe, palatable, digestible and nutritionally balanced foods for pet animals at prices affordable by the human owner. The food must also satisfy the human owner's expectation of wholesomeness, hygiene, texture, smell, colour and convenience in the required range and variety of products. Probably the most rigorous evaluation of prepared pet foods takes place in the commercial market place where competition between companies and individual brands is invariably fierce. A failure to combine biological and economic attributes for a particular prepared food according to animal and human expectations results ultimately in commercial failure. For example, unpalatable foods are quickly recognized by animals and humans alike and product franchise is lost by the manufacturer. Similarly, nutritionally imbalanced foods will make little long-term impact in the market place because of the negative product feedback from opinion leaders in response to feeding problems in individual animals or populations. However, the successful manufacturer will do his best to prevent such controls occurring and the best way to ensure this is by producing high quality, safe, nutritionally balanced foods backed up by sensible feeding advice. This means that foods will usually have been thoroughly tested for suitability under controlled scientific conditions prior to marketing and will also be subject to continuous and thorough appraisal throughout the life of the product. Without doubt the products having greatest long-term commercial success will be well fitted to meet the combined demands of the animal consumer and human purchaser consistently over a long time span.

THE DEMAND FOR PREPARED FOODS

Before the biological evaluation of prepared petfoods can be discussed in detail it is important to understand something of the history, growth and role of the petfood industry.

Most dogs and cats are almost entirely dependent on man for their food but it is only within the last few decades that there have been significant changes in the sources and supply of this food.

A number of factors affecting both pet animals and owners are associated with this change. Smaller family units have resulted in a decrease in the total consumption of food in each household, coupled with increased use of convenience human foods which require relatively little preparation. In both cases there is a corresponding decrease in the amount of left-over food.

The increased number of 'working' housewives has also resulted in less time being available for food preparation, whether for the family or the family pet.

Alongside these changes within the family there has been the rapid development of the self-service store in place of the local butcher, grocer and fishmonger which formerly provided a readily available source of 'off-cuts' for pets.

Legislation has also been a contributing factor. The Meat Sterilisation Regulations (1969) of the Food and Drugs Act (1955) reduced the availability of those cuts of meat which were unsuitable for human consumption but acceptable for sale for the dog or cat.

With today's emphasis on family health there is also a growing awareness of the importance of safety, hygiene and a balanced, nutritious diet for both the family and the animals in its care.

All these factors have created a growing demand for prepared foods for dogs and cats; indeed, it would now be difficult and most costly for many families to feed their pets in the absence of food manufactured specifically for them.

The pet food industry and the prepared foods it manufactures and distributes are therefore an almost inevitable consequence of the demand created by these changing social factors. In many ways the industry performs on a large scale the part played previously by the individual pet owner, by gathering food materials not destined for human consumption and using modern techniques and nutritional expertise to transform them into palatable and nutritious foods for pet animals. By centralizing this collection and preparation however, raw materials can be used and economies of scale achieved which are beyond the reach of the individual owner. Dogs and cats have thus retained their traditional role of using up surplus food materials in the environment while the pet food industry has taken up the job of making them available in a processed form which is nutritionally balanced, safe and requires the minimum of preparation.

RELATIVE IMPORTANCE OF PREPARED FOODS IN MEETING NUTRIENT REQUIREMENTS OF DOGS

Information on the overall contribution prepared foods make in meeting nutrient requirements of pet populations tends to be very general in nature because of the difficulties of obtaining reliable data from the home situation. Normally the nutritional penetration of prepared dog foods into the total population requirements is based on metabolizable energy (ME).

However the ME needs of dogs of different breeds, sizes, ages in the various physiological states are not precisely known, similarly weights of dogs in the population and their typical activity levels have not been accurately characterized. Similar difficulties arise in estimating ME needs of cats in home circumstances. The absence of this and other information allows only very approximate estimates of penetration of prepared pet foods to be made.

Evaluation for what purpose?

The nutrition of pet animals such as dogs and cats is a science with few practitioners compared with the nutrition of farm animals. Yet in many ways the nutritional standards which prepared pet foods have to meet are more exacting than those for farm animal or human foods.

Whilst some dogs do perform useful work, the majority of dogs and cats are kept as household pets. Like man but unlike most farm animals, pet dogs and cats are expected to attain a healthy old age. The main feeding objective is to maintain long-term physical and mental fitness. Thus, prepared pet foods must provide in a limited range or even in a single product, the nutrients which will attain the end — an aim which is demanded for few single animal foods and virtually no single human food. A broad spectrum of evaluatory study is therefore considered important in order to meet the demanding brief for a prepared dog food.

Prepared foods for dogs and cats should be toxicologically safe, palatable, digestible, nutritionally balanced and be accompanied by sensible and effective feeding guidance. These criteria will need to be qualified depending on the exact role of each product. For example, some products may be positioned as complete and balanced for all life stages, whilst others may be claimed complete and balanced for adult maintenance. The definition of terms like 'complete' and 'balanced' are often the source of some confusion. However, comprehensive definitions are provided by the Association of American Feed Control Officials (AAFCO 1981) and the U.K. Feedingstuffs Regulations (1981). The AAFCO definition of a complete food is 'a nutritionally adequate feed for animals other than man; by specific formula is compounded to be fed as the sole ration and is capable of maintaining life and for promoting production without any additional substance being consumed except water'. The U.K. Feedingstuffs Regulations (1981) define a 'complete feedingstuff' as a compound feedingstuff which by reason of its composition is sufficient to ensure a daily ration. Where 'daily ration' means the total quantity of feedingstuff, expressed on 12% moisture basis, required by an animal of a given kind, age group and level of production in order to satisfy its average daily nutritional needs.

Therefore both the AAFCO (1981) and U.K. Feedingstuffs Regulations (1981) definitions of complete feedstuffs mean the same thing. Some dog foods are not intended to form the whole diets for dogs and cats and are termed complementary foods, examples of these could be low protein dog biscuits or some meat-based canned foods. The U.K. Feedingstuffs Regulations (1981) defines 'complementary feedingstuff' as a compound feedingstuff which, by reason of its composition, is not sufficient to ensure a daily ration unless it is used in combination with other feedingstuffs.

The term 'balanced' is defined by AAFCO (1981) as a term that may be applied to a diet, ration or feed having all known recognized nutrients in proper amount and proportion based upon recommendations of recognized authorities in the field of animal nutrition, such as the National Research Council (NRC), for a given set of physiological animal requirements. The species for which it is intended and the functions such as maintenance or maintenance plus production (growth, foetus, fat, milk, eggs, wool, feathers or work) shall be specified. In the case of dog foods the most authoritative collection of published data on nutritional requirements is the NRC (1974) document, *Nutrient Requirements of Dogs,* No. 8. This document is widely used by formulators of dog foods to establish balanced nutrient profiles in products. It is currently under review and a revised version is expected to be available in 1982. A sister document (NRC 1978) and equally useful reference has been published for cats, entitled the *Nutrient Requirements of Cats,* Report No. 13.

Motivation for evaluation

The motivation for evaluating biological suitability of prepared pet foods rests firmly with the manufacturer, if only for the commercial reasons outlined earlier. However voluntary petfood industry codes of practice and formal legislation are important modulating influences in most countries. In the space available it is not possible to give a comprehensive international overview on how each country considers aspects of biological evaluation of prepared pet foods. Therefore most emphasis has been placed on the EEC and North American situations.

Legislation affecting how prepared foods are evaluated

At EEC and national levels, the basic legislation affecting the petfood industry is that which relates to farm animals and covers the manufacture and marketing of its products. This agrees with the industry's own view but it is important also that the EEC Commission and national governments take into account the special characteristics and requirements of the prepared petfood industry within the directives for food for farm animals. (Legislation for example should, and in large measure already does, take into account the standards established for the nutrition of pet animals, that prepared petfoods are purchased alongside and from the same distribution outlets as human food, that health/safety regulations affecting food-producing animals are not relevant to pet animals.)

Because only part of the basic legislation is specific to prepared pet foods, some countries have chosen to prepare codes of practice with the national authorities. Examples of this are codes of practice on ingredient designation and product descriptive terms agreed under the auspices of the U.K. Petfood Manufacturers' Association (PFMA).

Legislation at EEC and national levels is concerned with the health and safety of products, the use of additives, marketing practices and safety/health regulations governing the importation of raw materials. At EEC level the basic legislation affecting the industry is contained in the following four Directives.

1. *Additives* — which is concerned with the use of additives in prepared pet foods. November 23, 1970 (70/524/EEC).
   This directive has already been subject to amendments on 28 occasions.
   The main amendments are:
   The 6th: regulating the use of colourants for cats and dogs.
   The 15th: which establishes a permitted list with 2 annexes
   Annex 1 being a permanent list
   Annex 2 being a temporary list
2. *Undesirable substances* — concerned with the fixing of maximum permitted levels for undesirable substances and products in feedingstuffs. December 17, 1973 (74/63/EEC).

3. *Marketing and straight feedingstuffs* – concerned with the distribution of straight feedingstuffs. November 23, 1976 (79/101/EEC).

4. *Marketing of compound feedingstuffs* – concerned with the distribution of compound feedingstuffs, April 2, 1979 (79/373/EEC).

Other Directives which also affect the evaluation of prepared petfoods cover sampling and analytical methods; packaging materials; safety and health regulations relating to meat importations and consumer protection aspects common to all industries (which include directive 79/112/EEC concerned with the labelling and advertising of foods).

In the U.S.A., Official Pet Food Regulations have been prepared and approved by AAFCO in conjunction with industry's representatives under the auspices of the Petfood Institute (PFI) and are currently in official status under the new Uniform Feed Bill approved by AAFCO (1981). Comprehensive regulations exist governing definitions and terms (PF1), label format and labelling (PF2), brand and product names (PF3), expression of guarantees (PF4), ingredients (PF5), directions for use (PF6) and drugs and pet food additives (PF7).

In addition protocols for adequate testing of pet food products have been developed by a committee of nutritionists from the PFI at the request of AAFCO. This committee was concerned only with the testing of foods for normal healthy animals. Thus the protocols presented cover gestation/lactation, growth and maintenance of adult animals. It was considered that protocols for testing products intended for the dietary management of disease states lay outside the directive given to the committee.

The AAFCO protocols or variants thereof have tended to be used by reputable pet food manufacturers in many other countries to assess nutritional adequacy. However it is important to appreciate that AAFCO protocols are the minimum necessary to substantiate particular product nutritional claims and more complex testing is frequently undertaken by some manufacturers.

Evaluation of prepared pet foods in practice

1. TOXICOLOGICAL SAFETY

An assessment of the toxicological status of prepared pet foods is usually a complex procedure based on a knowledge of origin and analytical content of raw materials. Some toxicological examination of finished products and *in-vivo* screening may be done as a further check but only the detailed knowledge of raw materials allows predictive assessments to be made. Toxicological constraints on the use of raw materials may totally prohibit use or restrict levels; in the latter case most manufacturers will impose constraints on inclusion via raw material specification documents. Toxicological safety of prepared pet foods tends also to be an area where legislative controls operate strongly and internationally in comparison with, for example, nutritional assessment. Almost all such controls have been agreed following input from the petfood industry and it is clearly in the long-term interest of all that such controls are adhered to.

2. PALATABILITY

It is self-evident but worth restating that the nutritional quality of a food is of no consequence if the dog or cat will not eat it. Taste preferences in carnivores have been comprehensively reviewed by Mugford (1977). Making products which are consistently eaten well over extended periods requires a great deal of expertise and the ability to match a basic understanding of factors affecting appetite and food intake to available raw materials. Recipe development in this way is a key factor in both the commercial and biological success of a pet food, and it is important that the food technologist can measure the success of his efforts to maintain palatability. Therefore newly developed and existing products will be regularly tested with animals. Many different types of palatability test have been devised for dogs and cats. Different test methodologies have been reviewed in detail by Walker (1971, 1975) and Kitchell and Baker (1972).

Most methods used by the petfood industry reflect a behavioural approach to the problem of assessing palatability of prepared foods. This is an extremely difficult area in which to work, especially as preferences of individual dogs or cats may vary with time and previous dietary experiences both in the short- and long-term. Although most palatability tests are simple in concept, it requires great care to maintain proper scientific control over experiments.

Probably the most widely used test method is the 1- or 2-day preference test, where individually fed test animals are offered a choice of two or more products. The weight of each product offered is known in advance and the dogs or cats are offered sufficient of each food to exceed total appetite, so that the choice situation is always preserved.

At the end of a fixed time period of usually at least 1 h, the remaining food is re-weighed and the amounts eaten computed. It is usually necessary to repeat the test on the same animals later with the bowl positions reversed in an attempt to eliminate side bias. The data generated should be statistically analysed by at least an analysis of variance so that variation between individuals due to side bias, feeding occasions and interactions can be accounted for.

Some petfood manufacturers carry out in-home palatability tests either instead of or as an adjunct to kennel or cattery testing. The main advantage of the in-home testing is that both animal preference and human expectations can be monitored, whilst the main disadvantage is often the lack of control over experimental conditions which reduces test sensitivity.

3. NUTRITIONAL SUITABILITY

In order to make foods which are suitable for a particular class of animal, the following information is needed:

(a) qualitative and quantitative nutrient needs in any given physiological condition;
(b) palatability and toxicological status of available raw materials;
(c) nutrient content of available raw materials;
(d) validation of how well items (a), (b) and (c) have been combined to meet biological needs.

Item (a) has already been extensively reviewed in the earlier chapters of this book and item (b) has been briefly mentioned in the current chapter, therefore it is proposed to consider here only items (c) and (d) in any detail.

Evaluation of the nutrient content of raw materials is important so that blends can be produced which satisfy nutritional requirements of dogs or cats. Assessment of nutrient content of raw materials should combine both laboratory and in-vivo tests. Gross nutrient content of raw materials can be assessed by chemical analysis and comparison with tables of nutrient needs such as those included in the NRC (1974) for dogs and NRC (1978) for cats. However, chemical analysis alone does not reveal how well food can be broken down to release available nutrients. The availability of the nutrients to the animal can be measured by conducting digestibility or metabolism trials in which the raw material is fed as the only food or in a significant proportion with a basal diet of known nutrient digestibility. In this way overall nutritional value of a raw material to the dog or cat can be described together with effects on faeces bulk and water turnover if necessary. The effects of process variables on raw material nutrient availability can also be ascertained in such digestibility assays. The digestible energy (DE) and crude protein (DCP) content of some raw materials measured with dogs are given in Table 26. The same methods can also be used to measure the digestibility/availability of nutrients in finished products. At the Animal Studies Centre conducting research on behalf of the Mars Petcare Group each digestibility trial is conducted with six adult dogs or cats over 14- or 21-day periods. Typical apparent digestibility values for canned, semi-moist and dry prepared foods are outlined in Table 27. In general, canned and semi-moist dog foods have closely similar apparent digestibility percentages, except for nitrogen-free extract digestibility, which tends to be low in canned products. The nitrogen-free extract in canned foods tends to contain appreciable amounts of soluble fibre from gelling agents which is not digested in the small intestine but may be fermented by micro-organisms in the large intestine. Dry dog foods tend to have slightly lower average apparent digestibility percentages than either canned or semi-moist, this may partly reflect characteristics of raw ingredients and degree of processing.

Apparent digestibility of cat foods tends in general to be lower than dog foods (Kendall, 1981). However canned cat foods tend to have higher digestibility on

Table 26. *Digestible energy (DE) and digestible crude protein (DCP) values of raw materials on a dry matter (DM) basis, as measured* in-vivo *dog digestibility trials*

Raw material	DE (kcal/100 g DM)	DCP (% DM)	Apparent digestibility %		
			Dry Matter	Crude Protein	Gross Energy
Protein meals					
Defatted soya bean meal (50% CP)	337	46	74	85	71
Full fat soya flour (*n* = 4)	450	34	77	81	79
Ground extruded whole soyabeans	379	29	68	71	71
Textured soya protein (*n* = 2)	352	43	77	84	78
Vital gluten	512	84	83	96	93
Rape seed meal	310	31	64	82	77
Walnut meal	147	2	31	14	34
Almond meal	222	21	47	69	52
White-fish meal	388	66	72	90	85
Meat meal	464	72	81	92	91
Meat and bone meal (*n* = 2)	239	43	55	77	75
Poultry by-product meal (*n* = 2)	471	55	71	82	82
Cereals and by-products					
Whole ground wheat	366	11	79	78	83
Barley meal	361	9	80	78	81
Maize grits	324	7	73	65	73
Flaked maize	414	8	96	89	95
Rice	328	7	85	77	84
Refined flour	358	12	92	84	92
Wheat feed	280	11	60	70	62
Wheatgerm meal	338	16	73	72	73
Oatfeed	327	13	75	75	75
Other					
Cassava	275	0	73	NEG.	81
Dried molassed sugar-beet pulp	170	6	28	45	42
Potato by-product	338	7	86	65	85
Locust bean meal	192	5	51	96	46
Scotaferm (Distillery by-product)	307	12	57	42	62
Scotagran (Distillery by-product)	195	9	33	43	39

Values given are based on single samples unless otherwise indicated.

average than dry cat foods, thus agreeing with data from dog digestibility studies.

Digestibility trials are concerned with short-term effects rather than with providing information about long-term nutritional suitability. They are concerned with availability of specific, usually major organic, nutrients, but do not provide data on the ability of a particular product or family of products to support an animal in good health for an extended period. Product validation trials to provide this kind of information include gestation—lactation studies in which the food or feeds to be tested are given with water as

Table 27. *Typical proximate and gross energy analyses, apparent digestibility (%) and digestible nutrient contents for canned, semi-moist and dry prepared dog foods*

Number of samples	Canned 43	Semi-moist 27	Dry 40
Apparent digestibility %			
Dry matter	80	84	77
Organic matter	83	87	81
Crude protein	83	84	77
Acid ether extract	88	92	79
Nitrogen-free extract*	72	87	82
Gross energy	85	88	81
Digestible nutrients per 100 g			
Digestible energy (kcal)	102	345	331
Digestible crude protein (g)	7	17	15
Digestible acid ether extract (g)	4	11	6
Digestible nitrogen-free extract (g)	6	36	48
Analysis %			
Dry matter	23.3	79.1	91.8
Organic matter	20.8	73.0	84.5
Crude protein	9.0	19.8	19.6
Acid ether extract	4.4	12.0	7.0
Nitrogen-free extract	7.6	41.1	58.1
Gross energy (kcal/100 g)	120	392	409

*Estimated by difference and includes fibre component

the only source of nutrients, to a minimum of eight but usually 10 or 12 females throughout pregnancy and lactation until puppies or kittens are weaned at 6–8 weeks of age. These trials are usually followed by a growth study in which progeny from litters produced on the breeding study are fed for 3 months in comparison with a known satisfactory diet. Gestation–lactation studies may cover more than one reproductive cycle depending on the strength of nutritional reassurance sought. Such tests are usually costly yet still do not allow absolute proof of nutritional suitability to be made because some nutrients may take many years before clinical or even subclinical deficiency or toxicity signs appear. Probably the soundest approach to assessing nutritional suitability of prepared foods relies on a sequence of analytical, digestibility and longer-term feeding tests depending on the intended biological role of each product and how frequently recipes are adjusted.

Protocols intended to examine the suitability of prepared foods for various physiological states have been agreed between AAFCO and PFI in the U.S.A.

(AAFCO 1981). As indicated earlier, the procedures laid down tend to be the minimum compatible with satisfactory testing of foods and more detailed examination is desirable. To enable an exhaustive exploration of the biological suitability of a prepared food requires the use of considerable numbers of dogs or cats.

The large international manufacturers of prepared pet foods tend to have their own kennels and catteries where such work can be done. For example, the Mars Petcare Group conducts a substantial part of its nutritional testing at the United Kingdom Animal Studies Centre (Waltham-on-the-Wolds, Leicestershire, England). Usually about eight different breeds of dog and several hundred cats are kept and a wide range of behavioural and nutritional studies carried out under the supervision of a team of nutritionists, veterinarians and behaviourists. Some guidelines on how feeding protocols are planned, conducted and interpreted by the Animal Studies Centre are given in Appendices A–D.

Quality control and assurance

This discussion of how quality control is achieved in the manufacture of prepared pet foods is by necessity slanted at the Mars Petfood Group approach. It is likely that other reputable manufacturers will have broadly similar methods.

To provide products of consistently high quality, which meet the combined expectations of target consumer and human owner, requires a continuous and substantial effort on the part of the pet food manufacturer. Manufacturers therefore need to develop and maintain control systems which ensure that products achieve their objectives in terms of safety, palatability and nutritional suitability, as well as aesthetics and convenience for the human owner. Effective quality control programmes should be prospective rather than retrospective in outlook. Retrospective examination of finished products is certainly part of quality control but is quite insufficient on its own. The best quality control does not begin in the factory but at the abattoir or processing plant where materials for prepared pet foods are harvested. Thus a lot of potential problems concerned with contaminations, spoilage and foreign bodies can be minimized by consultation with the vendors of materials.

Many raw materials used in pet foods are perishable and variable in nature and are mainly by-products from the human food processing industry, therefore to get things right from the onset is of paramount importance. It is customary to buy each material against unique written specifications. The availability of rapid analytical methods, such as infra-red reflectance analysis permits determination of water, fat, protein and ash content of incoming materials at an early stage. In this way materials can be classified and used to best advantage or rejected as unsuitable.

Susceptible raw materials such as chilled fresh meats and meat by-products have codes of manufacturing procedure to ensure that they are properly handled and used within a specified time. Microbiological control is achieved by, for example, monitoring susceptible materials, cooling water used in canning operations and post-process handling equipment.

Quality assurance programmes are followed throughout the whole manufacturing cycle. In well run factories established standard manufacturing procedures are adhered to and each product has its own unique recipe of blended ingredients. Automatic and visual checks of product quality are made continuously or at frequent intervals during the process. Various devices are incorporated to further minimize the incidence of foreign bodies. For example, ferrous contaminants can be picked out by strong magnets. Above all, factories should be hygienic, clean and conscious of the fact that they are making food. There is no reason to accept lower standards of hygiene or quality for pet foods than those that are applied to human foods; in many ways the petfood manufacturers aim to set and achieve even higher standards because of the unpromising nutritional and microbiological status of many raw materials.

Quality control of finished products is also a multi-stage operation. At the end of each production run or shift, samples of finished product are visually, gravimetrically or physicochemically checked against specifications. Product outside specification is identified and will be held for further checks before release or rejection. Quality control procedures will continue to operate during all stages of distribution, in warehouses and ultimately on the store or supermarket shelf.

An efficient customer service department is also instrumental in monitoring and processing feedback from retailers and customers alike so that quality faults can be quickly diagnosed and measures initiated for elimination. Nutritional quality of products can only really be achieved effectively by the prospective approach which entails the setting of standards in product specifications. However the feedback loop must be completed and comprehensive analyses of all essential nutrients on statistically valid samples of finished product should be a regular feature of any programme. Studies on the shelf-life of susceptible nutrients also need to be arranged so that guarantees of nutrient content at various times after manufacture can be given. *In-vivo*, palatability, digestibility and longer-term feeding trials on standard samples of finished products obtained at random from factory, warehouse or shop should also be incorporated in the nutritional feedback quality loop.

Taken overall, quality control programmes are an indispensable part of the evaluation of prepared pet foods so that products released for sale comply with specifications in terms of safety, wholesomeness, appearance, colour, texture and nutrient content.

Appendices A—D describe in detail biological trial procedures carried out at the Animal Studies Centre.

APPENDIX A. BIOLOGICAL TRIAL PROCEDURES IN DOG AND CAT NUTRITION

Digestibility trials

The objective is to measure the availability to the animal of the nutrient content of a food product, complete diet or raw material (i.e. food ingredient). Examples of test procedures already in use are given.

Basis of method

The nutrient content of the test food is determined by analysis of representative samples. Measured amounts are individually fed to six dogs or cats for a minimum period of 14 days (dogs) or 21 days (cats). Faeces are quantitatively collected for the last 7 days (dogs) or 14 days (cats) of each feeding period and analysed for their nutrient content. The average daily amount of nutrient apparently absorbed into the animal's body is calculated from the difference between nutrient intake as food and nutrient output as faeces. This amount expressed as a proportion of intake is the digestibility percentage or availability percentage of the food as fed. Where the test product or raw material is not suitable to be fed as the only food because for example, of serious nutritional imbalance or because it is unpalatable, then a series of trials is necessary in which the test material is fed in different proportions with a basal diet. It is then possible to calculate the digestibility and the digestible nutrient content by 'difference' or by 'regression' methods.

Since faeces do not consist only of undigested, unabsorbed material but contain cell debris and material excreted into the digestive tract the difference between intake and output measured in this way is defined as apparent digestibility or absorption. To measure true absorption or digestibility it is necessary to use control diets free of the nutrient being studied to establish the size of output when intake is zero. For most practical purposes apparent digestibility is the measurement used as it measures the net amount of digestion.

Within a species, digestibility values are largely independent of the individual animal and are more a characteristic of the food. The digestibility value obtained with adults is very similar to that obtained with young growing animals and is equally appropriate for other stages of life of normal healthy animals. It is not therefore, necessary to conduct measurements on several classes of animal.

Metabolism or balance trials are extensions of digestibility trials in that urine output is collected as well as faeces. It is then possible to draw up a balance sheet showing intake of nutrients as the food or test material and total output as faeces and urine. The difference between these two is regarded as the amount of nutrient retained in the body. (There are losses other than faecal and urinary losses which have to be accounted for. These are mainly integumental losses such as skin and hair.)

In young growing animals the balance trial permits such estimates as the amounts of protein or mineral retention and provides a good method of estimating the protein quality of foods or ingredients. The technique is less valuable with adults which are not normally depositing or accumulating protein as a result of growth. The errors then become considerable. Metabolism trials also permit the measurement of energy lost in urine and of water turnover both of which are useful in comparing foods of different kinds such as fresh food, canned or dry products.

Use in nutritional evaluation of products and food ingredients

Digestibility trials with six animals provide reliable information on the availability of the major nutrients protein, fat and energy in a food. Additionally they indicate any adverse or beneficial effect on the amount and consistency of faeces produced.

Each trial takes a maximum of 21 days for the feeding of animals and so a large number of raw materials and types of food can be assessed.

Conduct of trials (dogs)

Dogs are fed once daily at 9.00 a.m. They are penned individually in concrete floored pens equipped with an automatic drinker and electrically heated bed. Faeces are collected first thing in the morning and then at regular intervals throughout the day, often within minutes of being voided. Faeces voided outside the working day are collected the next morning. Faecal collections are stored in a refrigerator to minimize spoilage.

At the end of the 7 day collection the faeces are mixed and representative samples obtained for freeze drying and analysis. Freeze dried samples are used for all chemical analysis and for energy determination by adiabatic bomb calorimetry. Food samples are prepared in the same way.

Conduct of trials (cats)

Essentially the same procedure is followed for cats. Cats are penned individually in glass fibre cages which are fitted with a separate small tray in which the cat has been trained to defaecate and urinate.

The amounts of food given are maintained constant for the whole of the trial period so that by the time faeces are collected after a 7 day run-in period a day's faeces can be related to a day's food. The amount fed is calculated to provide enough energy for adult maintenance (70 kcal/kg bodyweight).

Although a knowledge of food digestibility does not give a complete picture of its nutritional value it allows digestive and absorptive efficiency to be measured. Taken together with detailed analyses of micronutrient content this information gives a reliable indication of whether or not foods or combinations of foods are suitable for providing adequate nutrition for adult maintenance and evidence of their value for supporting growth or lactation.

APPENDIX B. GROWTH TRIALS

Biological trials are necessary because it is possible that foods or combinations of foods which on analysis would provide enough nutrients to meet the estimated requirements of an animal might prove to be unsuitable when fed over a long period. They may be unpalatable so that animals are not willing consistently to eat enough or they may have some unknown contamination or deficiency which affects their feeding value. An extended feeding trial with growing animals is able to determine a food's ability to support normal, healthy growth and development.

The basis of such tests and of the appropriate trial design is a statistical comparison with a contemporary control group fed a proven satisfactory diet. Each trial should be suitable for the number of foods or diets to be tested and ensure that the design, the selection of animals and the conduct of the trials as a minimum meet the requirements of protocols laid down by AAFCO (The American Association of Feed Control Officials).

Growth trials with dogs

ANIMALS

A minimum of 6 puppies per diet regime and usually 9 or 12 are used. More than one breed is used, the commonest being Labradors and Beagles. Dogs must be pure-bred.

TRIAL DESIGN

An appropriate design which will allow statistical evaluation of the results is necessary. Randomized block designs are used in which dogs on the test and control diets are matched by breed, age, initial weight, litter origin and sex whenever possible. Equal sex distribution is preferred but not essential. Trials usually begin at 7 weeks of age, one week after weaning. This seventh week is used to accustom the puppies to being fed individually and to train them to eat the appropriate test or control diet prior to the start of the trial.

FEEDING

No other food is given other than the appropriate control or test diet regime. Drinking water is available *ad libitum*. Although group feeding as in the AAFCO protocol, is permissible and easier to carry out it does not allow statistical comparison of food and nutrient intakes unless there are several groups on each diet. It is therefore less useful in interpretation of results and hence puppies are usually fed on an individual basis.

Control and test animals are fed in the same way. It may be *ad libitum*, to appetite 2—4 times a day or to a scale of intake based on the weight of the puppy with food to provide 335 kcal/kg$^{0.75}$ bodyweight daily. The latter method is usually adopted since it allows the effects of nutrient content to be studied independent of food palatability. Other feeding regimes that meet the needs of good husbandry would be acceptable provided that both control and test groups are treated in the same manner.

No nutritional supplements are given at any time. No medication is given except under the direction of a veterinary surgeon and all such medication is recorded. Routine vaccination and anti-worm preparations are administered as normal for the animal.

Trials normally continue for a minimum of 12 weeks.

RECORDS

Individual liveweight is recorded at the beginning of the trial and at least at weekly intervals (usually two weighings per week).

Measurement of body length (nose to rump) at 2 weekly intervals.

Food consumption daily for each dog when fed as individuals.

Blood characteristics, haemoglobin (Hb), packed cell volume (PCV), red and white cell count, mean corpuscular haemoglobin concentration (MCHC), mean corpuscular volume (MCV), mean cell haemoglobin (MCH) as a minimum are measured at 7, 12 and 19 weeks of age. Total plasma protein, urea, alanine transaminase and alkaline phosphatase are also measured at the beginning and end of each trial.

Each puppy is examined by a veterinary surgeon at the beginning and end of trial. The examinations cover eyes, ears, mouth, rectal temperature, skin and coat condition, congenital/hereditary defects, circulatory, respiratory, digestive, urino-genital systems and muscular-skeletal development.

A daily record of faeces consistency is maintained.

CRITERIA FOR EVALUATION OF RESULTS

Abnormal muscular or skeletal developments, abnormal hair loss, skin or coat condition observed in test animals but not controls would represent a failure of the food. The average weight gain or rate of weight gain of test dogs should not be significantly less than that of the control group as determined by an appropriate statistical test and should not in any event be less than 90% of the control group average. The control group must be within the normal range expected for its breed. Average Hb and PCV values should not be statistically significantly below those of the controls nor outside the normal range of dogs of similar age and breed.

Growth trials with cats

Kitten growth trials are basically similar to puppy growth trials in objective and design. Because cats are smaller and easier to keep, larger numbers of animals are used and with better statistical control. Kittens are usually weaned at a later age and so trials do not usually start until the animals are 10 weeks old.

A minimum of 8 kittens per diet group and normally 10 or 12 are used. Equal sex distribution is preferred but a balanced sex distribution between diet groups is acceptable. Randomized block designs are used with kittens within a block matched as far as possible for age, litter origin, weight and sex. All kittens are weaned at 8 weeks and usually begin growth trials by 10 weeks of age. The trials run for a minimum 10 week period and usually take 12 weeks.

FEEDING

No food is given other than the appropriate control or test diet regime. Drinking water is available *ad libitum*. As with puppies group feeding is allowed in the AAFCO protocol although it does not allow

statistical comparison of food and nutrient intakes unless there are several groups on each diet. It is therefore less useful in the interpretation of results and hence kittens are usually fed on an individual basis. In kitten growth trials it is the normal practice to allocate both the test and control foods *ad libitum* or to appetite at several meals. No medication should be given except under veterinary direction and then comprehensive records of the reason and effect of medication should be kept.

RECORDS

Individual liveweight is recorded at the beginning of the trial and at least at weekly intervals (usually two weighings per week).

Food consumption is recorded daily for each kitten when fed as individuals or the average per cat.

Blood characteristics, Hb, PCV, MCHC, MCV, MCH, red and white cell counts as a minimum are measured at the start and end of the trial and also on two other occasions during the trial. Total plasma protein, urea, alanine transaminase and alkaline phosphatase are also measured at the beginning and end of each trial.

Each kitten is examined by a veterinarian at the start and end of the trial. The examinations cover eyes, ears, mouth, rectal temperature, skin and coat condition, congenital/hereditary defects, circulatory, respiratory, digestive, uro-genital systems and muscular—skeletal development.

CRITERIA FOR EVALUATION OF RESULTS

The average weight gain and growth rate of the test group shall not be less than the control group by appropriate statistical analyses. It shall in any event be not less than 85% of the control group average.

The average Hb and PCV values of the test group shall not be less than the values for the controls by appropriate statistical analysis.

None of the test group kittens shall show abnormal muscular or skeletal development, loss of body, skin or coat condition which is ascribed to the diet. None shall have any of the characteristic signs of nutritional deficiencies.

APPENDIX C. REPRODUCTION TRIALS

The objective is to demonstrate that the food or feeding regime will support breeding females in good health and permit normal reproduction of healthy viable young when fed throughout pregnancy and lactation.

Dogs

As a minimum bitches should be fed the test food or regime from the beginning of oestrus until the puppies are weaned at 6–8 weeks of age.

Feeding for the trials usually begins a few weeks prior to oestrus and all puppies are weaned at 6 weeks. Rarely do trials extend over more than one parity.

ANIMALS

AAFCO protocols require a minimum of six pregnant females, four of which must perform satisfactorily. Dogs are pure-bred, usually Labradors or Beagles, and are between 1 and 8 years old. Whenever possible animals are used which have previously had at least one litter.

A control group is not necessary since the characteristics measured can be compared with data obtained previously, but a control group is desirable when animals are available for the purpose.

FEEDING

Each bitch is fed individually. No supplements are given and no medication except under veterinary direction; all such medication is recorded. Water is freely available, and the same formulation (though not necessarily the same batch of product) is fed throughout the trial.

After parturition the puppies are only fed the same food as the bitch. Food intake is recorded for each bitch plus puppies.

Bitches may be fed to appetite, to a feeding scale, by packet recommendation or *ad libitum*. Bitches during pregnancy are fed to a maintenance level for the first 35 days of pregnancy and then food is increased by 10% each week until parturition. In lactation, bitches may be fed *ad libitum* or to a scale dependent on bitch weight and the size and weight of her litter.

Detailed records of bodyweight of bitch and puppies are maintained together with records of daily food consumption and observations on health and behaviour. Blood samples are taken from the bitch on four occasions and from puppies at weaning to check on Hb and PCV values. A detailed physical examination is given to each bitch by a veterinary surgeon when blood samples are taken, i.e. in the week after mating, the last week of pregnancy, the first week of lactation, and at weaning. Puppies are examined at birth and given a detailed examination at weaning.

CRITERIA FOR EVALUATION OF RESULTS

When a control group is used the average of the test group for any record but particularly for weight changes of bitch, weight and numbers of puppies per litter and the veterinary assessment of health should not be significantly poorer than the average for the control group by an appropriate test of significance.

Usually there is no control group and the following criteria apply. AAFCO protocols demand that at least two-thirds of the bitches which became pregnant with a minimum of 4 have to meet the criteria. Individual bitches should gain weight steadily during gestation. The average weight at weaning should ideally equal the average weight at mating. Individual animals may not weigh less than 85% of their weight at mating. Each bitch must rear 75% of her day-old puppies to 6 weeks of age with a minimum number of 4 for large breeds and 3 for small and medium-sized breeds (less than 20 kg mature weight).

Any bitch with any abnormality or loss of condition ascribed to nutrient deficiency or excess is indicative of failure of the food. Haemoglobin and PCV values must not fall below the accepted normal values for animals in the unit where the test is done. These values will approximate to 12–13% for Hb and 30–40% for PCV.

The average birth and 6-week weight of puppies should be within the normal range for their breed. Puppies must appear normal on veterinary examination with no signs of nutritional deficiency.

Reproduction trials

CATS

The objective with cats, as for dogs, is to demonstrate the ability of a food or feeding regime to support good reproductive performance in normal healthy animals.

ANIMALS

Because cats are smaller and easier to keep, there are usually at least 12 animals in a control group and an equal number on one or two test diets or regimes. Testing may continue over more than one parity to obtain at least 12 litters per diet.

Simple randomized block designs are usually used with queens grouped into pairs or trios on the basis of age, weight, breeding record and litter origin, and one from each pair or trio allocated at random to the control or test groups.

FEEDING

Feeding is usually *ad libitum* with the appropriate food and water freely available.

During the mating period and the first six or seven weeks of pregnancy cats on the same food are housed together and fed as a group. Food is recorded as average intake per cat. After 6 or 7 weeks queens are penned individually until they have given birth and subsequently reared their kittens to 8 weeks of age. During this period individual records are kept of food intake for queen plus litter.

Weight records are kept for individual queens on a weekly basis throughout the feeding trials, and on the day of mating, the day after parturition and again weekly thereafter. Kittens are weighed at weekly intervals from birth.

Veterinary examinations are done at the beginning of the trial, during the first week of lactation, and 6 weeks after parturition and at weaning. Blood samples to check on haemoglobin and PCV are also obtained on these occasions except for 6 weeks after parturition. Veterinary examination and blood sampling of kittens is done at 6 weeks of age.

CRITERIA FOR EVALUATION OF RESULTS

All queens should gain weight steadily during gestation. Average weight gain of the test group should not be significantly less than that of controls.

Average weight of queens at 6 weeks should ideally be not less than the average at mating. Weight loss if any should not be significantly greater than any corresponding weight loss of the control group. Average number and weight of kittens born alive and at 6 weeks of age should not be significantly less than the control group. Each queen should rear at least 60% of her day-old kittens unless illness, diagnosed by a veterinarian as being unconnected with diet, is responsible for greater losses. None of the queens or kittens should show signs characteristic of nutrient deficiency.

APPENDIX D. ADULT MAINTENANCE

Maintenance of weight and condition of adults is nutritionally much less demanding than for growth and reproduction.

Feeding trials to demonstrate nutritional adequacy or suitability of foods for this purpose usually last for 6 months and are less reliable than growth or reproductive studies. This is because a well-nourished healthy adult will have quite large reserves of many nutrients which can be used whenever the diet is inadequate and these can mask a dietary insufficiency for long periods. It is impractical to expect regular feeding trials of test products to extend for periods of a year or more which would be necessary if marginal deficiencies in some nutrients, e.g. trace metals like zinc or iron, or major deficiencies in nutrients like vitamins A, D or E are to be revealed.

Therefore reliance is on digestibility tests of foods which can be done regularly and which give a good measure of the availability of most nutrients. Combined with the results of detailed chemical analysis of the nutrient content of foods, which show if known safe levels are present, good assessment of suitability for adult maintenance is obtained. A supporting and relatively short feeding trial to demonstrate adequate intake is usually available as a result of the digestibility trial.

BIBLIOGRAPHY

AAFCO (1981) Association of American Feed Control Officials, Official Publication. Copies may be obtained from Donald H. James, Department of Agriculture, State Capital Building, Charlestown, W. Virginia, U.S.A.

Kendall, P. T. (1981) Comparative evaluation of apparent digestibility in dogs and cats. *Proc. Nut. Soc.* **40**, 2, 45A.

Kitchell, R. L. and Baker, G. G. (1972) Taste preference studies in domestic animals. *University of Nottingham Conference for Feeding Manufacturers.* No. 6, pp. 157–202. Churchill Livingstone, London.

Mugford, R. A. (1977) External influences on the feeding of carnivores. *The Chemical Senses in Nutrition.* Academic Press, London.

NRC (1974) *Nutrient Requirements of Dogs,* Report No. 8. National Research Council, National Academy of Sciences, Washington.

NRC (1978) *Nutrient Requirements of Cats,* Report No. 13. Nutritional Research Council, National Academy of Sciences, Washington.

Walker, A. D. (1971) Nutritional studies in the domestic dog and cat. PhD Thesis, University of London, England.

Walker, A. D. (1975) Taste preference in the domestic dog and cat. *Proceedings of Small Animal Nutrition Workshop,* Gaines Dog Research Centre, White Plains, NY.

APPENDIX I
CALORIE GUIDE FOR DOGS AND CATS

Daily energy guide in kcal required for dogs at different physiological states

Body wt. in kg	Body wt. in lbs	Weaning to half grown	Late pregnancy	Peak lactation	Adult maintenance
1	2.2	274	188	470	132
2	4.4	466	320	799	224
3	6.6	630	432	1081	304
4	8.8	767	526	1316	370
5	11.0	904	620	1551	436
6	13.2	1041	714	1786	502
7	15.4	1178	808	2021	568
8	17.6	1315	902	2256	634
9	19.8	1425	978	2444	686
10	22.0	1534	1053	2632	739
11	24.2	1644	1128	2820	792
12	26.4	1781	1222	3055	858
13	28.6	1897	1287	3243	911
14	30.8	1973	1354	3384	950
15	33.0	2082	1429	3572	1003
16	35.2	2192	1504	3760	1056
17	37.4	2302	1579	3948	1109
18	39.6	2384	1636	4089	1148
19	41.8	2493	1711	4277	1201
20	44.0	2603	1786	4465	1254
21	46.2	2686	1842	4606	1294
22	48.4	2795	1918	4749	1346
23	50.6	2877	1974	4933	1386
24	52.8	2959	2030	5076	1426
25	55.0	3069	2106	5264	1478
26	57.2	3151	2162	5405	1518
27	59.4	3261	2237	5593	1571
28	61.8	3343	2294	5734	1610
29	63.6	3425	2350	5875	1650
30	66.0	3507	2406	6016	1690
31	68.2	3589	2463	6157	1729
32	70.4	3699	2538	6345	1782
33	72.6	3781	2594	6486	1822
34	74.8	3863	2651	6627	1881
35	77.0	3946	2707	6768	1901
36	79.2	4028	2764	6909	1940
37	81.4	4110	2820	7050	1980

Continued over

Body wt. in kg	Body wt. in lbs	Weaning to half grown	Late pregnancy	Peak lactation	Adult maintenance
38	83.6	4192	2876	7191	2020
39	85.8	4274	2933	7332	2059
40	88.0	4357	2989	7473	2099
41	90.2	4439	3046	7614	2138
42	92.4	4521	3102	7755	2178
43	94.6	4603	3158	7896	2218
44	96.8	4685	3215	8037	2257
45	99.0	4768	3271	8178	2297

Daily energy guide in kcal required for cats at different physiological states

Body wt. in kg	Body wt. in lbs	Weaning to half grown	Late pregnancy	Peak lactation	Adult maintenance
0.5	1.1	125	—	—	—
1.0	2.2	250	—	—	—
1.5	3.3	250	—	—	—
2.0	4.4	300	200	500	170
2.5	5.5	325	250	625	213
3.0	6.6	390	300	750	255
3.5	7.7	450	350	875	298
4.0	8.8	—	400	1000	340
4.5	9.9	—	450	1125	383
5.0	11.0	—	500	1250	425

APPENDIX II
FURTHER READING LIST

1. Abrams, J. T. (1962) *Feeding of Dogs*. Green, Edinburgh.
2. Anderson, R. S. (1973) Feeding cats and kittens. *Pedigree Digest*, **1**, (1), 2–3.
3. Anderson, R. S. (1973) Obesity in the dog and cat. *Veterinary Annual*, Vol. 14, pp. 182–186. Wright, Bristol.
4. Anderson, R. S. (1977) Nutrition and disease in the cat and dog. *Pedigree Digest*, **4**, (2), 9–10.
5. Anderson, R. S. (1979) Feline nutrition. *Pedigree Digest*, **6**, (3), 12–14.
6. Anderson, R. S. (1980) Dietary aspects of diabetes in the dog. *Pedigree Digest*, 7, (14), 5–7.
7. Anderson, R. S. (1980) *Nutrition of the Dog and Cat*. Pergamon, Oxford.
8. Anderson, R. S. (1980) Water content in the diet of the dog. *Veterinary Annual*, Vol. 21, pp. 171–178. Wright, Bristol.
9. Anon (1980) *Pedigree Chum Book of Dog Care*. Petfoods' Education Centre, Melton Mowbray, Leicestershire.
10. B.V.A. (1978) *Small Animal Nutrition* Suppl. *Vet. Rec.* B.V.A., London.
11. Baker, D. H. (1980) Some essentials of kitten diets. *Pet Fd Indu.* **22**, (1), 20.
12. Baird, I. McL. and Howard, A. N. (Editors) (1969) *Obesity, Medical and Scientific Aspects*. Livingstone, Edinburgh.
13. Barnett, K. C. and Burger, I. H. (1980) Taurine deficiency retinopathy in the cat. *J. Small Anim. Pract.* **22**, 521–534.
14. Blaza, S. E. (1981) How dogs digest food. *Pedigree Digest*, **8**, (1), 3–4.
15. Burger, I. H. (1979) Water balance in the dog and cat. *Pedigree Digest*, **6**, (1), 10–11.
16. Craddock, D. (1960) *Obesity and its Management*. Livingstone, Edinburgh.
17. Collins, D. R. (1972) *Collins Guide to Dog Nutrition*. Howell, New York.
18. Edney, A. T. B. (1972) Current trends in small animal nutrition. *Veterinary Annual*, Vol. 13, pp. 194–199. Wright, Bristol.
19. Edney, A. T. B. (1973) Dental health and hygiene in the dog. *Pedigree Digest*, **1**, (1), 4–6.
20. Edney, A. T. B. (1974) Poisoning in dogs and cats. *Pedigree Digest*, **1**, (3), 3–4.
21. Edney, A. T. B. (1974) Dietary management in small animal practice. *Vet. Rec.* **102**, 543–545.
22. Edney, A. T. B. (1978) Small animal nutrition, the present state. *Veterinary Annual*, Vol. 18, pp. 285–289. Wright, Bristol.
23. Edney, A. T. B. (Editor) (1979) *Diarrhoea in the Dog*. Animal Studies Centre, Waltham.
24. Edney, A. T. B. (Editor) (1980) *Over- and Under-Nutrition*. Animal Studies Centre, Waltham.
25. Edney, A. T. B. (1980) Rearing motherless puppies. *Pedigree Digest*, **7**, (3), 7–9.
26. Fiennes, R. (1981) Bothie in Antarctica. *Pedigree Digest*, **8**, (1), 7.
27. Gannon, J. R. (1981) Nutritional requirements of the working dog. *Veterinary Annual*, Vol. 21, pp. 161–166. Wright, Bristol.
28. Graham-Jones, O. (1965) *Canine and Feline Nutritional Requirements*. Pergamon, Oxford.
29. Griffiths, B. C. R. (1969) Nutrition of the greyhound. *Vet. Rec.* **84**, 645–646.
30. Harcourt-Brown, N. H. (1981) Nutritional problems of cage birds. *Veterinary Annual*, Vol. 21, pp. 219–223. Wright, Bristol.
31. Heath, J. S. (Editor) (1978) *Aids to Nursing Small Animals and Birds*, 2nd Ed., Chapter on Feeding, by A. T. B. Edney, pp. 2–12. Baillière Tindall, London.
32. Holme, D. W. (1974) Feeding the pregnant and lactating bitch. *Pedigree Digest*, **1**, (4), 4–5.
33. Holme, D. W. (1975) Vitamins and minerals in nutrition. *Pedigree Digest,* **2**, (1), 3–8.
34. Holme, D. W. (1981) Diets for growing dogs. *Veterinary Annual*, Vol. 21, pp. 157–160. Wright, Bristol.
35. Kendall, P. T. (1978) Nutritional management of the bitch and litter from conception to weaning. *Pedigree Digest*, **5**, (4), 6–7.
36. Kendall, P. T. (1980) Some nutritional differ-

ences between the dog and cat. *Pedigree Digest*, **6**, (5), 4–6.

37. Kendall, P. T. (1980) Too much supplementation can be harmful. *Pedigree Digest*, **7**, (2), 3–5.

38. Kendall, P. T. (1980) New developments in kitten nutrition and feeding. *Pedigree Digest,* **7**, (3), 10.

39. Lane, D. R. (1980) *Jones's Animal Nursing*, 3rd Ed. Chapter on Feeding by R. S. Anderson, pp. 167–189. Pergamon, Oxford.

40. Lewis, L. (1978) Obesity in the dog. *Pedigree Digest*, **5**, (2), 5–6; **5**, (3), 5–6 parts I and II.

41. M.A.F.F. (1976) *Manual of Nutrition*, 8th Ed. H.M.S.O., London.

42. McCay, C. M. (1949) *Nutrition of the Dog*. Comstock Publishing, New York.

43. McLean, J. G. (1981) Essential fatty acids in the dog and cat. *Veterinary Annual*, Vol. 21, pp. 167–170. Wright, Bristol.

44. Miller, H., (1977) *Basic Guide to Canine Nutrition*, 4th Ed. Gaines, White Plains, NY.

45. Mosier, J. E. (Editor) (1978) Canine paediatrics. *Vet. Clin. N. Amer.* **8**, (1). Symposium Edition.

46. National Research Council (1974) *Nutrient Requirements of Dogs*. Report No. 8, National Academy of Sciences, Washington.

47. National Research Council (1978) *Nutrient Requirements of Cats*. Report No. 13, National Academy of Sciences, Washington.

48. O.H.E. (1969) *Obesity and Disease*. Office of Health Economics, London.

49. Pearson, H. (1975) Gastric dilation and torsion. *Pedigree Digest,* **2**, (3), 6–7.

50. Tavernor, W. D. (Editor) (1971) *Nutrition and Disease in Experimental Animals*. Baillière Tindall, London.

51. Taylor, R. J. F. (1957) The breeding and maintenance of sledge dogs. *Polar Rec.* **8**, 429–440.

52. Turner, W. T. (1980) *How to Feed Your Dog*. Popular Dogs, London.

53. Walker, A. D. (1980) *Fit for a Dog*. Davis-Poynter, London.

54. Walton, G. S. (1976) Food allergies in the dog and cat. *Pedigree Digest*, **3**, (2), 5–10.

55. Watson, A. D. J. (1981) Nutritional Osteodystrophies in dogs. *Veterinary Annual*, Vol. 21, pp. 209–218. Wright, Bristol.

56. Wilkinson, G. T. (1966) *Diseases of the Cat*, Chapter on Nutrition by P. P. Scott, pp. 1–31. Pergamon, Oxford.

57. Wilkinson, G. T. (1981) Nutritional deficiencies in the cat. *Veterinary Annual*, Vol. 21, pp. 183–189. Wright, Bristol.

58. Wright, M. and Walters, S. (1980) *The Book of the Cat*. Pan Books, London.

59. Wyatt, H. T. (1963) Further experiments with sledge dogs. *Br. J. Nutr.* **17**, 273–279.

INDEX